Literacy Skills

for
the Knowledge
Society

Further Results from the
International Adult Literacy Survey

ORGANISATION FOR ECONOMIC CO-OPERATION AND DEVELOPMENT
HUMAN RESOURCES DEVELOPMENT CANADA

ORGANISATION FOR ECONOMIC CO-OPERATION AND DEVELOPMENT

Pursuant to Article 1 of the Convention signed in Paris on 14th December 1960, and which came into force on 30th September 1961, the Organisation for Economic Co-operation and Development (OECD) shall promote policies designed:

- to achieve the highest sustainable economic growth and employment and a rising standard of living in Member countries, while maintaining financial stability, and thus to contribute to the development of the world economy;
- to contribute to sound economic expansion in Member as well as non-member countries in the process of economic development; and
- to contribute to the expansion of world trade on a multilateral, non-discriminatory basis in accordance with international obligations.

The original Member countries of the OECD are Austria, Belgium, Canada, Denmark, France, Germany, Greece, Iceland, Ireland, Italy, Luxembourg, the Netherlands, Norway, Portugal, Spain, Sweden, Switzerland, Turkey, the United Kingdom and the United States. The following countries became Members subsequently through accession at the dates indicated thereafter: Japan (28th April 1964), Finland (28th January 1969), Australia (7th June 1971), New Zealand (29th May 1973), Mexico (18th May 1994), the Czech Republic (21st December 1995), Hungary (7th May 1996), Poland (22nd November 1996) and the Republic of Korea (12th December 1996). The Commission of the European Communities takes part in the work of the OECD (Article 13 of the OECD Convention).

HUMAN RESOURCES DEVELOPMENT CANADA

Human Resources Development Canada (HRDC) was created in 1993 to provide an integrated approach to Canada's national investment in people. It administers programs supporting the income of Canadians and human resources programs linked to the requirements of the national economy and labour market.

HRDC has three fundamental and complementary objectives:

- to help Canadians prepare for, find and keep work, thereby promoting economic growth and adjustment;
- to assist Canadians in their efforts to provide security for themselves and their families, thereby preventing or reducing poverty among Canadians;
- to promote a fair, safe, healthy, stable, cooperative and productive work environment that contributes to the social and economic well-being of all Canadians.

Within HRDC, the National Literacy Secretariat (NLS) has a mission to contribute to the development of a literate Canada in which every citizen is able to participate fully in social, cultural, political and economic life.

STATISTICS CANADA

Statistics Canada, Canada's central statistical agency, has the mandate to "collect, compile, analyse, and publish statistical information relating to the commercial, industrial, financial, social, economic and general activities and condition of the people of Canada." The organization, a federal government agency, is headed by the Chief Statistician of Canada and reports to Parliament through the Minister of Industry Canada.

Statistics Canada provides information to governments at every level and is the source of statistical information for business, labour, academic and social institutions, professional associations, the international statistical community, and the general public. This information is produced at the national and provincial levels and, in some cases, for major population centres and other sub-provincial or "small" areas.

The Agency fosters relations not only within Canada but also throughout the world, by participating in a number of international meetings and professional exchanges. Statistics Canada was responsible for managing the design and implementation of the International Adult Literacy Survey in co-operation with the Educational Testing Service and national research teams.

Publié en français sous le titre :

Littératıe et Société du Savoir

Nouveaux résultats de l'Enquête internationale sur les capacités de lecture et d'écriture des adultes

Published by authority of the Secretary-General of the Organisation for Economic Co-operation and Development, Human Resources Development Canada and the Minister responsible for Statistics Canada

Photo credit: Galien Gavignet

Editorial

*L*iteracy Skills for the Knowledge Society, the second report from the International Adult Literacy Survey (IALS), builds on the data analysis for seven countries presented in the first IALS publication, *Literacy, Economy and Society*, released in December 1995. Literacy data have been collected in five additional countries – Australia, Belgium (Flanders), Ireland, New Zealand and the United Kingdom – and results for them are included in this comparative report. This wider data pool permits more in-depth analysis of the results, as well as more conclusive interpretation. The report is addressed to OECD Member countries and other interested parties; its primary aim is to encourage the development of policies to raise skill levels. The countries included in the report together represent approximately 7 per cent of world population and 55 per cent of world GDP.

The key finding, echoing that of the first report, is that there are significant literacy skill gaps in every country. At least one-quarter of the adult population of the countries surveyed fails to reach the third of five literacy levels. Level 3 is regarded by many experts as the minimum level of competence needed to cope adequately with the complex demands of everyday life and work; after all, knowledge societies will dominate the twenty-first century.

This has profound social and economic implications. Jobs in knowledge societies require high levels of literacy skill for which demands are expected to increase. The fact that many members of the population possess only low skills poses problems for both countries and individuals, and affects families, communities and employers. The title of this publication was chosen to convey the notion that literacy is an essential condition for the active and equitable participation of citizens in social, cultural, political and economic life. Participation is the very premise upon which social stability and economic development are based.

Literacy has long been a key element in education policy. This report suggests its importance to a broader array of policy domains, relating to youth, senior citizens, employment, welfare programmes, social affairs, health, immigration and the administration of justice – to mention just a few.

The search for solutions requires a commitment to concerted action. Governments cannot do it all alone; they can formulate strategies for improvement, but delivering those strategies requires partnerships. Improving education is part of the solution. The IALS results have shown, however, that while high educational attainment improves the chances of achieving high literacy, there is no guaranteed correlation. The active use of literacy skills throughout life is essential. That cannot be legislated, but requires changes in behaviour by individuals and institutions. What is needed is the development of a culture committed to learning. Rather than the separate development of pre-school, primary, secondary and adult education policies, the research suggests a convergence of policy and practice towards comprehensive approaches to lifelong learning for all.

The agenda for a new partnership to raise adult literacy levels would include: improving curricula; strengthening incentives to continue learning throughout the life-span; ensuring that measures to improve literacy are built into strategies for community development; building the capacity of employers to create and offer jobs that both call on and enhance literacy; and encouraging everyday practices which use literacy skills to the full. That last objective calls in particular for the commitment of employers, given their daily opportunity to promote literacy and learning in the workplace.

Literacy Skills for the Knowledge Society should be taken not as the last word on literacy, but rather as a contribution to an evolving body of policy-relevant research. IALS results for some 25 OECD countries will become available over the next two years. Much is already known about the consequences of low levels of literacy; all countries need to address the problem as a matter of priority.

Note to Readers

This publication combines text and figures to present the results of the data analyses and to illustrate differences and similarities among countries. Readers are encouraged to consult Annex C, which contains the data values used for the figures.

The data presented in this report for the United Kingdom are based on combined estimates for Great Britain and Northern Ireland, where separate surveys were conducted. Data for Belgium (Flanders) are representative of the Flemish Community excluding the population of Brussels.

Table of Contents

List of Figures

List of Tables

Introduction

Literacy is a powerful determinant of an individual's life chances and quality of life. The same holds true in the wider context of countries: Overall literacy has a demonstrable effect on the well-being of economies and societies. Previously, policy emphasis was placed on the deleterious effects of "illiteracy" – an approach that proved unhelpful, since it fails to alert the reader to the important facts that all people are literate to a degree, and that no single standard of literacy can be set. The question asked of individuals by the International Adult Literacy Survey (IALS) was not "Can you read?" but rather, "How well do you read?"

The ability to read and write with increased competence is a highly prized job and life skill.

The ability not only to read and write, but to do so with increased competence, is a modern requirement with origins in economic and social changes that are by now familiar: the reach of global money markets; the shift to knowledge-dependent, information-based economies and societies; the stunning increase in the use of computers and other information technologies; the growth of the Internet; and the liberalisation of world trade, to cite a few examples. Forces such as these are changing the nature of both life and work across the OECD area. The result, at least in the advanced OECD economies, is that the number of low-skill jobs is expected to diminish – which means that higher levels of literacy are needed now more than at any time in the past. And the demand for literacy in the future can only increase.

The IALS highlights the strong links between economic growth and labour force skill. Its findings suggest that industrial sectors experiencing growth tend to have a highly literate and highly skilled workforce. The rates of return to education and literacy, reported in Chapter 2, also suggest that what countries, communities, employers and workers spend on literacy should be seen as an investment with long-term pay-off, rather than simply as a cost.

The contribution literacy makes to social well-being is also beginning to be better understood.

The profound importance of literacy for social well-being is also beginning to be better understood. Greater exposure to reading material can provide preschool children with a "formative skill" in their initial development, which will later affect vocabulary, the communication of ideas and experience, the establishment of thinking skills, and healthy social interaction and emotional expression. In school, literacy competence offers an essential foundation for acquiring other, higher-order, cognitive skills. The IALS has amply demonstrated that literacy is an essential work skill; beyond that, it is a life skill that enables social, cultural and political participation. Finally, literacy is the key facility senior citizens require in order to live their later years with dignity and self-confidence even though they see their familiar landscapes altered by social, technological and economic change.

The challenge thus issued is for policy-makers to enable all citizens to have access to environments that both call for and enhance literacy and learning – in their homes, in their communities and at work. Even if we *have* left behind the old paradigm equating learning with schooling, this challenge calls for far more: a commitment to literacy and learning in every aspect of daily life ("life-wide") and continuously throughout the life-span ("lifelong").

The Goals of the Survey

The IALS sought to compare the demonstrated literacy skills of people across countries, cultures and languages.

The IALS venture started out with two underlying goals. The first was to develop measures and scales that would permit useful comparisons of literacy performance among people with a wide range of ability. If such an assessment could be produced, the second goal was to describe and compare the demonstrated literacy skills of people from different countries. The latter objective presented the challenge of comparing literacy across cultures and languages.

The purpose of this report is to extend the analysis initially presented in the publication, *Literacy, Economy and Society: Results of the First International Adult Literacy Survey* (OECD and Statistics Canada, 1995)[1] and in national reports published subsequently.[2] It seeks to do so in two ways. First, it incorporates data for several new countries, previously unavailable. Findings are presented for Australia, Belgium (Flanders), Canada (French- and English-speaking), Germany, Ireland, the Netherlands, New Zealand, Poland, Sweden, Switzerland (French-and German-speaking), the United Kingdom[3] and the United States. Second, it presents the results of new studies and analyses of the IALS dataset; these analyses offer a number of new insights concerning the economic and social importance of literacy in OECD countries.

Organisation of the Report

This introduction presents an overview of new key findings and policy directions suggested by the study. It also reviews the conceptual framework and the definitions of literacy employed in the study, information necessary for an understanding of the literacy levels and performance scales used in the data analysis.

Chapter 1 outlines the overall levels of proficiency as well as the distributions of adult literacy in each country, highlighting the complex ways in which these distributions vary across countries and according to specific factors.

Chapter 2 offers new evidence concerning the economic and wider social benefits of literacy. It includes an analysis of the heretofore unrecognised contributions that literacy makes to productivity and earnings, quality of life, health, and voluntary engagement in community activities. The chapter also presents new findings with respect to the returns to human capital, as measured by assessed literacy skill.

Chapter 3 examines the relationships between literacy and a range of individual characteristics – such as home background, age and gender – and explores how the socio-economic differences observed relate to interactions within families, schools and the workplace.

---

[1]   This first report, published in December 1995, presented comparative data for seven countries: Canada, Germany, the Netherlands, Poland, Sweden, Switzerland and the United States.

[2]   These national reports are from, *inter alia*, Canada (1996), Sweden (1996), United Kingdom (1997), Australia (1997), Switzerland (1997), and Belgium (Flanders) (1997). Results for the Netherlands are given in van der Kamp and Scheeren (1997).

[3]   Separate samples were used for Great Britain and Northern Ireland.

Chapter 4, finally, presents the results of an analysis of adults' readiness to learn in a variety of settings: formally in adult education institutions, non formally in the workplace, and informally at home and in the community. The findings indicate that there are differences among countries in the extent to which a culture of lifelong learning is already established. These differences have important implications for policies to make lifelong learning a reality *for all*, a goal to which OECD education ministers are strongly committed (OECD, 1996).

Annex A describes in detail the definitions of literacy performance on the five levels and three scales employed in the survey. It also presents sample tasks which illustrate the types of materials used for the test, and the demands made on the respondents at the levels of proficiency established for each scale.

Annex B describes how the survey was conducted in each country. It reports on survey coverage, language, and sample yields. Information about the response rates achieved, deviations from the recommended design, and the quality of the datasets is also provided.

Annex C is the Statistical Annex. It presents, for each figure in the main body of text that is based on IALS data, the underlying data values plus, where applicable, the standard errors associated with those values.

Finally, Annex D lists the participants in the project, notably the national study managers, the international study team, and the authors of this report.

As is the case in any household survey, the IALS results contain a degree of error, although the standard errors of the estimates are typically quite small.

Data Quality and Comparability

The task pool developed for the IALS was large, and the materials were selected from everyday tasks judged to be culturally appropriate and relevant by all countries represented in the survey. Once the selection of test items was agreed, with nearly half of the items coming from European countries and the other half from North America, each country adapted the materials to their own languages using a set of standard guidelines. This ensured that the psychometric properties (such as layout, design and print size) of the materials were identical for everyone.

The pool of test items was developed collaboratively and piloted in each country to ensure that each item functioned in the same way across languages and cultures. 175 literacy tasks were constructed for the field test. Of the tasks that proved valid across cultures, 114 were selected in a way that ensured a range of difficulty and adequate representation of different contexts, such as home, work and community.

Subtle differences in survey design and implementation, and in the pattern of non-response across languages and cultures, do introduce some error into the literacy estimates. Standard errors of estimates are therefore included in the Statistical Annex to this report (Annex C). Statistics Canada, the Educational Testing Service, and the national study teams have performed exhaustive data analyses to understand the nature and extent of error associated with the differences in design and implementation. Notes to figures and tables are used to alert readers whenever errors may have occurred that introduce bias and affect interpretation.

Detailed information about all aspects of survey design, implementation and the quality of data obtained is presented in Murray et al. (1997).

The Definition of Literacy

Throughout this report, the term "literacy" is used to refer to a particular skill – namely, the ability to understand and employ printed information in daily activities at home, at work and in the community – to achieve one's goals, and to develop one's knowledge and potential. In denoting a broad set of information-processing competencies, this conceptual approach points to the multiplicity of skills that constitute literacy in advanced industrialised countries. In contrast, a term such as "illiteracy", which is still widely used in many countries, fails to alert the reader to the important facts that people are literate to a degree, and that no single standard of literacy can meaningfully be set.

The IALS was designed to measure adult literacy skills, as determined by assessed proficiency levels, using test materials derived from specific contexts within countries. The conceptual framework is based on a theory of adult reading that links levels of reading difficulty to attributes of the text and the tasks the reader must perform; the theory also acknowledges the various uses of literacy in everyday life (Kirsch and Mosenthal, 1990). The IALS reported on three literacy domains instead of a single measure:

- *Prose literacy* – the knowledge and skills needed to understand and use information from texts, including editorials, news stories, poems and fiction;

- *Document literacy* – the knowledge and skills required to locate and use information contained in various formats, including job applications, payroll forms, transportation schedules, maps, tables and graphics; and

- *Quantitative literacy* – the knowledge and skills required to apply arithmetic operations, either alone or sequentially, to numbers embedded in printed materials, such as balancing a cheque-book, figuring out a tip, completing an order form, or determining the amount of interest on a loan from an advertisement.

The IALS employed a sophisticated testing and scaling method developed and applied by the Educational Testing Service of Princeton, New Jersey, to derive proficiency scores for populations. The method employs Item Response Theory[4] to estimate both item difficulty and proficiency, and has been used successfully in several large-scale studies of literacy performance and educational achievement.[5] The proficiency scores for each scale ranged from 0-500, with 0 representing the lowest ability. Each scale was then grouped into five empirically determined literacy skill levels.[6] With the help of a common yardstick, the proficiency scores provide detailed portraits of the skills of the population. In addition, skill profiles can be estimated for specific sub-populations. Thus, the skill levels of those aged 16-25 can be compared with those of adults aged 56-65 or, for the countries that collected such data, for senior citizens aged 66-74.

---

[4]   Annex A presents a detailed description of the testing and scaling methodology used in the assessment.

[5]   Notably the National Adult Literacy Survey undertaken in the United States in the early 1990s, as well as the Third International Mathematics and Science Study undertaken in 1994 and 1995 under the auspices of the International Association for the Evaluation of Educational Achievement (IEA).

[6]   Levels 4 and 5 are grouped together for the purpose of the analyses presented in this report. The reason is that there are few people at the highest skill level in some countries, and so reliable estimates cannot be obtained in those cases.

Figure I.1 illustrates the scale range, and the numerical values that define the five skill levels. These values are the same across the three scales. The five proficiency levels are determined by the qualitative shifts in the skills and strategies required to succeed at various tasks along the scales, ranging from simple to complex. This scaling method takes account of the "distance" between successive levels of information-processing skills, and allows for an analysis of performance along a range of literacy tasks.

FIGURE I.1

IRT scale: Range and skill level values

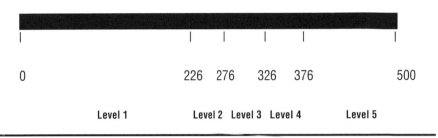

| 0 | 226 | 276 | 326 | 376 | 500 |

Level 1 Level 2 Level 3 Level 4 Level 5

IRT = Item Response Theory.

All test items used in the assessment required each level respondents to work with materials derived from everyday applications; multiple-choice was not used. These items included labels from medicine bottles, simple invoices and receipts, directions for assembling things, transportation maps, prose articles from newspapers and magazines, and items that require basic mathematical calculations. Scale score ranges and task characteristics are described in Figure I.2. Collectively, the items can predict with a high degree of accuracy whether a respondent would be able to handle unfamiliar texts with similar attributes of difficulty. To be placed at a particular skill level, respondents have to consistently perform tasks correctly at that level. The threshold for consistent performance was set at 80 per cent. It is this predictability of the respondent's ability to deal with the unfamiliar that makes literacy such a strategic asset for individuals and countries.

The survey does not challenge the reality that the great majority of adults in OECD countries can read, but it does question whether a proportion of them can read well enough to obtain consistently the correct answers on test items that represent the range of difficulty found in tasks most people encounter in their daily lives. The ability to read printed materials carefully and critically, while looking for key pieces of information, is a highly prized workplace skill.

FIGURE I.2
Scale score ranges and task samples

	Prose	Document	Quantitative
Level 1 (0 to 225)	Most of the tasks at this level require the reader to locate one piece of information in the text that is identical to or synonymous with the information given in the directive. If a plausible incorrect answer is present in the text, it tends not to be near the correct information.	Most of the tasks at this level require the reader to locate a piece of information based on a literal match. Distracting information, if present, is typically located away from the correct answer. Some tasks may direct the reader to enter personal information onto a form.	Although no quantitative tasks used in the IALS fall below the score value of 225, experience suggests that such tasks would require the reader to perform a single, relatively simple operation (usually addition) for which either the numbers are already entered onto the given document and the operation is stipulated, or the numbers are provided and the operation does not require the reader to find the numbers.
Level 2 (226 to 275)	Tasks at this level require the reader to locate one or more pieces of information in the text, but several distractors may be present, or low-level inferences may be required. Tasks at this level also begin to ask readers to integrate two or more pieces of information, or to compare and contrast information.	Document tasks at this level are somewhat more varied. While a few still require the reader to match on a single feature, more distracting information may be present or the match may require a low-level inference. Some tasks at this level may require the reader to enter information onto a form or to sift through information in a document.	Tasks at this level typically require readers to perform a single arithmetic operation (frequently addition or subtrac-tion) using numbers that are easily located in the text or document. The operation to be performed may be easily inferred from the wording of the question or the format of the material (for example, a bank deposit form or an order form).
Level 3 (276 to 325)	Tasks at this level direct readers to search texts to match pieces of information that require low-level inferences or that meet specified conditions. Sometimes the reader is required to identify several pieces of information that are located in different sentences or paragraphs rather than in a single sentence. Readers may also be asked to integrate or to compare and contrast information across paragraphs or sections of text.	Tasks at this level are the most varied. Some require the reader to make literal or synonymous matches, but usually the matches require the reader to take conditional information into account or to match on multiple features of informa-tion. Some tasks at this level require the reader to integrate information from one or more displays. Other tasks ask the reader to cycle through a document to provide multiple responses.	Tasks at this level typically require the reader to perform a single operation. However, the operations become more varied – some multiplication and division tasks are involved at this level. Sometimes two or more numbers are needed to solve the problem, and the numbers are frequently embedded in more complex displays. While semantic relation terms such as "how many" or "calculate the difference" are often used, some of the tasks require the reader to make higher-order inferences to determine the appropriate operation.
Level 4 (326 to 375)	These tasks require readers to perform multiple-feature matching or to provide several responses in cases where the requested information must be identified through text-based inferences. Tasks at this level may also require the reader to integrate or contrast pieces of information, sometimes presented in relatively lengthy texts. Typically, these texts contain more distracting information and the information that is requested is more abstract.	Tasks at this level, like those in the previous levels, ask the reader to match on multiple features of information, to cycle through documents, and to integrate information; frequently, however, these tasks require the reader to make higher-order inferences to arrive at the correct answer. Sometimes, conditional information present in the document must be taken into account by the reader.	With one exception, the tasks at this level require the reader to perform a single arithmetic operation where typically either the quantities or the operation are not easily determined. That is, for most of the tasks at this level, the question or directive does not provide a semantic relation term such as "how many" or "calculate the difference" to help the reader.
Level 5 (376 to 500)	Some tasks at this level require the reader to search for information in dense text that contains a number of plausible distractors. Some require readers to make high-level inferences or to use specialised knowledge.	Tasks at this level require the reader to search through complex displays of information that contain multiple distractors, to make high-level inferences, process conditional information, or to use specialised knowledge.	These tasks require readers to perform multiple operations sequentially, and they must disembed the features of the problem from the material provided or rely on background knowledge to determine the quantities or operations needed.

Survey Administration

The survey was conducted in homes by experienced interviewers who administered the test in a neutral manner. The survey design combined educational testing techniques with those of household survey research.[7] Respondents were first asked a series of questions to obtain background and demographic information on variables such as educational attainment, literacy practices at work and at home, labour force status, adult education participation, and literacy self-assessment. Once this background questionnaire was completed, the interviewer presented a booklet containing six simple tasks. If the respondent failed to complete at least two of these correctly, the interview was adjourned. Respondents who completed two or more tasks correctly were then given a much larger variety of tasks, printed in a separate booklet. The assessment was not timed, and respondents were urged to try each exercise. Respondents were thus given maximum opportunity to demonstrate their skills.

The IALS represents a first, systematic attempt at fielding a large-scale assessment of adult skills across different countries. The survey is unique, but it also has limitations.

The IALS represents a first attempt at undertaking a large-scale assessment of adult skills at the international level. The need to generate valid and reliable estimates over a wide range of languages and cultures demanded much of both theory and statistical process for quality assurance. The study finally furnished a body of empirical evidence that validated the conceptual framework underlying the project and has, in certain respects, set a new standard for quality assurance (see Murray *et al.,* 1997). Most importantly, however, the IALS has demonstrated that literacy does matter, both economically and socially, and that its population distribution can be changed through policy.

Like any other survey-based assessment, the IALS also has its limitations. First among these is the limited sample size available for most countries. Testing of the sort employed for the IALS is expensive, and the survey budgets provided in many countries were insufficient to field very large samples. Second, the response rates are not as high as one would have hoped – Australia excepted. Several aspects of the survey methodology can be improved – and indeed have been as new rounds of data collection have been undertaken. Finally, the IALS offers data on a single, albeit important, skill. Until similarly credible data are collected for other major skill areas, such as problem solving or team work, it will not be possible to examine the relationships that may exist between literacy and these other skills.

Key Findings and New Perspectives

The results, published in *Literacy, Economy and Society* (OECD and Statistics Canada, 1995), can be summarised in eight points:

- Important differences in literacy skill exist, both within and among countries. These differences are large enough to matter both socially and economically.

- Literacy is strongly associated with economic life chances and well-being. It affects, *inter alia*, employment stability, the incidence of unemployment and income.

- In North America and several European countries, scores on the quantitative scale show the strongest correlation with income. There is a large "wage premium" in Canada, Ireland, the United Kingdom and the United States for those whose literacy proficiency is at the highest level (level 4/5).

---

[7] Details about the survey administration procedures, achieved sample sizes and response rates are provided in Annex B.

- Literacy levels are clearly linked to occupations and industries; some occupations call for high-level skills, others intermediate skills.

- The relationship between literacy proficiency and educational attainment is complex. Although the association is strong, there are some surprising exceptions. For example, many adults have managed to attain a relatively high level of literacy proficiency despite a low level of education; conversely, there are some who have low literacy skills despite a high level of education. Objective skill testing is a tool for more rigorous evaluation of workforce skills.

- Low skills are found not just among marginalised groups, but among significant proportions of adult populations in the countries surveyed. The data show that adult education and training programmes are less likely to reach those with low skills, who need them most.

- Adults with low literacy skills do not usually consider that their lack of skills presents them with any difficulties. When asked if their reading skills were sufficient to meet everyday needs, respondents replied overwhelmingly that they were, regardless of tested skill levels. This may reflect the fact that many respondents are in jobs that do not require them to use literacy, a situation that is likely to change as the knowledge society matures.

- Literacy skills, like muscles, are maintained and strengthened through regular use. While schooling provides an essential foundation, the evidence suggests that only through using literacy skills in daily activities – both at home and at work – will higher levels of performance be attained.

This new report offers a number of additional insights into how literacy is related to economic and social well-being.

This report builds on the analysis presented in *Literacy, Economy and Society*, and offers important additional insights into the economic and social dimension of literacy in a range of OECD countries. Among these are the following:

- *Literacy plays an important role in the determination of wages in all countries except Poland. The contribution of literacy comes on top of the effect of education on earnings.* Economists have long argued that the labour market functions as a market for skill, a market in which the demand for skill in work organisations and production processes is matched with the supply of skill offered by the labour force. Traditionally, educational attainment and experience – as measured by age or employment history – have been used as proxy measures of skill in the estimation of wage equations. The IALS data suggest that these analyses have been based on two mistaken assumptions: that data on initial educational attainment provide equivalent measures of skill across countries, and that national labour markets offer and value experience in the same way. Data presented in this publication show clearly that educational attainment is a poor proxy for skill, that economies differ greatly with regard to skills demanded, and that experience and skills are rewarded differently in different OECD countries.

- *The role literacy plays in the determination of wages is greater in economies that are more flexible and open.* As measured by wage premiums, the IALS data reveal that the economic returns to literacy, when controlling for education, are largest in "open" economies such as Canada and the United States. This fact has important implications for other OECD countries engaged in making their labour markets more flexible and efficient. First, steps must be taken to ensure an adequate supply of skill, given the demand of the economy. OECD countries have long relied on the educational system to provide the requisite supply of (increasingly) skilled workers. With OECD labour forces replenishing themselves at a rate of roughly 3 per cent per annum, countries can no longer rely on schools only but need to target low-skill adults, the majority of whom are currently in the labour force. Second, as part of the move towards more efficient markets for skill, policy-makers must encourage employers to demand and reward high skills while at the same time, ensuring that adequate learning opportunities are available to those economically or socially at risk because of their low skills.

- *Literacy outcomes vary considerably according to socio-economic status in some, but not all, of the countries investigated.* Public policy in most OECD countries aims to reduce social disparity in economic opportunity. Economic inequality has tended to rise over the past two decades in most countries, despite massive investment in education. Results indicate that literacy outcomes in some countries vary considerably by socio-economic status, with youth from disadvantaged backgrounds performing more poorly than could be expected, given education and experience. These disadvantaged individuals will bear large reductions in lifetime earnings as a result. Not only is this unfair, but there is a large cost to society as well, for example, in terms of tax revenue forgone. The absence of disparity in some countries suggests that the problem can be addressed through policy.

References

AUSTRALIA (1997), *Aspects of Literacy: Assessed Skill Levels*, Australian Bureau of Statistics, Canberra.

BELGIUM (Flanders) (1997), *Hoe geletterd en gecijferd is Vlaanderen? Functionele taal- en rekenvaardigheden in internationaal perspectief*, Garant, Leuven.

CANADA (1996), *Reading the Future: A Portrait of Literacy in Canada*, Statistics Canada and Human Resources Development Canada, Ottawa.

KIRSCH, I.S. and MOSENTHAL, P.B. (1990), "Exploring document literacy: Variables underlying the performance of young adults", *Reading Research Quarterly*, Vol. 25, pp. 5-30.

MURRAY, T.S., KIRSCH, I.S. and JENKINS, L.B. (Eds.) (1997), *Adult Literacy in OECD Countries: Technical Report on the First International Adult Literacy Survey,* National Center for Education Statistics, United States Department of Education, Washington, DC.

OECD (1996), *Lifelong Learning for All*, Paris.

OECD and STATISTICS CANADA (1995), *Literacy, Economy and Society: Results of the First International Adult Literacy Survey*, Paris and Ottawa.

SWEDEN (1996), *Grunden för fortsatt lärande: En internationell jämförande studie av vuxnas förmåga att förstå och använda tryckt och skriven information*, National Board of Education, Skolverket, Stockholm.

SWITZERLAND (République et Canton de Genève) (1997), *La Littératie à Genève: Enquête sur les compétences des adultes dans la vie quotidienne en lecture, écriture et calcul*, Service de la Recherche en Education, Département de l'instruction publique, Genève.

UNITED KINGDOM (1997), *Adult Literacy in Britain*, Office for National Statistics, London.

VAN DER KAMP, M. and SCHEEREN, J. (1997), *Functionele taal- en rekenvaardigheden van oudere volwassenen in Nederland*, Max Goote Kenniscentrum, University of Amsterdam, Amsterdam.

Chapter 1

Distributions of Adult Literacy

The distribution of literacy skills in the adult population differs from country to country.

1.1 Introduction

Two straightforward messages emerge from the survey: the distribution of adult literacy skills differs from country to country; and these skills really do matter, at work and in everyday life. The purpose of this first chapter is to present the survey's findings regarding literacy distribution and its links with individual characteristics. Subsequent chapters examine the sources and consequences of differences in skill, between individuals and countries.[1]

1.2 Basic Distributions

The range of literacy scores is wide in all countries, as Figure 1.1 shows. Even though some countries have higher mean scores than others, all have some proportion of their population with low scores. Figure 1.1 indicates that countries differ in how literacy skills are distributed. On the quantitative scale, for example, the difference between the score at the 25th percentile and that at the 75th percentile in Germany and the Netherlands is small compared to the difference between these points in Ireland, Poland, the United Kingdom and the United States. The average score thus offers only partial information about adult literacy in a country, since it can be relatively high even when there are many in the population with quite low scores. Such is the case with both language groups in Switzerland; where the average score is among the highest on the document and quantitative scales, yet the 5th percentile is among the lowest.

Because the distribution of literacy is as important as the average, the survey findings concerning the literacy scores are reported in levels of proficiency (see Annex A for a detailed description). Figures 1.2a-c, show significant numbers of adults with literacy skills no higher than level 1 in all countries. Also to be found in all countries are significant numbers at the highest skill level. Figures 1.2a-c also show that literacy comparisons across countries are not simple, because the distribution differs from country to country in several respects.

---

[1] In most of the participating countries the data were collected in 1994. In some the data collection occurred in 1995 or 1996. These minor differences in timing do not affect comparability, given that the surveys covered the entire population aged 16-65 in all countries.

FIGURE 1.1

Distribution of literacy scores

A. Mean scores with .95 confidence interval and scores at 5th, 25th, 75th and 95th
percentiles on the **prose** literacy scale, 1994-1995

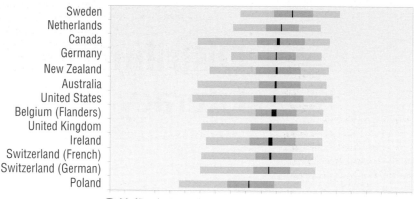

Mean scores for prose, document and quantitative skills do not differ by a large amount for most of the countries, but there are important differences in the way skills are distributed. In some countries, the score difference between the 5th and 95th percentile is rather small, indicating little variation of skills within the country (Germany is an example on the prose scale). Other countries show greater variation through a wider percentile gap (Ireland is an example on the prose scale).

The figures show the mean score in each country with the confidence interval for this average as well as the scores at several percentiles, illustrating how countries differ both in mean score and in the distribution of prose, document and quantitative literacy skills.

B. Mean scores with .95 confidence interval and scores at 5th, 25th, 75th and 95th
percentiles on the **document** literacy scale, 1994-1995

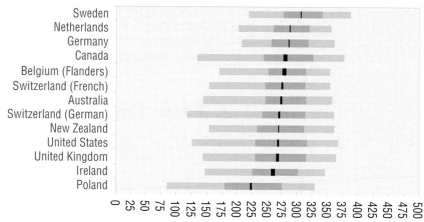

C. Mean scores with .95 confidence interval and scores at 5th, 25th, 75th and 95th
percentiles on the **quantitative** literacy scale, 1994-1995

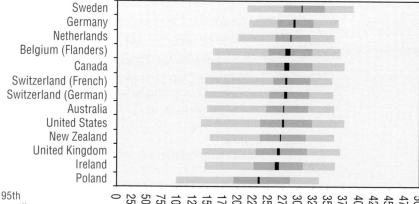

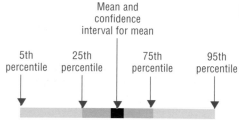

Countries are ranked by mean score differences.
Source: International Adult Literacy Survey, 1994-1995.

Box 1A   Reading the Figures

Figure 1.2 displays information in a novel way. The bars for each country are stacked; each section represents the proportion at a particular level. Rather than being stacked from the zero point, the bars are anchored between literacy levels – allowing much readier comparison of the relative proportions of the population found to be at particular levels across countries. For example, the bars are lined up so that the proportions at levels 1 and 2 are below the reference line and those at levels 3 and 4/5 above the line. The order of countries is based on the proportion of the population above the reference line. In Figure 1.2b, for example, Sweden's bar is furthest left, since that country has the largest proportion of its population at levels 3 and 4/5 on the document scale.

On the prose scale, Ireland, the United Kingdom and the United States have a comparatively large proportion at level 1 (see Figure 1.2a). But the United States also has a larger proportion at level 4/5 compared with Belgium (Flanders), Germany and the Netherlands. The countries also differ in their ranking from scale to scale. On the prose scale, the German-speaking Swiss population has a relatively small proportion at level 4/5 (see Figure 1.2a) – smaller than Australia, Ireland or New Zealand, for example. Yet on the quantitative scale at level 4/5 (see Figure 1.2c), the Swiss-German group has a larger proportion than Ireland or New Zealand, one that is the same as that of Australia. Only Sweden (highest on all scales) and Poland (lowest on all) have a consistent relationship to the other countries. Thus, aside from these two, it is not very useful to attempt to rank countries using the IALS results; the relationships are too complex, varying from scale to scale and yielding different comparisons from level to level. Rather, it is important to look at how literacy is related to important social and economic factors.

It is useful to look briefly at the skill distributions within each country:

- Australia has the same skill distribution across the three scales. The overall pattern of literacy proficiency in Australia is close to those of Canada and New Zealand, especially on the prose scale, with relatively large proportions of the population scoring at levels 1 and 4/5.

- Flanders in Belgium is similar in many ways to the Netherlands, but there are somewhat larger proportions at level 1 and smaller proportions at level 4/5, especially on the prose and quantitative scales. The distributions for these two groups are very close on the document scale. And, as is the case in the Netherlands, there is a relatively large proportion at level 3 on the prose and document scales.

- Canada has relatively large proportions at both low and high levels. In this it is similar to Australia and, on prose, to New Zealand.

- In Germany, as in the Netherlands, there are only small numbers at level 1 on any scale. However, on the prose and document scales, there are relatively large proportions at levels 2 and 3. Only on the quantitative scale does Germany have a large population share at level 4/5.

- Ireland has relatively large proportions at levels 1 and 2 compared to the other countries. On all scales the proportion at level 1 is second largest, and that at level 4/5 second smallest.

- The Netherlands has, like Sweden, relatively fewer adults at the lowest levels on all three scales, but only the document scale shows a comparatively large number at level 4/5. On all scales, there are large numbers at level 3.

FIGURE 1.2
Comparative distribution of literacy levels

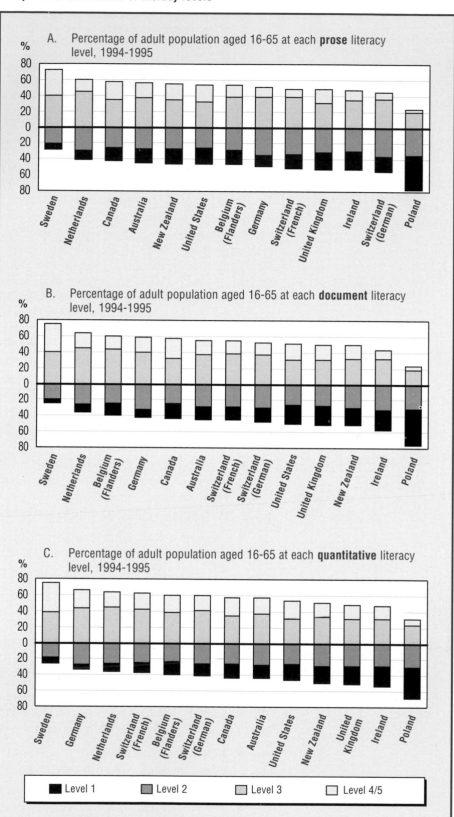

All countries have some proportion of their adult population at each literacy level on the prose, document and quantitative scales, but there are substantial differences between countries in the proportions at a given level. For example, while the Netherlands has a large proportion of its population at prose skill levels 3 and 4/5, the proportion at the highest level is considerably smaller than the proportion at this level in Sweden.

The figure shows the estimated proportion of the adult population at each of the prose, document and quantitative literacy levels for each country. Proportions at levels 1 and 2 are represented by the bar segments below the reference line and the proportions at levels 3 and 4/5 by the bar segments above the line.

A. Percentage of adult population aged 16-65 at each **prose** literacy level, 1994-1995

B. Percentage of adult population aged 16-65 at each **document** literacy level, 1994-1995

C. Percentage of adult population aged 16-65 at each **quantitative** literacy level, 1994-1995

Level 1   Level 2   Level 3   Level 4/5

Countries are ranked by the proportion in levels 3 and 4/5.

Source: International Adult Literacy Survey, 1994-1995.

- New Zealand has relatively fewer adults at level 4/5 on the quantitative scale compared with the prose and document scales. On prose and document, New Zealand has a similar distribution to that observed in Australia. But on the quantitative scale, there are comparatively fewer adults at level 4/5 in New Zealand than Australia.

- Poland has large proportions at lower levels on all scales. The Polish distribution reflects the history of social and economic change in that country.

- Sweden has comparatively fewer adults at level 1 on all three scales – but though smaller than in other countries, that number is not negligible. The proportions at level 4/5 are also comparatively large on all three scales.

- The two language groups in Switzerland are similar at all levels on all three scales. On all scales, but especially on document and quantitative, the proportions at level 1 are small.

- The United Kingdom and Ireland have very similar proportions above level 2 and below level 3, but the distribution in the United Kingdom is always somewhat higher. That is, there is a larger population share at level 4/5 and fewer at levels 3 and 1 in the United Kingdom.

- The United States has relatively large proportions at level 1 on all scales, but the numbers at level 4/5 are also large on the prose and quantitative scales. Thus, there is a wide spread of performance in this country. Indeed, as Figures 1.1a-c show, the spread between the 25th and 75th percentile (the interquartile range) on the prose scale is larger in the United States than in any other country, and the country's interquartile range is second largest on the other two scales.

Despite the considerable variation in distribution, literacy in each country has an impact on social and economic life. Chapters 2 and 3 will explore the ways in which literacy affects how people live and work. Meanwhile, the remainder of this chapter examines relationships between literacy proficiency and other individual characteristics.

1.3 Education, Age and Literacy

There is a strong connection between educational attainment and literacy performance, but the relationship is not straightforward.

Older age groups have, on average, received less education than younger age groups, and the differences show up also in literacy proficiency.

Most people learn to read in school, a setting that can also offer ongoing opportunities to use and improve literacy. It is therefore not surprising that there are strong connections between educational attainment and adult literacy. Some may attribute the differences in literacy displayed in Figures 1.1 and 1.2 to differences in the quality of education, but the IALS data suggest that the picture is considerably more complicated.

First, the countries differ significantly in the proportion of their adult population by age group who have different levels of education (see Figure 1.3). For example, half or more of those aged 25-64 in Australia, Belgium and Ireland had not completed upper secondary education in 1994, but a much smaller proportion, only 16 per cent, had not completed this level of education in Germany. It is not surprising, then, that fewer Germans than Australians, Belgians and Irish are at level 1. On the other hand, 12 per cent of that age group in the United Kingdom had completed university, against 21 per cent in the Netherlands and 24 per cent in the United States (OECD, 1996). Again, that a larger proportion of the adult population in the Netherlands or the United States is at level 4/5 should therefore not be surprising. Figure 1.3 shows, moreover, that older age groups have received less education than younger age groups – a fact that is reflected in differences in literacy proficiency between age groups.

However, differences in educational attainment are not the only factors underlying differences in adult literacy. Figures 1.4a-c show the average score in each country for successive levels of education for the prose, document and quantitative scales. While in every country the average score increases as education increases, there are still marked differences between countries at a given level. More telling are the inconsistencies in relative position across levels of educational attainment. While the average for those with less than completed upper secondary education in the United States is among the lowest of the countries, the average in that country for those who have obtained some tertiary-level education is among the highest.

In some countries, respondents with low levels of initial education do more poorly than predicted, given the performance of their fellow citizens with higher levels of education. Questions of whether specific policies led to this and whether the discrepancy should be addressed, while raised by the IALS data, cannot be answered by them. What the data do suggest, however, is that if literacy is important to social and economic success, then those with low levels of education in some countries may be at more of a disadvantage than those with low education in other countries. This calls perhaps for more focused effort to enable those with low education to acquire more skills.

Countries differ widely with regard to the educational attainment of their adult populations. For example, Belgium and Ireland have relatively small proportions in all age groups above 35 who have completed secondary school, in contrast to Germany, Switzerland and the United States, where large proportions in all age groups have at least this level of education. There are also considerable within-country differences in educational attainment. While overall attainment is high in Canada, Poland and the United Kingdom, there is a large difference between older and younger adults. In contrast, there is little age difference in attainment in Australia.

The figure shows the proportion of adults in an age group who have received at least upper secondary education, including those who have acquired tertiary education, for each country.

FIGURE 1.3

Educational attainment by age

Percentage of population aged 25-64 with upper secondary education, by age group, 1994

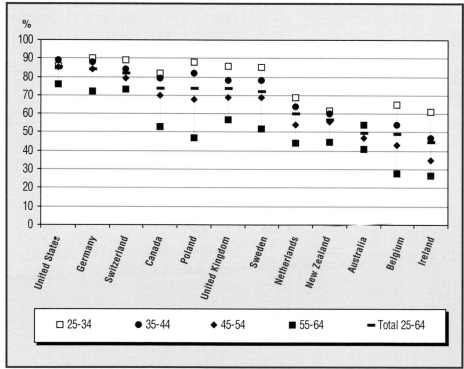

Countries are ranked by the proportion of persons aged 25-64 who completed upper secondary education.

Source: OECD, *Education at a Glance: OECD Indicators* (1996).

FIGURE 1.4

Educational attainment and literacy proficiency

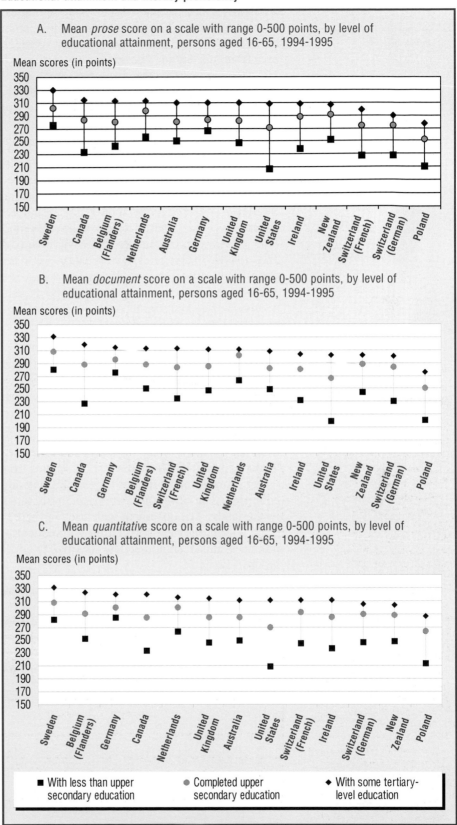

A.   Mean *prose* score on a scale with range 0-500 points, by level of educational attainment, persons aged 16-65, 1994-1995

B.   Mean *document* score on a scale with range 0-500 points, by level of educational attainment, persons aged 16-65, 1994-1995

C.   Mean *quantitativ*e score on a scale with range 0-500 points, by level of educational attainment, persons aged 16-65, 1994-1995

■ With less than upper secondary education   ● Completed upper secondary education   ◆ With some tertiary-level education

Countries are ranked by the mean prose literacy score of those with some tertiary education.
Source: International Adult Literacy Survey, 1994-1995.

Individuals who have not completed secondary school score lower, on average, than those who have completed secondary school. Those who have only graduated from secondary school have, in turn, lower average scores than those who completed some tertiary education. In most countries, the difference between those without and with secondary graduation is greater than the difference between the latter and those with some tertiary education.

This figure shows the mean literacy score of persons at three different levels of educational attainment: less than upper secondary education; secondary school graduation; and completion of some form of tertiary education.

In some countries those with little schooling find ways to acquire literacy skills that are not so easily found in others.

Figure 1.4 also shows that countries differ most at the lowest education levels. The range of country average scores for those who have not completed upper secondary school is much larger than the range of scores for those who received education at the tertiary level. For example, on the document scale the difference between the lowest and highest country averages for those with low education is over 80 points, but for those with some tertiary education the difference is near 55. The differences on the other two scales are not as large, but still notable. This suggests that in some countries those with low education find ways to acquire literacy skills that are not available, or so easily found, in others. It also suggests that countries whose overall average scores are low might best invest in strengthening adult education, rather than expanding the intake capacity of tertiary education.

Figure 1.5 also indicates that there are marked differences among the countries in the extent to which adults with low education may nonetheless obtain high levels of literacy skill. In Belgium (Flanders), Germany, the Netherlands and Sweden over 40 per cent of those who have not completed upper secondary school nevertheless have literacy scores at level 3 or 4/5 on the document scale. At the other extreme, in Ireland, Poland, Switzerland and the United States, fewer than 25 per cent of those with low education are in these two highest levels. Ranking similarities between overall document literacy (Figure 1.2b) and on the literacy of adults with low education (Figure 1.5) suggest that much of the difference in average literacy skills from country to country is due to differences among the least, rather than most, educated.

It is quite possible to acquire high levels of literacy skills by other means than through education.

That large numbers of adults are able to reach high levels of literacy without high levels of education clearly suggests that while education is the most common route to skill, it is quite possible to acquire literacy skills via other means. Chapter 4 looks at some of the ways in which education beyond formal schooling plays a role in skill development.

Because young people have, on average, received more initial education than older age groups, it would logically follow that there are larger proportions of young adults with higher literacy skills. As Figure 1.6 shows, 16-25-year-olds do have larger proportions at higher literacy levels compared to 46-55-year-olds in all countries. The differences are particularly large in Belgium (Flanders) and the Netherlands. The document scale used in Figure 1.6 is deliberately chosen as the scale with the lowest correlation with education and the highest with literacy practices, and so should be less sensitive to educational differences between age groups.

As younger, more highly skilled workers enter the labour force, governments will have to develop policies to respond to the need for programmes targeting lower-skilled older workers, many of whom may reasonably expect to continue working for many years. Chapter 3 provides further analysis and information on the role of age in literacy skill development.

Countries differ markedly in population percentages who have acquired medium to high document literacy skills even though their formal educational attainment is low. In Sweden and Germany over 50 per cent of those with low education have high literacy skills. In contrast, fewer than 25 per cent of those with low education in Ireland, Poland, French- and German-speaking Switzerland and the United States have skills at this level. The ranking of countries in this figure is similar to that in Figure 1.2b, which suggests that much of the overall difference between countries is explained by the differences in literacy skills of the least educated.

Each bar represents the proportion of adults who have not completed upper secondary education but who have medium to high literacy skills.

FIGURE 1.5

Document literacy levels among low-educated adults

Proportion of adults aged 16-65 who have not completed upper secondary education, but who nevertheless score at levels 3 and 4/5 on the document scale, 1994-1995

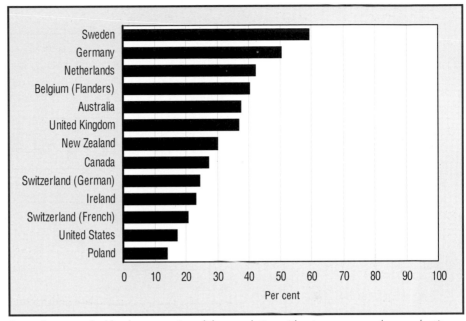

Countries are ranked by the proportion of the population without upper secondary graduation who are at levels 3 and 4/5.
Source: International Adult Literacy Survey, 1994-1995.

1.4 Parents' Education and Socio-economic Status

Research findings show consistently that parents with higher levels of education and literacy are in a better position to build a strong foundation for literacy in their children[2]. Because enhanced literacy and education translate into higher incomes, parents in this category may be able to provide a richer home environment and send their children to better schools. Higher literacy skills also facilitate literacy practices, so well-to-do parents are likely to offer literacy-rich environments for their children. Because there is such a close connection in literacy across generations, improvements in the literacy of adults benefit children as well.

Figure 1.7 compares the average socio-economic index of the 14-year-old students who scored in the lowest 15 per cent on the IEA Reading Literacy Study with the average of the whole 14-year-old population in their country[3]. In every country the low-scoring students generally came from households with reduced economic and social resources. The difference in the socio-economic index score for all students and for students scoring in the lowest 15 per cent was relatively smaller in British Columbia (Canada) and larger in Germany and Switzerland.

---

[2]   For a general source, see Haveman and Wolfe (1994). Reviews of research literature and results of specific analyses involving mother-child interactions and development of literacy skills using experimental field trials are presented in Leibowitz (1974) and Gross *et al*. (1997).

[3]   The socio-economic index is based on student reports of parental education and home possessions and is standardised within each country. For all student populations participating in the IEA Reading Literacy Study (which included more than the 14-year-old students included here) in a country, the mean is 0 and the standard deviation is 1. Note that the Canadian data represent only students in the province of British Columbia and are therefore not representative of the country as a whole.

FIGURE 1.6

Literacy proficiency and age

Proportion of persons aged 16-25 and 46-55 who are at each document literacy level, 1994-1995

In all countries the literacy skills of the younger age group are higher than those of the older group. In some, Belgium (Flanders) and the Netherlands, for example, the difference in skill is large.

The left bar of each pair represents the proportion of persons aged 16-25 at each document literacy level and the right bar the proportion of those aged 46-55 at each proficiency level. The reference line lies between level 2 and level 3.

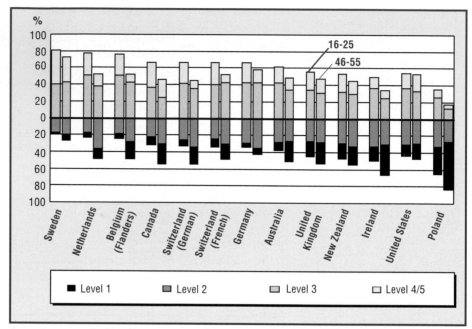

Countries are ranked by the proportion of the population aged 16-25 who are at levels 3 and 4/5.

Source: International Adult Literacy Survey, 1994-1995.

FIGURE 1.7

Socio-economic status of 14-year-old students with low reading scores

Mean of socio-economic index score for all students and for students scoring in the lowest 15 per cent, 1990-1991

In all countries the mean socio-economic index for low-scoring students is significantly lower than the overall mean. This indicates that there is a strong relationship between skill and socio-economic status.

This figure compares the mean socio-economic index for 14-year-old students who scored low on the IEA Reading Literacy Study with that for all 14-year-old students. Bars above the zero point show the mean socio-economic index for all students; bars below that point show the index for the students scoring in the lowest 15 per cent in reading achievement.

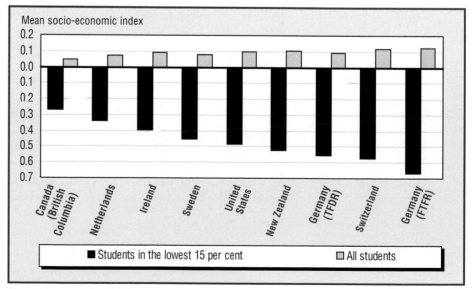

Countries are ranked by the mean socio-economic index for the lowest-scoring 15 per cent of students.

Source: IEA, Reading Literacy Study, 1991.

Figure 1.8 shows a similar connection between parental education and the performance of 8th-grade students in mathematics on the IEA Third International Mathematics and Science Study (TIMSS). Here, too, there is a large and significant difference between the scores of children whose parents received some tertiary education and those of children whose parents did not complete upper secondary school. Eighth-grade mathematics achievement is high in Belgium (Flemish Community) compared with the United States, where there are large differences in achievement between children whose parents have high and low levels of education.

Effects of parental education are also found for the adults who participated in the IALS. As Figure 1.9 shows, even when individuals have received the same level of education (here all are secondary school graduates), differences in the father's educational background still have an impact on the patterns of performance in prose literacy[4]. In every country except Canada and New Zealand, there is a noticeably larger proportion above level 3 when the father has completed secondary education or more. Even in Canada, the proportion of secondary school graduates at level 4/5 is larger when the father has at least graduated from secondary school. The differences between the comparison groups are small in Germany and high in Switzerland and the United Kingdom. Chapter 3 examines further the role parents' education plays in developing literacy skills. For the moment, it is sufficient to point out that lifelong learning is of tremendous value, both to increase an individual's own skill and to provide a firmer foundation for the skills of the next generation (see Box 1B).

FIGURE 1.8

Parental education and mathematics achievement

Mean mathematics achievement scores on a scale range 0-1 000 for 8th-grade students by level of parental education, 1994-1995

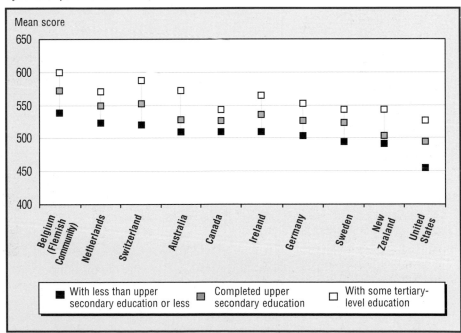

Countries are ranked by the average score of those whose parents have lower secondary education or less.

Source: IEA, Third International Mathematics and Science Study, 1994-1995.

---

4   The same pattern is found for document and quantitative literacy; only the prose pattern is presented for clarity.

Box 1B   Literacy and Lifelong Learning

One of the clearest messages conveyed by the results of the International Adult Literacy Survey is that literacy is not simply the result of schooling. Literacy acquisition can, and in many instances does, continue after schooling stops. Unfortunately, the study also shows that skills can be lost after leaving school. One of the most important policy priorities is to identify and support those features that enhance the growth of skill while also working to eliminate the conditions that lead to loss.

FIGURE 1.9

Father's education and respondents' literacy performance

Proportion of adults at or above prose literacy level 3, by father's educational attainment, adults 16-65 whose own highest educational attainment is upper secondary graduation, 1994-1995

In all countries but Canada and New Zealand, adults whose fathers have obtained upper secondary education or better are found at the higher levels of literacy skill in greater numbers than those whose fathers have less education.

This figure compares upper secondary school graduates, at prose level 3 or above. The left-hand bar represents those whose fathers have not completed upper secondary education, and the right-hand bar represents those whose fathers have completed upper secondary education.

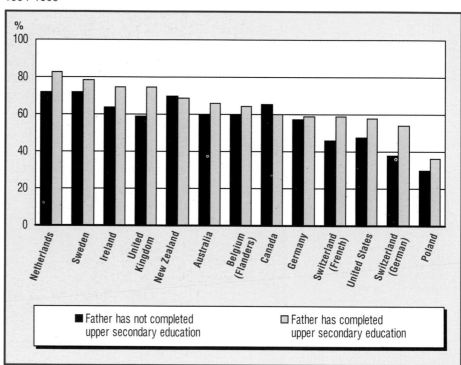

Countries are ranked by the proportion of level 3 adults whose fathers have completed upper secondary education.

Source: International Adult Literacy Survey, 1994-1995.

1.5 Gender

Studies of reading achievement consistently show an advantage for girls over boys at a young age.

Until recently, men typically obtained more education than women; to the extent that education influences literacy, there are also likely to be differences in the literacy skills of men and women. However, studies of school reading typically show a consistent advantage for girls during the early years of schooling. In later years this advantage is maintained in most, but not all, countries. On the test administered as part of the IEA Reading Literacy Study, girls scored higher than boys at both 9 and 14 years of age in all the participating countries[5] (Elley, 1992 and 1994).

---

[5]   Australia, Belgium (Flemish Community), Poland and the United Kingdom did not participate in the study. Only one Canadian province, British Columbia, took part.

Comparative surveys of student achievement in school mathematics, on the other hand, often show an advantage for boys. In all but three of the countries[6] boys outscored girls on the 8th-grade mathematics test, and in all but two boys outperformed girls in the 4th-grade assessment (Beaton *et al.*, 1996).

Figure 1.10 compares the differences in standard score units between boys and girls on the reading (age 14, derived from the IEA Reading Literacy Study) and mathematics (8th-grade, derived from TIMSS) tests. Typically, girls have a consistently higher average score than boys in reading, while boys outperform girls in mathematics in all but three countries [Australia, Belgium (Flemish Community) and Canada]. However, the size of the boys' advantage in mathematics is notably smaller than the girls' advantage in reading. Boys have a large advantage over girls in mathematics in Ireland and Scotland.

FIGURE 1.10

Gender differences in reading and mathematics achievement

Standard score differences between boys and girls in reading (age 14, 1990-1991) and mathematics (8th-grade, 1994-1995) achievement

Girls outperformed boys in reading in all countries, and by a considerable margin in some. Differences of 0.1 and larger are particularly noteworthy. In most countries boys outperformed girls in mathematics, but the differences are not as large as for reading. In only two countries is the boys' advantage over 0.1 and nowhere is it over 0.2.

This figure shows the difference in standard score units between the average for boys and girls on the IEA Reading Literacy assessment (14-year-old population) and on the TIMSS mathematics assessment (8th-grade population). The difference is calculated by subtracting the boys' average score from the girls' average and dividing this difference by the pooled standard deviation. Different countries participated in the two studies, and in some cases only part of a country may have participated.

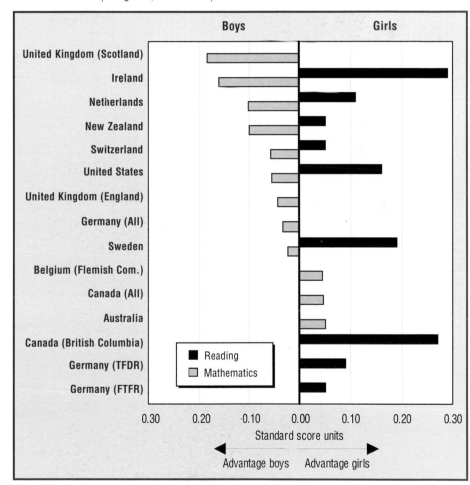

Countries are ranked by the advantage of boys in mathematics.

Source: IEA, Reading Literacy Study, 1991, and IEA, Third International Mathematics and Science Study, 1994-1995.

---

[6] Poland did not take part in the TIMSS assessment, and only part of the United Kingdom was involved (England and Scotland). Girls outperformed boys in mathematics in both the 4th and the 8th grades in Australia and Belgium (Flemish Community). In Canada, 8th-grade girls outscored boys.

Figure 1.11 sets out the difference between men's and women's average scores on each of the IALS scales for each country. The data show some consistency in the gender patterns observed for reading and mathematics achievement among young children and the patterns found for literacy proficiency among the adult population.

In all countries men outscore women on the quantitative scale, and in some countries – Belgium (Flanders), the Netherlands and the United Kingdom – by a significant amount. Women do better than men in prose literacy in 8 of the 12 countries, with particularly large differences in Canada and New Zealand. The gender differences in literacy performance are the smallest in the United Kingdom for prose and in Canada for the document and quantitative scales.

FIGURE 1.11

Gender differences in adult literacy

Standard score differences in mean literacy proficiency between men and women aged 16-65 on the prose, document and quantitative scales, 1994-1995

Women did not score higher than men in all countries on the prose scale, the literacy scale most closely reflecting the tasks in the majority of school reading assessments. However, with one exception (the United States), men had higher average document literacy scores than women and in all countries had higher averages on quantitative literacy. Further, even when there was a female prose advantage, the difference was small – less than or close to 0.1 – except in Canada and New Zealand. In contrast, the advantage of men on the other scales was often large, especially for quantitative tasks.

This figure shows the difference in standard score units between the averages for men and women on the three IALS literacy scales. The difference is calculated by subtracting the average score for men from the average score for women and dividing this difference by the pooled standard deviation.

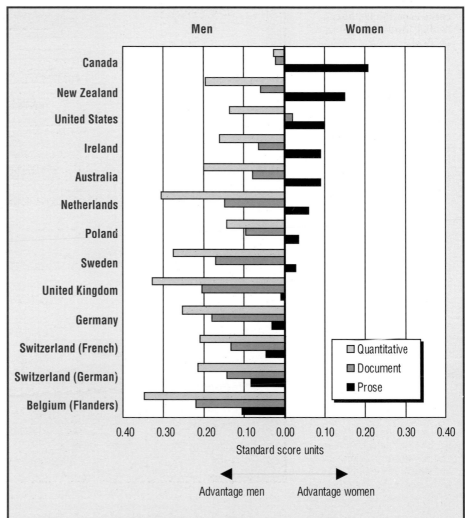

Countries are ranked by the difference in standard score units on the prose scale.

Source: International Adult Literacy Survey, 1994-1995.

The advantage found for young girls in the IEA Reading Literacy Study is not uniformly reflected in the patterns of performance observed for the adult population. The unadjusted data values in Figure 1.11 indicate that women outscore men on the prose scale in Belgium (Flanders), Germany and Switzerland, and only in the United States do they outscore men on the document scale.

FIGURE 1.12

Gender differences in adult literacy, controlling for differences in education

Standard score differences in mean literacy proficiency of men and women aged 16-65 on three scales, for population with completed upper secondary education, 1994-1995

When initial educational attainment is held constant women score higher than men in all but one country (Poland) on the prose scale, the literacy scale most closely reflecting the tasks in the majority of school reading assessments. Men had higher average document literacy scores than women except in the United States, and higher averages on quantitative literacy. The female prose advantage, once the effect of educational differences is removed, is larger even though it is still smaller than the male advantage on the other scales.

This figure shows the difference in standard score units between the average scores of men and women on the three literacy scales for those whose highest level of education is upper secondary graduation. This permits a comparison of the performance of men and women while controlling for the effects of differences in initial education. The difference scores are calculated by subtracting the average score for men from the average score for women and dividing this difference by the pooled standard deviation.

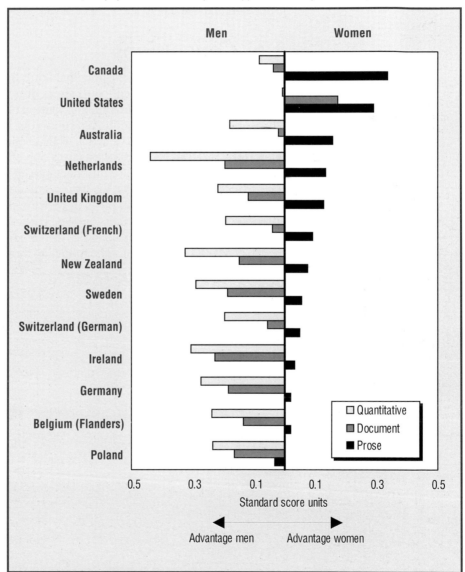

Countries are ranked by the difference in standard score units on the prose scale.

Source: International Adult Literacy Survey, 1994-1995.

The absence of a female advantage in adult prose literacy may be due, at least in part, to the generally higher level of educational attainment of men.

The differences in performance between adult men and women might be attributed to differences in educational attainment. However, Figure 1.12 shows that the gender patterns observed for the document and quantitative scales still show an advantage for men even when the level of education – here secondary graduation – is the same. The school reading pattern, showing a female advantage, is repeated for the prose scale when educational differences are controlled (compare Figures 1.10 and 1.12). This suggests that the absence of a female advantage in adult prose literacy is a consequence of the generally higher education of men and that – whatever the cause of the female advantage in school reading – it persists into adult life, as does the male advantage in mathematics.

Why these gender differences exist has been the subject of considerable research. A common finding is that the differences frequently reflect differences in course enrolment and training (Linn and Hyde, 1989), and that some of the differences may be due to a test effect (Ryan, 1996).[7]

1.6 Conclusions

This chapter has attempted to show that adult literacy differs in complex ways among the countries surveyed. Skill levels differ from country to country, but – more importantly – the population distribution of literacy skills within countries differs as well. In some countries relatively large proportions of the adult population have skills at levels 2 and 3, while in others there are comparatively large proportions at the highest and lowest levels of performance on all three scales. The patterns in literacy performance differ not only among countries but also from one scale to another, suggesting that the three scales do measure different, albeit closely related, skills. Gender differences in performance on the three scales are also apparent. These relationships are complex; the findings must be analysed carefully if a full understanding of why countries differ, or of the lessons to be learned from the IALS data, is to be gained. The following three chapters provide that analysis.

---

[7]   The articles in the special issue of *Educational Measurement: Issues and Practice* edited by K. Ryan (1996) discuss some of the test effect issues in gender differences. Ever since Maccoby and Jacklin's (1974) pioneering analysis of gender effects, there have been numerous studies on gender differences. Hyde (1990) presents a recent meta-analysis. Tartre and Fennema (1995) report that differences in spatial ability are related to differences in mathematics achievement among women, but not among men. On the other hand, differences in verbal ability are related to male differences in achievement, but not to female differences. Whatever the causes of the differences, they are relatively small and declining, and as Linn and Hyde (1989) point out: "Gender differences in height, physical strength, career access, and earnings power are much larger and more stable than gender differences on cognitive and psycho-social tasks".

References

BEATON, A.E., MULLIS, I.V.S., MARTIN, M.O., GONZALES, E.J., KELLY, D.L., and SMITH, T.A. (1996), *Mathematics Achievement in the Middle School Years*, TIMSS International Study Center, Boston College, Chestnut Hill, MA.

ELLEY, W.B. (1992), *How in the World do Students Read?*, Grindeldruck GMBH, Hamburg.

ELLEY, W.B. (Ed.) (1994), *The IEA Study of Reading Literacy: Achievement and Instruction in Thirty-two School Systems*, Pergamon Press, Oxford.

GROSS, R.T., SPIKER, D., and HAYNES, C.W. (1997), *Helping Low Birthweight Premature Babies: The Infant Health and Development Program*, Stanford University Press, Stanford, CA.

HAVEMAN, R. and WOLFE, B. (1994*), Succeeding Generations on the Effects of Investment in Children*, Russell-Sage Foundation, New York.

HYDE, J.S. (1990), "Meta-analysis and the psychology of gender differences", *Signs: Journal of Women in Culture and Society,* Vol. 18, pp. 35-72.

LEIBOWITZ, A. (1974), "Home investment in children", *Journal of Political Economy*, Vol. 82, pp. 111-131.

LINN, M.C. and HYDE, J.S. (1989), "Gender, mathematics, and science", *Educational Researcher,* Vol. 18 (8), pp. 17-19, 22-27.

MACCOBY, E.E. and JACKLIN, C.N. (1974), *The Psychology of Sex Differences,* Stanford University Press, Stanford, CA.

OECD (1994), *Education at a Glance: OECD Indicators*, Paris.

OECD (1996), *Education at a Glance: OECD Indicators*, Paris.

OECD and STATISTICS CANADA (1995), *Literacy, Economy and Society: Results of the First International Adult Literacy Survey*, Paris and Ottawa.

RYAN, K.E. (Ed.) (Winter, 1996), "Special issue: Gender and mathematics performance", *Educational Measurement: Issues and Practice,* Vol. 15 (4).

TARTRE, L.S. and FENNEMA, E. (1995), "Mathematics achievement and gender: A longitudinal study of selected cognitive and affective variables [grades 6-12]", *Educational Studies in Mathematics,* Vol. 28, pp. 199-217.

Chapter 2

The Benefits of Literacy

2.1 Introduction

To be literate is to be connected with the language and culture of a society, and to be able to participate in that society's political and economic life. Although the importance of literacy is certainly recognised in all Member countries, the full range of benefits deriving from a literate population is often not recognised.

The purpose of this chapter is to analyse the relationships between literacy skills and a number of economic and labour market variables, and to suggest a broad set of documented economic and social benefits. These can serve as incentives to develop and reinforce literacy, not only in schools but also in workplaces and other settings.

2.2 Economic Benefits

This section looks at the relationship between education, literacy, and three sets of indicators of labour market outcomes: productivity and earnings; labour force participation and unemployment; and the distribution of jobs in the emerging knowledge society.

Productivity and earnings

Early work on the impact of people's knowledge and skills, or "human capital", pointed to the important role of schooling in influencing productivity and earnings. At that time it was assumed that much of the apparent impact of educational qualifications on earnings was due to the greater levels of knowledge and skills which more highly educated persons bring to their jobs. Literacy and numeracy skills were thought to figure importantly, but there was little direct evidence on their role in raising productivity and earnings.

As distinct from early work, a substantial body of empirical research has emerged showing the statistical connections between educational attainment and earnings. In these studies, educational attainment is considered not only as a qualification that offers access to certain jobs and careers in the labour market, but also – in the absence of variables that measure skills directly – as an indicator of people's knowledge and skills. Hence the connection between educational attainment and earnings can be interpreted in several ways: as an effect of qualification, self-selection or screening in the labour market, and/or as an effect of knowledge and skill. Whichever interpretation is correct, the positive relationship between educational qualifications and earnings is unquestionable (see Figure 2.1).

This chapter presents evidence on a range of social and economic benefits associated with high literacy.

The positive relationship between educational qualifications and earnings is unquestionable.

Rates of return to university education are particularly high in Ireland and the United Kingdom.

Figure 2.1 shows the economic rates of return to education calculated using the short-cut method (see Box 2A). The findings indicate that the rates of return to university education as opposed to upper secondary schooling are substantial, with rates exceeding 10 per cent for university education in all countries, although there are significant differences both between countries and between men and women. Rates of return to university education are particularly high in Ireland and the United Kingdom. It should be noted, however, that these returns do not take account of the public and private costs of providing and acquiring education.

Box 2A   Rates of Return Measures

The short-cut method for calculating rates of return to schooling is used when cross-sectional or longitudinal earnings data are not available, but mean earnings by level of schooling are. The results presented in Figure 2.1 were obtained using the method developed by Psacharopoulos (1981). Mean earnings for various levels of schooling are derived from the OECD Education Database. Summary data are presented in OECD (1995 and 1996a).

Even if the relationship between education and earnings is not in doubt, questions continue to be asked about how the link should be interpreted. Can the findings be taken as *prima facie* evidence that more highly educated people earn more simply because they have better skills? This question can be addressed properly only if educational attainment and skill measures are both specified in the wage equation. In recent years, economists examining the separate influences of initial qualifications and direct measures of skills on earnings have controlled for variables such as gender, occupation and work experience. For example, Murnane, Willett and Levy (1995), using longitudinal data for US high school seniors, show that for women the increase in the returns to cognitive skills between 1978 and 1986 accounts for all of the increase in the wage premium associated with tertiary education.

Another empirical study that took account of initial educational attainment, work experience, geographic location and country of origin found a 12 per cent increase in earnings attributable to fluency in language for Canadians in 1981; a 17 per cent increase in the United States; and an increment rising from about 5 per cent in 1981 to 8 per cent in 1986 in Australia, suggesting the rising importance of literacy over time (Chiswick and Miller, 1995). The study concluded that investments in intensive literacy training – such as that offered in Israel – would have economic rates of return considerably higher than those for most other investments: between 9 and 18 per cent in Australia; 12 to 24 per cent in Canada; and 17 to 34 per cent in the United States. Dustmann (1994) obtained similar results for immigrants in Germany, with an 11 per cent difference between those with good or very good speaking and writing skills and those with poor communication skills. Carliner (1996) found that from 6 to 18 per cent of the gap in the earnings of native and foreign-born persons in the United States during the 1950s and 1960s was attributable to the difference in English proficiency.

Rates of return exceeding 10 per cent can be considered high in comparison with many other types of investment. The figure shows that gains exceed this threshold for most countries. Returns tend to be higher for women than for men, particularly at higher levels of educational attainment.

The figure shows the economic rate of return for obtaining a university education as opposed to upper secondary only. Estimates are based on gross earnings, converted to US dollars, and are adjusted using purchasing power parities.

FIGURE 2.1

Rates of return to education

Rates of return to education, university degree vs. upper-secondary, men and women, short-cut method, 1994

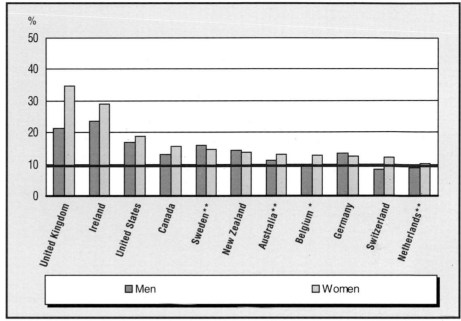

Countries are ranked in descending order by the returns for women.

* 1992 data.

** 1993 data.

Source: Calculated from data published in OECD (1995 and 1996*a*) by Cohn and Addison (1997).

Figure 2.2 shows the relationship between literacy skills and income for the three scales, prose, document and quantitative. In this report income quintiles are used for analysing the relationships between earnings, literacy and other variables of interest. This is in part because the focus is on distributional relationships. Another reason is that most countries collected pre-tax income data, whereas both Germany and Switzerland asked about after-tax earnings. The use of quintiles rather than real dollar values adjusted for purchasing power parities implies some loss of information value but facilitates the comparative analysis.

The data clearly indicate that the percentage of people with relatively high incomes mounts with increasing levels of proficiency. The wage premium associated with good literacy skills is comparatively high in Canada, the United Kingdom and the United States. Conversely, the wage penalty associated with low performance is both consistently larger across all countries and more variable. For example, penalties exceed 30 per cent for individuals at level 1 on the quantitative scale in Australia, Canada, Ireland, Netherlands, New Zealand, United Kingdom and United States. The data also show a larger return to quantitative skill compared with reading skill in some countries, notably Poland. This finding is consistent with the emerging research literature on differential returns to various types of skill as an explanation for growing wage gaps.[1]

---

[1]   See Bishop (1988 and 1995); Murnane, Willett and Levy (1995); Rivera-Batiz (1994*a*); and Leuven, Oosterbeek and van Ophem (1997). Trend data on earnings growth and wage dispersion are reported in OECD (1997*a*).

**Workers with higher
literacy skills generally earn
more than those with lower
literacy skills, even though
the effect is not uniform
across all levels or across
countries.**

The range covered by each
income quintile includes
20 per cent of wage-earners
in each country. The
comparison across
countries takes into account
the distribution of income
within countries. The
association between
literacy and income tends
to be stronger in countries
with wide wage dispersion
and weaker in countries
with a compressed wage
structure.

FIGURE 2.2

Adult literacy and earnings

Proportion of employed people aged 25-65 at each literacy level who are in the top
60 per cent of earners: percentage points difference from level 3, 1994-1995

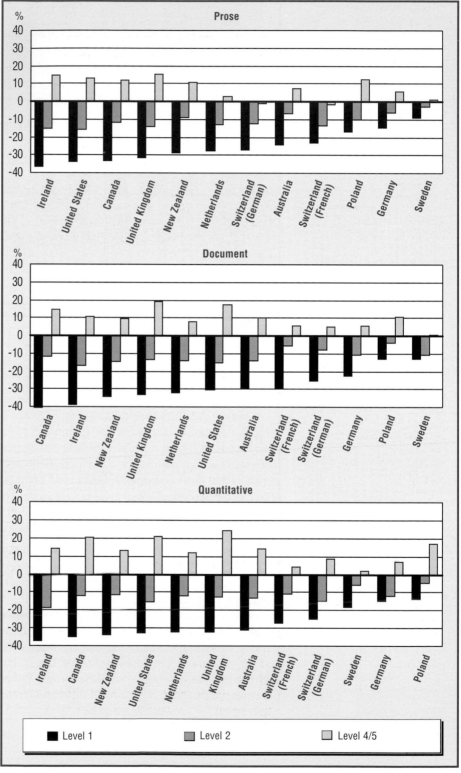

Countries are ranked by the relative income disadvantage of workers with level 1 skills.

Source: International Adult Literacy Survey, 1994-1995.

These findings are particularly important given the high levels of migration into a number of OECD countries. Working from a survey of immigrants in 1976, Kossoudji (1988) found that Hispanic immigrants to the United States who were deficient in English experienced 18 to 35 per cent lower pay than comparable non-immigrants; losses among professionals were the largest, proportionally twice those of other workers. Many sophisticated statistical studies on immigrant populations have found that Hispanics in the United States pay a particularly high price in terms of lower earnings if they have low levels of literacy.[2] Indeed, at least one study finds that virtually all of the wage differentials normally associated with Hispanic ethnicity, schooling abroad, citizenship in the United States and time spent in that country, show no statistically significant relationship with earnings when taking account of English language deficiency (Grenier, 1984).

Figure 2.3 suggests there to be a considerable loss in earnings associated with a lack of language proficiency among immigrants and the general population. There is some evidence that reading and writing literacy are more important than speaking literacy in studies concerning the United States and Germany (Chiswick, 1991). Communication skills have been shown to be very important in developing countries (Snow and Tabors, 1993). In addition, there is considerable evidence, from the IALS as well as other data sources, that quantitative literacy has an important impact on earnings, even when taking account of language literacy (Rivera-Batiz, 1994a).

FIGURE 2.3

Earnings of native-born vs. foreign-born population by literacy levels

Proportion of native-born vs. foreign-born employed population aged 25-65 in top 60 per cent of earners, by literacy level, document scale, selected countries, 1994-1995

Immigrant populations generally face a wage penalty in the labour market which appears to be associated with their lower-than-average reading skills. The wage penalty is particularly pronounced in Canada and the United States.

This figure shows the percentage of the employed native- vs. foreign-born population who are in the top three quintiles of earnings by low and medium to high levels of literacy skills.

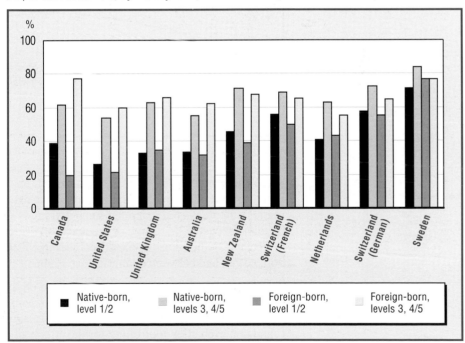

Countries are ranked by the wage differential for immigrants with low and medium to high literacy skills.

Source: International Adult Literacy Survey, 1994-1995.

2   For example, see McManus (1990); McManus, Gould and Welch (1983); Murnane and Levy (1996); Rivera-Batiz (1990; 1991); and Tainer (1988).

43

The results presented in Figures 2.2 and 2.3 illustrate the connection between literacy skills and income for all age groups and at one point in time. Figure 2.4 introduces an age scale, showing – for Canada – the estimated age-earnings profiles of men and women with low (level 1) and high (level 4/5) literacy skills (Bloom *et al.*, 1997). Peak life-time earnings occur at age 44 for men with high document literacy skills and age 39 for men with low skills. For women, peak earnings are at age 47 for those with high skills and 45 for those with low skills. For Canada, it has been calculated that a man with high literacy skills can expect to earn $1.743 million (pre-tax income) over a working lifetime, compared with $1.158 million for a man with low skills. The wage premium for high vs. low skills is thus in the order of $585 000 for Canadian men. Although the lifetime incomes of women are on average lower than those of men, the difference between the expected income of women with high literacy skills still exceeds by far that of low-skill women. The difference in this case is $683 000 (Bloom *et al.*, 1997).

FIGURE 2.4

Lifetime employment income profiles for men and women, Canada

Expected lifetime pre-tax income from employment by document literacy level and age, 16-64, undiscounted 1994 dollar values

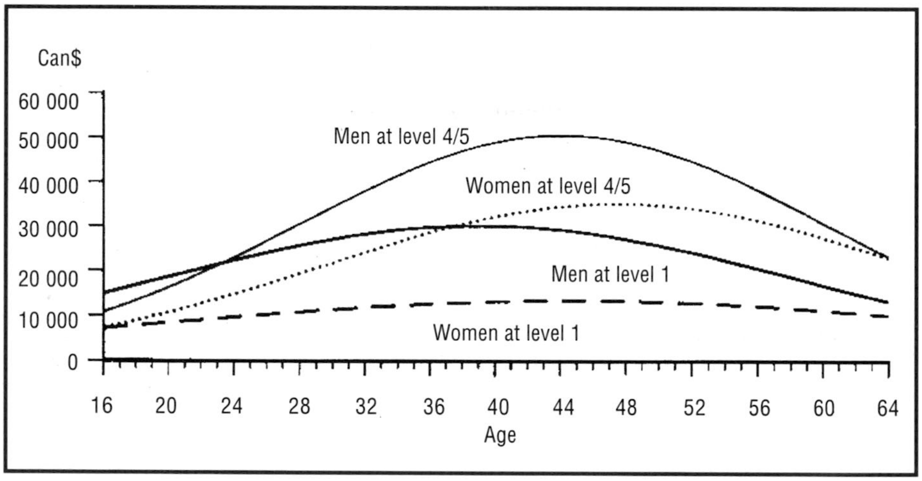

There is a considerable earnings gap between men and women with low and high literacy skills. Women can expect to have lower lifetime earnings than men. Moreover, the earnings gap is larger for women than for men.

The figure shows typical age-earnings profiles for Canadian men and women with low (level 1) and high (level 4/5) literacy skills.

Source: International Adult Literacy Survey, 1994-1995; and Bloom *et al.* (1997).

Some of the apparent effect of literacy on income may be attributable to differences in educational attainment.

The simple, bivariate analysis presented above does not take into account the other variables that are known, from previous research studies, to influence labour market outcomes. For example, since literacy is related to educational attainment, it can be expected that some of the apparent effect of literacy on income is in fact attributable to the considerable differences in educational attainment in populations, both within and between countries (see Figure 1.3).

One of the best sources of information on the net impact of literacy skills on earnings is found in a study conducted by Raudenbush and Kasim (1996), who work with data collected for the United States' National Adult Literacy Survey. They found that even after controlling for the effects of parental education, respondents' education, labour market experience, gender and ethnicity, an increase in combined literacy performance (document, prose and quantitative) of one standard deviation (i.e., from the 50th to the 80th percentile) is associated with an increase in hourly wages of about 18 per cent. This result is buttressed by studies of economic growth that have found that the faster-growing developing economies are those with above-average performance in literacy (Hicks, 1996).

Figure 2.5 presents estimates of the magnitude of the net direct effects of educational qualifications and literacy proficiency on pre-tax income for a group of OECD countries. The effect coefficients are obtained in models that account for the influences of other variables such as gender, parental education and occupation (see Box 2B). The coefficients indicate that educational attainment is the more important determinant of the two in all countries but Ireland. It can readily be seen that literacy proficiency has an independent and substantial effect on income, net of the influence of educational qualifications, in all countries except Poland, where the influence of literacy skill is negligible compared with the overwhelming impact of educational credentials.

Box 2B   Understanding Effect Coefficients

The effect coefficients are obtained in Linear Structural Equation (LISREL) models using the maximum likelihood method, standardised solution. The measurement models underlying the structural equations minimise the error introduced by the presence of multicollinearity in the effect estimates of educational attainment and literacy proficiency. Identical models are specified for each country, using only common variables measured in similar ways. The results can be compared between countries even though different samples are employed for the data analysis because the structural and measurement models are specified identically across countries.

FIGURE 2.5

Net direct effects of education and literacy on income

Regression coefficients showing the strength of the direct effect of education on income and of literacy on income net of the effects of background variables, 1994-1995

Educational attainment has a large effect on income in all countries studied. The effect is largest in Belgium (Flanders), Canada and Poland and weakest in Sweden, which has a compressed wage structure. Literacy produces a wage effect that comes on top of that of education. The literacy wage premium is largest in Ireland and the United States; there are similar wage effects in Canada, Germany, the Netherlands and Switzerland.

The effect of literacy on income is net of the combined influences of gender, parental education and respondents' education.

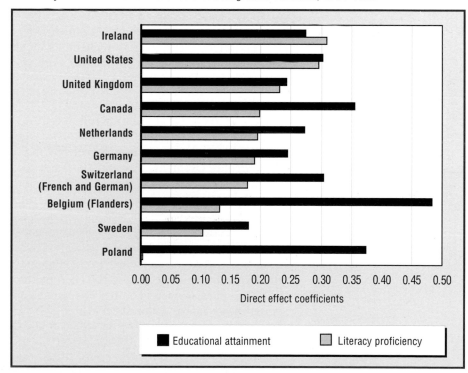

Countries are ranked by the net direct effect of literacy on income. See notes to Table 2.5.

Source: International Adult Literacy Survey, 1994-1995.

The magnitudes of the literacy coefficients vary across countries. In Ireland the returns to literacy skills outweigh those accruing to educational qualifications. The United States and the United Kingdom labour markets rewards literacy skill almost as much as educational credentials. In Canada, Germany, the Netherlands and Switzerland both qualifications and skills are rewarded with substantial returns in the labour market, although education dominates. Thus the results confirm that there is a measurable and substantial return to literacy skills in most of the countries surveyed; a return that brings social benefits as well (see Box 2C).

High literacy generates both private and social benefits.

Box 2C   Higher Tax Revenues

In all Member countries tax revenues for support of government services are derived directly or indirectly from income. In most societies taxes are levied on household income, consumption, profits, and wealth. In the long run all of these are tied to household income because consumption rises with income, profits contribute to income, and wealth is derived from income. This means that higher income generated through improved skills and greater productivity will contribute to higher government revenues to support social services. This is not a trivial concern at a time when Member countries are pursuing policies to curb public spending and reduce deficits. Even a relatively small increase in national productivity through improved literacy will have a relatively large impact on public revenues. For example, a 2 per cent increase in wages and earnings from improvements in national literacy would provide approximately a 1.8 per cent increase in revenue in a country that is dependent primarily on value-added tax, and where 90 per cent of such income is used for taxed consumption.

Labour force participation and unemployment

Literacy skills are important for success in the labour market.

The level of educational attainment is an important factor in a country, influencing both labour force participation rates for men and women and people's relative position in the labour market. Literacy proficiency is also related to labour force participation and success in the job market. Persons who are more literate are not only likely to have jobs with higher productivity and increased earnings; they are also less vulnerable to long-term unemployment. Higher levels of literacy make learning more efficient and, thus, allow workers to more easily adapt to changing job requirements (see Chapter 4).

Figure 2.6a-c contrasts the rates of labour force participation[3] for those with literacy skills at level 2 and below with those at levels 3 and 4/5. Overall participation rates vary substantially across countries. For the highly skilled on the document scale, rates vary from 87 per cent in Poland and the United Kingdom to 72 per cent in Germany. Participation rates for the low-skilled vary from 74 to 78 per cent in French- and German-speaking Switzerland to a low of 52 per cent in the Netherlands. These wide variations in rates that cover both men and women are mostly due to differences in participation rates for women (OECD, 1996a), which are highly correlated with educational attainment and literacy proficiency. However, gender differences in participation rates also have to do with age. In most European countries studied, women aged 25-34 demonstrate substantially higher rates of employment than those 45 and above; younger women also have better literacy skills than older women. For men and women alike, those with low skills are at a serious disadvantage with respect to access to the labour market.

---

[3]   The labour force participation rate is calculated as the percentage of the population who are economically active, either employed or unemployed, in accordance with ILO guidelines.

FIGURE 2.6

Labour force participation and literacy performance

Rates of labour force participation for population aged 25-65 by low (levels 1-2) and medium to high (levels 3-5) literacy proficiency, 1994-1995

Labour force participation rates increase with increasing levels of literacy proficiency.

The figures show labour force participation rates by prose, document and quantitative literacy levels.

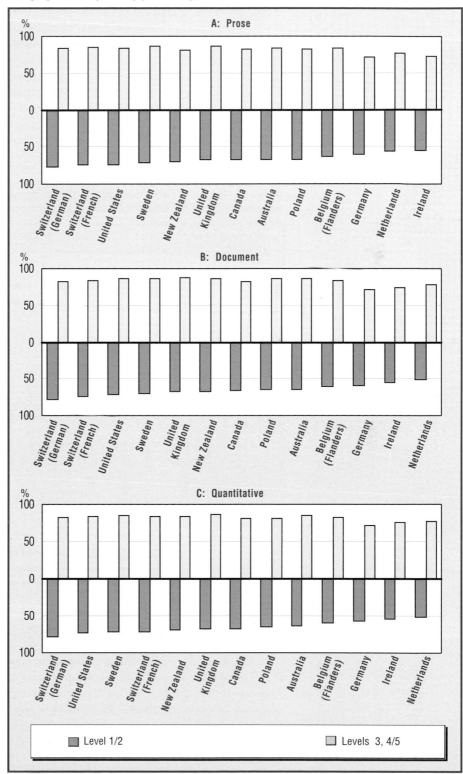

Countries are ranked by the participation rates of those with low literacy skills.

Source: International Adult Literacy Survey, 1994-1995.

Figure 2.7 presents data on the quantity of employment obtained by adults with very low literacy levels in comparison with those at level 2 or higher. Again, countries vary considerably with respect to the average number of weeks worked during the year preceding the interview. The labour forces of countries such as Belgium (Flanders), Germany, Switzerland and the United Kingdom are relatively successful in obtaining paid work and in working many weeks in a year, compared to the labour forces of Australia, Canada and New Zealand. Compared with those at levels 2 and above, low-literate adults work two or more weeks less per year in these three countries. Additional results indicate no systematic relationship between skills and whether a person has full- or part-time employment. In some countries, full-time workers have slightly higher representation at higher skill levels; in others, there are also large proportions of part-time workers at the higher skill levels.

FIGURE 2.7

Employment disadvantage of low-skill adults

Mean number of weeks worked for people who worked during the year preceding the interview, by literacy level on the quantitative scale, population aged 25-65, 1994-1995

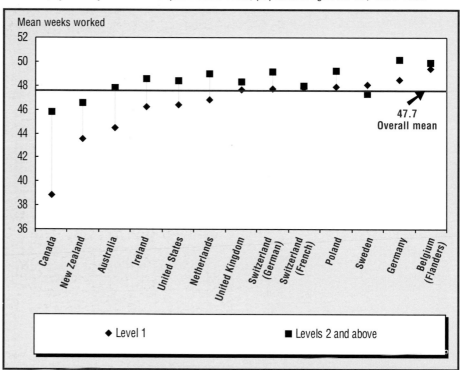

Countries are ranked by the employment disadvantage of people with very low literacy skills.
Source: International Adult Literacy Survey, 1994-1995.

Employed persons work on average 47.7 weeks per year. In all countries but Sweden, those with high skills tend to work more, and those with low skills less.

The figure shows mean weeks worked for the two groups compared with the overall mean for all countries.

Figure 2.8 highlights the variation in unemployment experienced by workers at different skill levels. Cumulated unemployment duration can be seen as a measure of the extent of labour market demand for different levels of skill. The adequacy of worker skills and the capacity of the labour market to supply jobs that match those skills are issues of significant policy interest. In 1996 there were about 36 million persons actively searching for work in the OECD area – an unemployment rate of 7.5 per cent. Low-skill and less-experienced workers have been particularly hit by adverse labour market developments: their participation rates have dropped in most countries, absolutely and relatively, particularly among older men, but less so among older women.

Employment and unemployment are strongly related to literacy proficiency: low-skilled adults have a greater chance of being unemployed than high-skilled adults.

Figure 2.8 shows the proportion of the labour force actively seeking paid work during the year preceding the interview.

FIGURE 2.8

Unemployment and literacy

Unemployment incidence (rate) by level of literacy proficiency for the labour force aged 16-65, document scale, 1994-1995

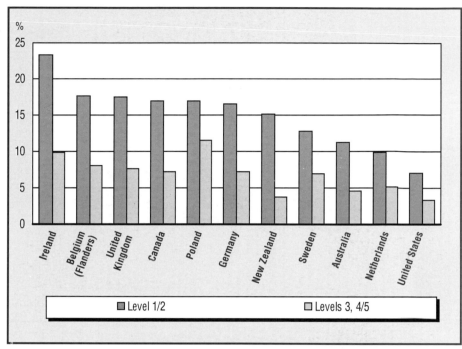

Countries are ranked by the incidence of unemployment of those with level 1 and 2 skills.

Source: International Adult Literacy Survey, 1994-1995.

Figure 2.8 suggests that unemployment tends to decrease as the level of literacy proficiency of workers increases. Overall unemployment appears to be related to the capacity of economies to create and sustain employment opportunities for those with low skills. This phenomenon appears to hold across all the countries studied, despite the differences in economic structures as well as in the population distribution of literacy skill. Continuously upgrading workforce skills through strategies for lifelong learning should, evidently, be part of the policy response to tackle low-wage jobs and persistent unemployment (OECD, 1996*b*).

Of course, in addition to lower levels of literacy, those with higher levels of unemployment might have less work experience, less education, and other characteristics that make them less employable. Recent studies that control for these influences still find a strong association between lower levels of literacy and unemployment. A study based on the 1985 Young Adult Literacy Survey of persons aged 21-25 in the United States – an age group that is highly vulnerable to unemployment – found that quantitative literacy is a major factor raising the probability of full-time employment (Rivera-Batiz, 1994*b*; Berlin and Sum, 1988). Figure 2.9 presents the results of a study comparing unemployment rates for white and black men in the United States, before and after adjustment for parental education, age, respondents' educational attainment and literacy proficiency. The results show that these variables explain a good portion, but not all, of the variance in unemployment. Low literacy has a significant and negative effect on employment opportunities for both white and black men, even after controlling for social origins, schooling and experience. But the risk of being unemployed in the United States is still substantially larger for black men compared to white men!

Low literacy skills have a significant and negative effect on employment opportunities for both white and black men, even after controlling for social origins, educational attainment and experience.

Effect estimates are obtained in a hierarchical linear model that controls for variation attributable to the state in which a respondent resides. Estimates are based on data for 12 894 US respondents.

FIGURE 2.9

Unemployment comparison between white and black men

Unemployment predicted by social origin, educational attainment, age and literacy proficiency for white and black men aged 25-59 who are in the labour force, United States, 1992

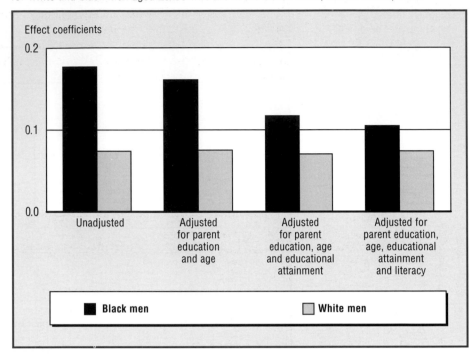

Source: Raudenbush, Kasim, Eamsukkawat and Miyazaki (1996).

Literacy is not the sole determinant of employment – it makes a labour force more productive and employable over the long run, and thus provides incentives to invest capital and create jobs. Given the serious unemployment problem in many countries, the IALS results suggest that effective strategies to raise workforce literacy should be included in the mix of policies required to counter unemployment (see also OECD, 1997*b*).

Internal labour markets and the knowledge economy

The evidence presented above highlights the important role literacy plays in the allocation of economic opportunities in OECD countries. But this evidence may understate the impact of literacy in two important ways – one concerning the role of credentials in labour market entry, and the other related to the wage premium paid for high-level skills in the emerging knowledge economy.

Rewarding credentials versus skills

The data analysed above include young people aged 16-25 – the group who entered the labour market most recently. Initial selection for jobs by employers is largely based on educational credentials. Job skills and productivity potential can be evaluated only after young people have moved beyond the transition stage and have been with the same employer awhile. Thus, with an increase in labour market experience one would expect to see evidence of a drop in the direct effect on income of educational attainment, which is used by employers as a screening and job-matching device, and an increase in the rewards accruing directly to knowledge and skills.

Figure 2.10 presents estimates of the net direct effect on income of labour market experience, with controls for both educational qualifications and literacy proficiency.[4] In every country, experience has a large and positive effect on income, with standardised regression coefficients ranging from a high of 0.35 in Belgium (Flanders) and the Netherlands to lows of 0.12 in Germany and 0.09 in the United Kingdom. These coefficients are large enough to matter, especially since they are estimated in models where the influences of other variables predicting income are held constant. Thus the net positive effect of labour market experience on income is over and above those of the net effects of educational qualifications and literacy skills examined in the previous section.

FIGURE 2.10

Income and experience, controlling for education and literacy skills

Adjusted effect coefficients indicating the size of the effect of labour market experience on income, relative to the effects of educational attainment and literacy proficiency, 1994-1995

Some countries reward labour market experience and to an extent years of education; others place relatively more value on skill.

The figure shows the magnitude of the adjusted effects of educational attainment, literacy proficiency and labour market experience on income.

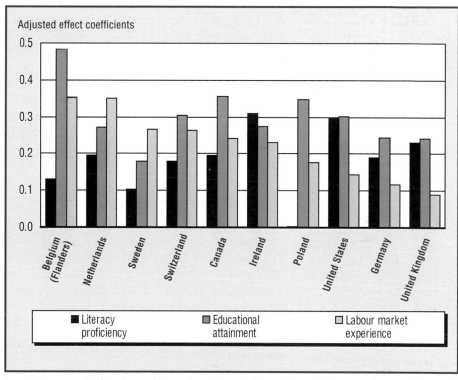

Countries are ranked in descending order of the net direct effect of labour market experience on income.

Source: International Adult Literacy Survey, 1994-1995.

---

[4]   For the purposes of this data analysis, labour market experience – or seniority – is a derived variable that is equal to (age - education - 5). It is centred around its mean for each country. The effect of labour market experience on income is estimated in linear structural equation models specifying identical control variables for all the countries studied. These controls include parental education, age, gender, educational attainment and literacy proficiency. The regression coefficients shown in Figure 2.10 are maximum likelihood estimates obtained in a standardised model solution, adjusted by the amount of variance explained in income, the dependent variable. See Box 2B.

In the United Kingdom and the United States, the return accuing to labour market experience is relatively unimportant while the net return to skill is large and in the same order of magnitude as the return to formal educational qualifications. Ireland is the only country where the return to skill exceeds that attributable to either education or experience. Hence selection and screening are important, but skills carry a tangible reward. The Netherlands and Sweden are the two countries where experience or seniority exerts the more important influence on income. The benefits accruing to both educational qualifications and workforce skills outweigh those accruing to labour market experience – even in Belgium (Flanders), where experience is as important as in the Netherlands. A possible explanation for these findings may be that the comparatively large variation in literacy skills in Ireland, the United Kingdom and the United States facilitates differential recognition by employers. In the Netherlands and Sweden, where the rewards to both education and literacy skill are modest in comparison with the effect of labour market experience, the explanation may be that literacy skills are higher on average and more uniformly distributed in the population, so that differences in skill are smaller and more difficult to detect, evaluate and reward.

It can be postulated that labour markets which reward experience and skill more than they pay for qualifications are more efficient – better able to match individuals with the range of jobs available. The Irish, UK and US labour markets pay a large premium for skill, and in terms of performance on indices such as employment, mobility and turnover rates, job creation and worker productivity, these countries stand out among the OECD Members (OECD, 1997*a*). As countries attempt to make their labour markets more flexible in line with the recommendations of the *Jobs Study* (OECD, 1994), there is a need to examine anew the interrelationships among educational qualifications, actual skills and work experience, and their effects on income – and, indirectly, on issues such as earnings inequality and poverty.

Returns to knowledge jobs

There is a second reason why the impact of literacy on income may grow in the medium term. The evidence on the returns to labour market experience obscures the fact that internal labour markets offer differential rewards for low-skill and high-skill jobs. In many countries in the OECD area, low-skilled workers have experienced an increase in unemployment and job instability, as measured by unemployment and turnover rates, since 1980. In Canada, the United Kingdom and the United States, low-skill workers also experienced a significant drop in relative or real earnings over that period (OECD, 1996*a*). There is evidence of a weakening in the supply of low-skill jobs in the European Union, even though the gap in earnings between unskilled and skilled workers remained fairly stable in the majority of countries. International trade, technological change and structural adjustment may be expected to contribute to a further deterioration in the labour market position of low-skill workers in certain sectors of the economy, while gains in employment opportunities and real earnings can occur for highly qualified workers in knowledge-intensive labour markets.

Jobs with high knowledge and skill content are coveted in all countries, in part because of the above-average wages they offer. Raudenbush, Kasim, Eamsukkawat, Liu and Miyazaki (1996) have extended, for the United States, the analyses presented previously in this report regarding the differential effects of experience, education and skill on income, by comparing the effects for different occupational groups. As expected, the data reveal substantial wage premiums associated with knowledge jobs.

As illustrated in Figure 2.11, OECD economies vary significantly in the proportion of the labour force employed in mostly high-wage and white-collar jobs.[5] The share of such jobs in total employment is influenced by a range of factors, including trade, technology and adjustment in industrial and occupational structures. The evidence presented in Figure 2.11 suggests that the supply of literacy skills may be another contributing factor. As expected, workers in "good" jobs with above-average pay possess high literacy skills, as demonstrated by high proportions at levels 3 and 4/5 compared with the balance of the employed population.

FIGURE 2.11

Employment in the knowledge economy

Proportion of labour force aged 16-65 employed in white-collar jobs, which are mostly high-skill and high-wage, 1994-1995

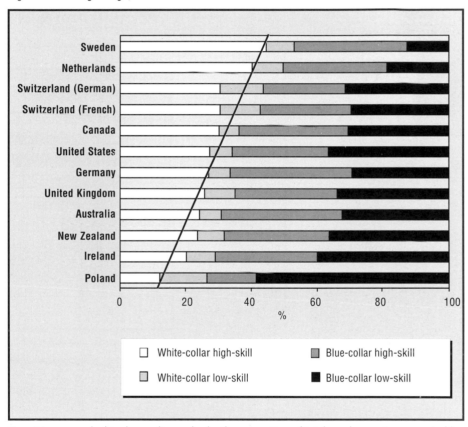

Countries are ranked in descending order by the proportion of total employment represented by high-skill white collar jobs.

Source: International Adult Literacy Survey, 1994-1995.

Countries differ greatly in the share of high-wage, high-skill jobs in total employment. The share of such jobs is comparatively low in Ireland and Poland.

This figure shows the share in total employment of mostly high-skill and high-wage white-collar workers by the proportions at literacy levels 1 and 2 versus levels 3, 4 and 5.

---

5   These jobs include administrators, managers, a wide range of professionals and technicians. Clerks and
     service workers are excluded from the definition.

The data presented in Figure 2.12 show that a significant proportion of blue-collar workers possess medium to high levels of literacy skills. This can be interpreted in at least two ways. First, it could be an indication of overqualification for the current job. This would mean that a substantial number of people in the labour market would have received a level of education, or alternatively developed a level of skill, that is higher than the level deemed socially and economically efficient. The other explanation might be that these workers are insufficiently challenged by their jobs. To the extent demand for skill is the issue, these workers represent a large pool of talent which can be tapped in a growing knowledge economy. Figure 2.12 shows that there are large differences in the skills reserve available to the OECD countries surveyed.

FIGURE 2.12

Blue-collar workers at medium to high skill levels

Proportion of skilled craft workers and machine operators at literacy levels 3-5, document scale, selected countries, 1994-1995

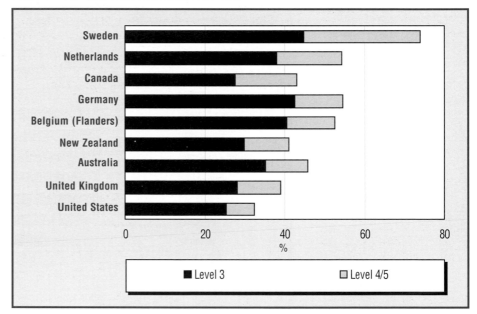

Countries are ranked by the proportion of blue-collar workers at literacy levels 4 and 5.

Source: International Adult Literacy Survey, 1994-1995.

Up to 75 per cent of Swedish craft workers and machine operators, and more than half of the craft workers and machine operators in Belgium (Flanders), Germany and the Netherlands, have good literacy skills, but the vast majority of them report that they have little use for these skills at work. Many do not consider themselves to be over-educated or overqualified for their jobs. Rather, these people tend to indicate that they are not sufficiently challenged at work.

The graph shows the proportions of skilled craft workers and machine operators who are at a medium to high level of literacy skill. See notes to Table 2.12.

2.3 Wider Social Benefits

Private rates of economic return to education and skill, while important, do not capture other benefits which have measurable economic value for society – for example, in terms of increased tax revenue. In addition to these returns, there exist wider social benefits, which are much harder to quantify but no less important. Primary among these are considerations of social cohesion and democracy (OECD, 1997*b*).

This final section examines some of these wider social benefits. Special attention is paid to the relationships between improved literacy and crime, public assistance, health and community participation.

Public assistance and welfare

As noted above, persons who have low levels of literacy on average earn lower wages and experience more frequent spells of unemployment. In this way, inadequate levels of literacy can contribute to poverty. When individuals or families are unable to support themselves through productive employment, they must rely upon other alternatives. All OECD countries have instituted social welfare in the form of various public assistance programmes – a humane and essential government function, but one that is costly to society.

An indication of the connections between low levels of literacy and both crime and public assistance is given in a study conducted by Barton and Coley (1996), where it was found that 79 per cent of 19-23-year-old Americans on public assistance, and 68 per cent of those who were arrested in the previous year, had lower-than-average basic skills. A good summary of the theories explaining how it is that people choose to pursue criminal alternatives and the potential links to educational attainment and educational results is found in Witte (1997).

Figure 2.13 shows that the US prison population has a substantially lower average literacy score than the general household population. In particular, prisoners in this country are heavily over-represented at the lowest literacy level and only slightly represented at the higher levels. A similar pattern is found when the population receiving public assistance is compared with the general population (Barton and Jenkins, 1995). Again, the population receiving public assistance is over-represented at the lower levels of literacy, but show only about one-third the representation of the general population at the higher levels.

The literacy scores of the prison population are significantly below those of the general population in the United States. Improving the literacy skills of prisoners can be an important element in successful rehabilitation.

The figure shows the mean literacy scores on the test of the two comparison populations. The area shaded dark corresponds to levels 1 and 2 and the area shaded light corresponds to levels 3, 4 and 5.

FIGURE 2.13

Literacy proficiency and crime

Mean literacy proficiency of prison and general household population aged 16-65, mean scores on prose scale with a range of 0-500 points, United States, 1992

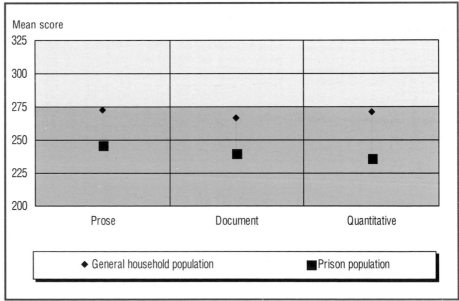

Source: Haigler *et al.* (1994).

There is no doubt that public assistance recipients and those in prison differ from the general population in more than just their levels of literacy. But their lower-than-average skill levels make finding jobs and stable employment more difficult. It would therefore seem reasonable to assume that a significant portion of public expenditure for welfare could be saved if the population at risk were to have access to, and make full use of, opportunities for developing literacy skills. But there is a cost attached to such developments, for households, communities, employers and society. Sufficient resources will only be forthcoming if literacy programmes are considered not simply as a cost but also as an investment which yields large and tangible, albeit long-term, returns (OECD, 1996*a* and 1997*b*).

Health and community participation

Literacy is also related to health (see Grossman and Kaestner, 1997), for two main reasons. First, literate persons may be able to gain access to information and obtain better health results through their ability to understand and process that information. Good examples of this are preventive health practices and the early detection of problems, so that they can be treated in their incipient, less costly stages. Second, more literate persons may make better choices in allocating health resources – i.e. in deciding what types of household and institutional resources are required to address health needs.

The IALS did not collect health data from the respondents, so the relationship, if any, between literacy and health cannot be examined directly using this source.

Numerous studies have shown a positive link between education, on the one hand, and health status and longevity on the other. In general, it is assumed that a key connecting factor is the effect of education on improving literacy skills. As was shown in Chapter 1, literacy is powerfully related to educational attainment. Unfortunately, few studies link education directly to the understanding of specific information pertinent to preventive health measures or specific health challenges (see Kenkel, 1991). Studies undertaken in a number of developing countries have shown a specific positive relationship between women's literacy and health (see Grosse and Auffrey, 1989; Comings, Smith and Shrestha, 1994; and LeVine *et al.*, 1994). Some of those findings must be assumed to have relevance for the OECD countries as well.

Beyond health care and crime prevention, social cohesion and democracy depend to a large extent on engagement in the broader society outside the paid labour market. One indicator of such engagement is the degree to which individuals participate in voluntary community activities. Figure 2.14 illustrates the relationship between literacy proficiency and voluntary participation in community activities at least once a month in the year preceding the interview. For all countries the results suggest a positive relationship between literacy and community work, although other variables must be assumed to influence this relationship as well.

FIGURE 2.14

Literacy proficiency and community participation

Proportion of the population aged 16-65 who participated in voluntary community activities at least once a month during the year preceding the interview, by prose literacy level, 1994-1995

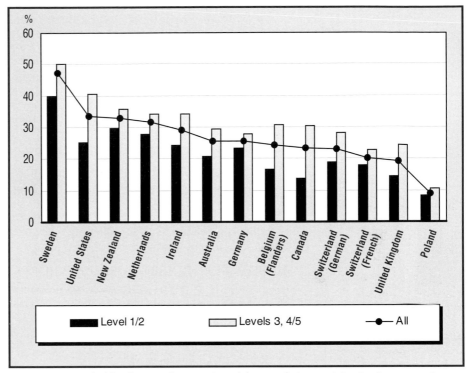

Countries are ranked by the overall proportion of the population participating in community activities regularly.

Source: International Adult Literacy Survey, 1994-1995.

Literacy is associated with voluntary community engagement in some countries.

The figure shows the proportion taking part in community activity by prose literacy level.

Literacy skills are necessary for community participation, citizenship and social cohesion.

2.4 Conclusions

All societies consider high levels of literacy desirable for all of their citizens, as a means of sustaining widespread participation in economic and social life. Literacy is important for communication, and is an element in making informed decisions. It is a necessary ingredient for citizenship and community participation. Yet the "quiet" contributions that literacy makes to the economy are not as fully appreciated. These can take the form of higher worker productivity, income and government revenues; a better quality of life in terms of reduced poverty, unemployment, crime and public assistance; and improved health and child-rearing – the private and social benefits that have been examined in this chapter. And, there are other contributions which have not yet been studied in terms of their connection to literacy, such as political participation and broad adjustment to technological change. Even if the quantifiable evidence is lacking, however, these contributions are logically connected to literacy, in providing the ability to address complex issues or to understand how to use evolving information technologies. The net payoffs to investments in raising literacy, whether private or social, are probably beyond calculation, but they are clearly substantial and manifold.

References

BARTON, P.A. and COLEY, R.L. (1996), *Captive Students: Education and Training in American Prisons,* Policy Information Center, Educational Testing Service, Princeton, New Jersey.

BARTON, P.A. and JENKINS, L. (1995), *Literacy and Dependency: The Literacy Skills of Welfare Recipients in the United States,* Policy Information Center, Educational Testing Service, Princeton, New Jersey.

BERLIN, G. and SUM, A. (1988), "Toward a more perfect union: Basic skills, poor families", *Occasional Paper No. 3,* Ford Foundation Project on Social Welfare and the American Future, The Ford Foundation, New York.

BISHOP, J.H. (1988), "Is the test score decline responsible for the productivity growth decline?", *American Economic Review*, Vol. 79 (1), pp. 178-197.

BISHOP, J.H. (1995), "The impact of curriculum-based external examinations on school priorities and student learning", Special issue of the *International Journal of Educational Research,* Vol. 23 (8), pp. 653-752.

BLOOM, M.R., BURROWS, M., LAFLEUR, B. and SQUIRES, R. (1997), *The Economic Benefits of Improving Literacy Skills in the Workplace*, The Conference Board of Canada, Ottawa.

CARLINER, G. (1996, September), "The wages and language skills of US immigrants", *Working Paper Series, No. 5763*, National Bureau of Economic Research, Cambridge, MA.

CHISWICK, B.R. (1991), "Speaking, reading and earnings among low skilled immigrants", *Journal of Labor Economics,* Vol. 9 (2), pp. 149-170.

CHISWICK, B.R. and MILLER, P.W. (1995), "The endogeneity between language and earnings: International analyses", *Journal of Labor Economics,* Vol. 13 (2), pp. 246-288.

COHN, E. and ADDISON, J. (1997), "The economic returns to lifelong learning", Mimeo, prepared for the OECD, forthcoming in a special 1998 issue of *Education Economics.*

COMINGS, J.P., SMITH, C. and SHRESTHA, C.K. (1994), "Women's literacy: The connection to health and family planning", *Convergence*, Vol. 27 (2/3), pp. 93-101.

DUSTMANN, C. (1994), "Speaking fluency, writing fluency and earnings of migrants", *Journal of Population Economics,* Vol. 7 (2), pp. 133-156.

GRENIER, G. (1984), "The effects of language characteristics on the wages of Hispanic-American males", *The Journal of Human Resources,* Vol. XIX (1), pp. 35-52.

GROSSE, R.N. and AUFFREY, C. (1989), "Literacy and health status in developing countries", *Annual Review of Public Health,* Vol. 10, pp. 281-297.

GROSSMAN, M. and KAESTNER, R. (1997), "Effects of education on health", in J.R. Behrman and N. Stacey (Eds.), *The Social Benefits of Education,* University of Michigan Press, Ann Arbor, Michigan.

HAIGLER, K.O., HARLOW, C., O'CONNOR, P. and CAMPBELL, A. (1994), *Literacy Behind Prison Walls: Profiles of the Prison Population from the National Adult Literacy Survey,* National Center for Education Statistics, United States Department of Education, Washington, DC.

HICKS, N. (1996), "Is there a trade-off between growth and basic needs?", *Finance and Development,* Vol. 17 (2), pp. 17-20.

KENKEL, D.S. (1991), "Health behavior, health knowledge, and schooling", *Journal of Political Economy,* Vol. 99, pp. 287-305.

KOSSOUDJI, S.A. (1988), "English language ability and the labor market opportunities of Hispanic and East Asian immigrant men", *Journal of Labor Economics,* Vol. 6 (2), pp. 205-228.

LEUVEN, E., OOSTERBEEK, H. and VAN OPHEM, H. (1997), "International comparisons of male wage inequality: Are the findings robust?", Tinbergen Institute Discussion Paper No. 97-059/3, University of Amsterdam, Amsterdam.

LEVINE, R.A., DEXTER, E., VELACO, P., LEVINE, S., JOSHI, A.R., STUEBING, K.W. and TAPIA-URIBE, F.M. (1994), "Maternal literacy and health care in three countries: A preliminary report", *Health Transition Review*, Vol. 4 (2), pp. 183-229.

McMANUS, W.S. (1990), "Labor market effects of language enclaves: Hispanic men in the United States", *Journal of Human Resources,* Vol. XXV (2), pp. 228-252.

McMANUS, W.S., GOULD, W. and WELCH, F. (1983), "Earnings of Hispanic men: The role of English language proficiency", *Journal of Labor Economics,* Vol. 1 (2), pp. 101-130.

MURNANE, R.J. and LEVY, F. (1996), *Teaching the New Basic Skills*, Free Press, New York.

MURNANE, R.J., WILLETT, J.B. and LEVY, F. (1995), "The growing importance of cognitive skills in wage determination", *Review of Economics and Statistics,* Vol. 77 (2), pp. 251-266.

OECD (1994), *The OECD Jobs Study: Evidence and Explanations, Part II: The Adjustment Potential of the Labour Market*, Paris.

OECD (1995), *Education at a Glance: OECD Indicators,* Paris.

OECD (1996a), *Education at a Glance: OECD Indicators,* Paris.

OECD (1996b), *Lifelong Learning for All,* Paris.

OECD (1997a), *Employment Outlook,* Paris.

OECD (1997b), "Literacy skills: Use them or lose them", Chapter 3 in *Education Policy Analysis*, Paris.

PSACHAROPOULOS, G. (1981), "Returns to education: An updated international comparison", *Comparative Education,* Vol. 17 (3), pp. 321-341.

RAUDENBUSH, S.W. and KASIM, R.M. (1996, October), "Adult Literacy, Social Inequality, and the Information Economy: Findings from the National Adult Literacy Survey", Mimeo, College of Education, Michigan State University, East Lansing, Michigan.

RAUDENBUSH, S.W., KASIM, R.M., EAMSUKKAWAT, S. and MIYAZAKI, Y. (1996), "Social Origins, Schooling, Adult Literacy, and Employment: Results from the National Adult Literacy Survey", Mimeo, College of Education, Michigan State University, East Lansing, Michigan.

RAUDENBUSH, S.W., KASIM, R.M., EAMSUKKAWAT, S., LIU, X.F. and MIYAZAKI, Y. (1996), "Human Capital, Labor Market Segmentation, and Social Inequality: Results from the US National Adult Literacy Survey", Mimeo, College of Education, Michigan State University, East Lansing, Michigan.

RIVERA-BATIZ, F.L. (1990), "English language proficiency and the economic progress of immigrants", *Economic Letters,* Vol. 34, pp. 295-300.

RIVERA-BATIZ, F.L. (1991), "The effects of literacy on the earnings of Hispanics in the United States", in E. Melendez, C. Rodriguez, and J.B. Figueroa (Eds.), *Hispanics in the Labor Force,* Plenum Press, New York.

RIVERA-BATIZ, F.L. (1994*a*), "Quantitative skills and economic success in the labor market", *IUME Briefs,* Teachers College, Institute for Urban and Minority Education, Columbia University, New York.

RIVERA-BATIZ, F.L. (1994*b*), "Quantitative literacy and the likelihood of employment among young adults in the United States", *Journal of Human Resources,* Vol. XXVII (2), pp. 313-328.

SNOW, C.E. and TABORS, P. (1993), "Language skills that relate to literacy development", in D. Tannnen (Ed.), *Spoken and Written Language: Exploring Orality and Literacy*, Ablex, Norwood, New Jersey.

TAINER, E. (1988), "English language proficiency and the determination of earnings among foreign-born men", *Journal of Human Resources*, Vol. XXIII (1), pp. 108-122.

WITTE, A.D. (1997), "Crime", in J.R. Behrman and N. Stacey (Eds.), *The Social Benefits of Education,* University of Michigan Press, Ann Arbor, Michigan.

Chapter 3

Literacy Acquisition during a Lifetime

3.1 Introduction

The IALS study findings convey at least three important messages. First, countries differ in the distribution of literacy skills (Chapter 1) and in the economic and social factors that generate high literacy (Chapter 2). Second, literacy is not an integral quality one does or does not possess, but a broad continuum of skill. Third, literacy is everyone's concern because of the economic and social opportunity it offers. This chapter argues that raising a country's overall level of literacy requires an inter-disciplinary and cross-sectoral approach to policy-making. Among the factors determining literacy skills, in all of the countries studied, are a person's socio-economic background, educational attainment and labour force experience. Therefore, understanding the production of a country's stock of human capital, as gauged by the literacy skills of its population, requires an analysis of how these skills are acquired, distributed and maintained during a lifetime. Analyses of data along social class lines and by age groups within countries can help decision-makers clarify where limited resources are best invested.

3.2 Literacy and Age

Age is a factor in explaining differences in the literacy profiles of populations. However, the influence of age does not operate singularly but acts in conjunction with effects attributable to different experiences in early childhood, schooling, school-to-work transition, and labour market experience. This section examines some of these age-related processes in literacy acquisition; the focus is not on economic but on social and cultural variables.

Literacy in early childhood

Age is strongly related to literacy proficiency in all countries, with younger persons tending to do better than older adults, but its effect is confounded with the influences of other important factors such as educational attainment, labour market experience and engagement in literacy activities at work and in daily life.

Children are born into a world of language. They are surrounded by the talk of their parents, their siblings and others who care for them. Speech emerges naturally as they learn to appreciate the reactions of adults around them. Children copy speech and create new sounds in an effort to make language work for them. Most children, at some point during their second year, say their first coherent words, and soon thereafter their vocabulary begins to grow exponentially. Literacy builds as children learn to communicate in a variety of contexts. These early years of language acquisition provide a critical foundation that affects children's school experience – and eventually, their life chances and well-being.

Not all children develop at the same rate. By the time they reach compulsory school age there are significant differences in their skills, including verbal skills and literacy proficiency. These differences are largely attributable to the effects of socialisation, particularly within the family; evidence of heredity effects is relatively slim (Husén and Tuijnman, 1991; Scarr and Weisberg, 1978). For example, studies of mother-child interactions during the preschool years clearly indicate that the rate of vocabulary growth and the emergence of language structures are directly related to the quality and quantity of language to which children are exposed (Huttenlocher *et al.,* 1991). Figure 3.1 suggests, for Canada, how school readiness relates to the quality of learning experiences in the home in the early years. Moreover, interventions aimed at improving parents' skills have profound effects on children's language development, and these effects can have long-term consequences for their future health and well-being (Deutsch *et al.*, 1983; Levenstein *et al.*, 1983; Schweinhart *et al.*, 1993).

FIGURE 3.1

School readiness and parental stimulus

Percentage of children aged 4 and 5 from homes with low and high parental education who face developmental delays, Canada, 1994-1995

Children who do well in school often approach school ready to learn. School readiness is influenced by the parents' level of education.

The figure shows school readiness as measured on the *Peabody Picture Vocabulary Test* or *l'Echelle de vocabulaire en images Peabody*. Education level is based on that of the parent with the highest education level.

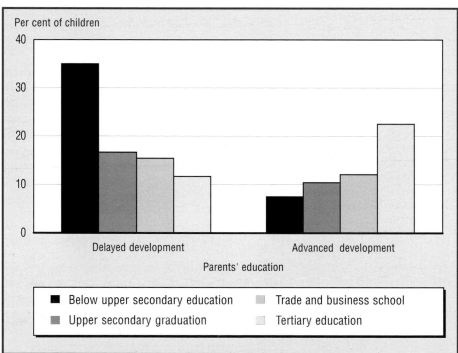

Source: National Longitudinal Survey of Children and Youth; HRDC Bulletin, 1997.

Literacy development during school age

Parenting continues to be an important influence on children's literacy during the schooling years, but the quality of school that the child attends also plays a critical role. Large-scale studies in a number of countries have demonstrated that schools vary considerably in their effects on children's literacy (Gray, 1989; Luthgart *et al.*, 1989). Children with the same parental background and initial verbal ability can attain the equivalent of as much as two additional years of achievement if they attend a particularly good school (Willms and Jacobsen, 1990). These studies attribute most of the effects to aspects of school "culture". In successful schools, teachers project the belief that *all* students can master the curriculum. Their high expectations are manifest in a number of classroom practices and school routines that differ from the ordinary in terms of the use of instructional time and resources, the content and pace of the curriculum, rules and norms for behaviour, and the type and amount of homework. These high norms for academic success are supported by the parents, who reinforce the schools' efforts through volunteering their time, participating in school activities, and complementing learning activities at home (OECD, 1996a). This research suggests that although the level of resources spent on schooling contributes to achievement, their effects are small compared with the cultural aspects of schooling related to high expectations and parental support (Willms, 1992; Wenglinsky, 1997).

For example, Figure 3.2 depicts the relationship between schools' average eighth-grade reading achievement and socio-economic status, observed in data from the United States National Educational Longitudinal Study. The figure demonstrates three findings. First, there are large differences between schools in their mean level of reading achievement – more than one full standard deviation at every level of socio-economic status. Second, the extent of parental engagement in school activities is related to parents' socio-economic status. Third, schools with high levels of parental engagement had, on average, higher levels of achievement, even after taking into account the level of family socio-economic status: increased levels of parental participation were associated with reading gains of about 8 per cent of a standard deviation (Ho-Sui Chu and Willms, 1996).

FIGURE 3.2

Reading achievement and parental engagement

Mean reading scores for schools with high and low levels of parental engagement in school activities, 8th-grade students, United States, 1988

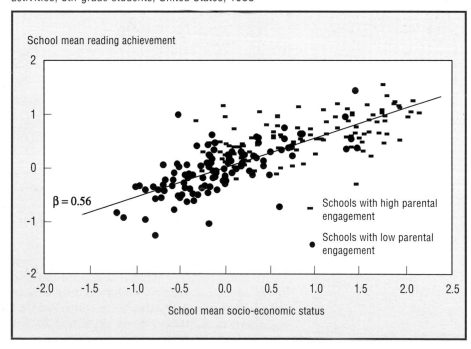

> There are large differences among schools in their reading achievement – more than one standard deviation at every level of socio-economic status. Parental engagement in school activities is related to parents' socio-economic status. Schools with high levels of parental engagement, on average, have higher levels of achievement, even after taking into account the level of family socio-economic status.

> Each symbol indicates the mean reading score and mean socio-economic status for 8th-grade students in a United States middle school. Socio-economic status is a composite measure describing the educational level and occupational prestige of the child's parents, and family income. Schools with the highest scores (top 10 per cent) on a measure of parental engagement (volunteering and attending parent-teacher association meetings) are denoted with a small bar: schools with the lowest scores (bottom 10 per cent) are denoted with a circle.

Source: National Educational Longitudinal Study, 1988.

Literacy skill comparisons among countries for children at age 14 have been derived from the Reading Literacy Study conducted by the International Association for the Evaluation of Educational Achievement (IEA). Given that literacy skills begin developing early, and that strong cultural forces contribute to that development, one would expect the IALS scores of young adults aged 16-25 to correlate with the IEA results for younger children. Figure 3.3 shows the relationship between average scores on the document literacy tests for the IALS and the IEA Reading Literacy Study, for eight OECD countries that participated in both studies. For most countries, there does indeed seem to be a positive link between the achievement of young children and that of young adults. New Zealand is an exception, with high document scores for the 14-year-olds, but comparatively low scores for the 16-25 year old group.

FIGURE 3.3

Early reading scores and adult literacy performance

Mean document literacy scores for IALS youth aged 16-25 and IEA students aged 14

Early literacy results foreshadow literacy results for youth and young adults.

Each dot denotes a country's mean IALS document literacy score and its mean score on the IEA reading literacy document scale at age 14. Because of a sampling anomaly in the IALS youth data in the United States, National Adult Literacy Survey (1992) data has been substituted for the United States IALS data in this figure.

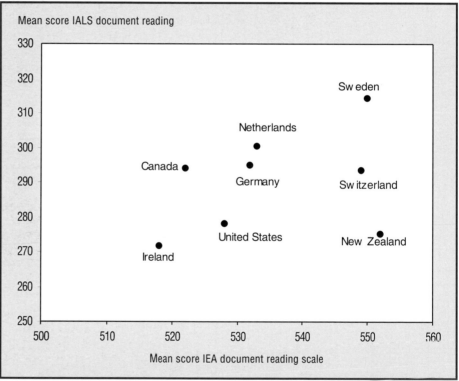

Source: International Adult Literacy Survey, 1994-1995, and IEA Reading Literacy Study, 1991.

Literacy and transition from school to work

In most OECD countries, graduation from upper secondary school is considered a minimum threshold qualification level for all youth. However noble this goal, the reality is that in many Member countries, large numbers of young adults leave the formal education system without this level of qualification or the requisite literacy skills. Figure 3.4 illustrates the considerable variation in net enrolment and graduation rates in upper secondary education among the countries surveyed. Net enrolment rates for 17-year-olds are at or close to 100 per cent in some countries, but drop to below 75 per cent in others.

FIGURF 3.4

Enrolment at age 17 and graduation in upper secondary education, selected countries

Net enrolment rates at age 17 and graduation rates at the typical age of graduation, percentage point difference from the OECD mean, 1994

Enrolment rates vary from 100 per cent of 17-year-old Belgians to 78 per cent of 17-year-olds in New Zealand. Differences among countries are larger for graduation than for enrolment rates.

The figure shows the differences in enrolment and graduation from the OECD mean for 25 countries.

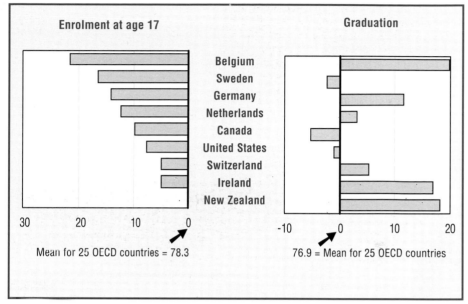

Countries are ranked by the rate of enrolment at age 17.

Source: OECD Education Database.

The levels of literacy attained by children during their years of primary and secondary schooling directly affect their opportunities to pursue further education, as well as their transition from school to work. Literacy has an influence on the types of jobs individuals hold, but these will affect levels of literacy in turn. Figure 3.5 shows the prose literacy proficiency levels of young adults aged 20-29, for selected countries. The mean performance level of those without high school graduation is significantly lower than the level attained by graduates in all five countries shown in Figure 3.5. In many cases, the lack of skill observed for those who did not obtain an upper secondary qualification can be thought of as both a cause and a consequence of the decision to leave school, in that their lower scores may have contributed to the decision to leave school without graduating.

Policy discussions about shortages of skilled workers and rising youth unemployment, in some countries, concentrate on the large number of students who drop out of school before graduation. In 1994, the average rate of unemployment was 19 per cent among youths aged 20-24, and 13 per cent among young adults aged 25-29 (OECD, 1996*b*). Figure 3.6 displays the 1994 unemployment rates for those aged 25-29, for the countries studied. In every country, young persons who had not completed upper-secondary schooling were more likely to be unemployed.

Moreover, the penalty for low educational attainment is greater for youth, as they generally lack work experience and seniority – assets which, for some older workers, compensate for low qualifications. For the 12 countries, the average unemployment rate for the age group 25-29 was 9.5 per cent in 1994-1995. In contrast, it was 17.7 per cent for those who had not completed upper-secondary schooling. In Ireland, Poland and the United Kingdom, where unemployment was highest for this age group, about one in four low-educated young persons was unemployed.

FIGURE 3.5

Literacy skills of school-leavers and young adults

Mean literacy scores on prose scale of young people aged 20-29 with and without upper secondary graduation, selected countries, 1994-1995

Young people who did not graduate have significantly lower prose literacy skills than graduates. The difference is especially large in Canada. Smaller differences exist in Australia and Germany.

The figure shows the mean score differences in prose literacy of young people who graduated from secondary school and those who did not.

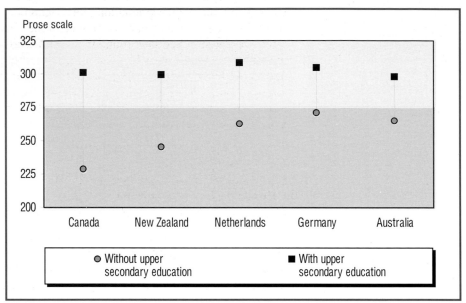

Countries are ranked by the mean score difference between the comparison groups.

Source: International Adult Literacy Survey, 1994-1995.

FIGURE 3.6

Unemployment and education

Unemployment rates by level of educational attainment for persons 25-29 years of age, 1994

Those without a full cycle of secondary education show high rates of unemployment.

The figure shows unemployment rates for each of three levels of educational attainment. The line shows the total unemployment rates for people aged 25-29.

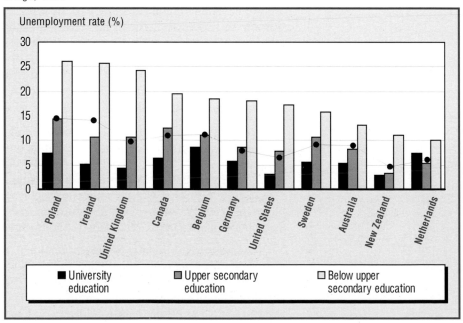

Countries are ranked by the unemployment rate of those without upper secondary education.

Source: OECD Education Database.

Despite the strong relationship between formal educational attainment and employment within countries, youth unemployment rates are not consistently related to graduation rates among countries. The Netherlands and the United States, for example, had graduation rates of 80 and 76 per cent in 1994, but their unemployment rates for all young persons aged 25-29 were 7.1 and 7.4 per cent; whereas Ireland, with a graduation rate of 93.8 per cent, had an unemployment rate of 14.2 per cent. This can be explained somewhat by the "discouraged worker" effect: research in Scotland found that youth who were faced with the prospect of unemployment were more likely to remain in school beyond the compulsory period and complete their upper-secondary education (Raffe and Willms, 1989). Also, high rates of youth unemployment cannot be attributed to low levels of literacy skills among upper secondary graduates because, as shown previously in Chapter 1, young persons are, on average, no less literate than persons above 45.

The results presented in Figure 3.7a-g suggest that the literacy skills of youth who are completing their formal schooling are, on average, comparable to, and in some countries higher than, the skills of adults who completed their schooling in the 1970s or 1980s. In most countries, literacy skills has a weak relationship with age until around ages 40-45, when they begin to decline substantially.

Literacy scores could decline with age because of three types of effects: *age effects* – people acquire skills through education and experience, but their skills deteriorate through lack of use or the ageing process; *period effects* – there may be more emphasis on acquiring literacy skills now than in an earlier period; and *cohort effects* – the cohort of adults who were born between 1947 and 1956 (the so-called "baby-boomers" who were aged 38-47 when the IALS data were collected) had more opportunities for education, housing and good jobs than the cohort born between 1957 and 1966 (Foot and Stoffman, 1996).

Figures 3.7a-g show the relationship between literacy and age after controlling for the differential effects of educational attainment for selected countries. It is impossible to separate the three types of effects when working with cross-sectional data. However, the figures also display, for each of the six countries, the literacy-age relationship after taking into account the level of educational attainment of the respondents (see Box 3A). The results suggest that the decline in literacy skills is associated mainly with differing life experiences (i.e. cohort effects), and are not due to the ageing process. Results presented later in this chapter suggest that people can lose some of their literacy skills if these are not maintained through regular and demanding practice at home and at work.

The literacy scores of older adults are lower than those of younger adults. In some countries differences in educational attainment play a role, but in others this influence is minor. In general, the lower scores are associated with differing life experiences and not with the ageing process.

Box 3A   Reading the Figures

The graphs in Figures 3.7a-g show the effect of age on literacy scores compared to the international mean score on the prose scale. Scale scores below the 0.0 reference line indicate how far below the international mean, in standard score units, the mean score at an age would be. Similarly, scale scores above the reference line represent standard scores above the international mean. Standard score units are the result of subtracting the mean from a score and dividing that result by the standard deviation. The values plotted in the graphs are those predicted by a regression equation reflecting the country-specific relationship between age and prose literacy proficiency. The unadjusted line shows the values obtained when the differences in educational attainment between age groups are ignored; the adjusted line shows values that take these differences into account.

In Australia differences in educational attainment have a large impact on differences in literacy scores, but other life factors play a role too, as scores decline with age even when educational differences are accounted for.

The solid line indicates the mean literacy scores at each age; the thin line indicates the mean literacy scores for persons aged 16-65, controlling for educational attainment.

Much of the differences in literacy scores by age in Canada are due to differences in educational attainment. However, even when these differences are accounted for, older Canadians still score lower than younger Canadians.

FIGURE 3.7A

Literacy and age in Australia

Relationship between prose literacy scores and age, with and without adjustment for level of education,1994-1995

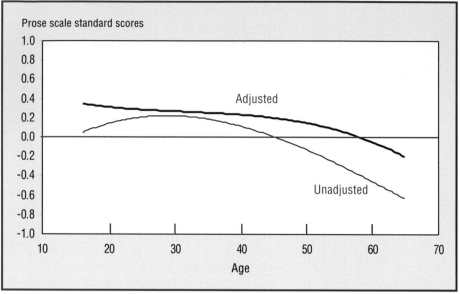

Source: International Adult Literacy Survey, 1994-1995.

FIGURE 3.7B

Literacy and age in Canada

Relationship between prose literacy scores and age, with and without adjustment for level of education, 1994-1995

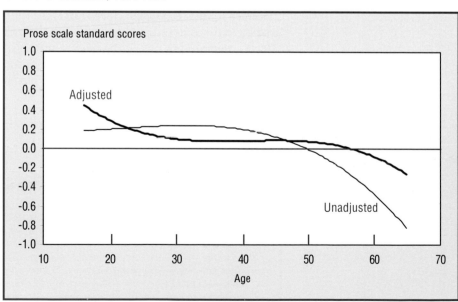

Source: International Adult Literacy Survey, 1994-1995.

FIGURE 3.7C

Literacy and age in the Netherlands

Relationship between prose literacy scores and age, with and without adjustment for level of education, 1994-1995

In the Netherlands there is a sharp decline in literacy scores after the age of 40. This appears to be due more to differences in life experiences than to variation in educational attainment.

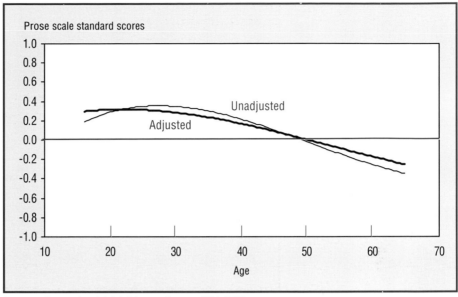

Source: International Adult Literacy Survey, 1994-1995.

FIGURE 3.7D

Literacy and age in United Kingdom

Relationship between prose literacy scores and age, with and without adjustment for level of education, 1994-1995

The United Kingdom is one of the few countries where young adults score lower than those aged 30 to 40, even after the data have been adjusted for differences in educational attainment. There is also a particularly sharp decline in literacy scores among older adults.

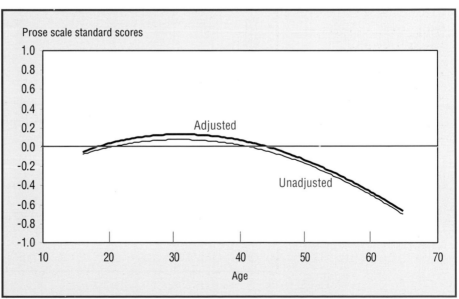

FIGURE 3.7E

Literacy and age in French-speaking Switzerland

Relationship between prose literacy scores and age, with and without adjustment for level of education, 1994-1995

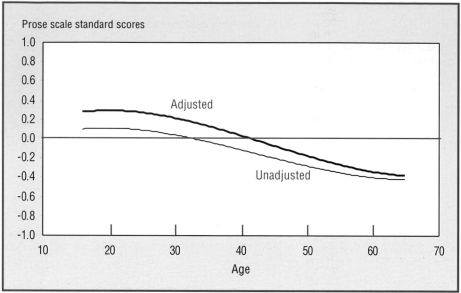

Source: International Adult Literacy Survey, 1994-1995.

In both French- and German-speaking Switzerland there is a sharp and regular decline in average literacy scores across the age groups even when educational attainment is held constant.

FIGURE 3.7F

Literacy and age in German-speaking Switzerland

Relationship between prose literacy scores and age, with and without adjustment for level of education, 1994-1995

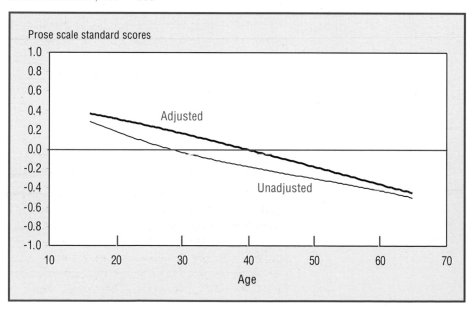

There are few differences in literacy scores by age in the United States once differences in educational attainment are taken into account. This graph shows how important it is to factor in education when examining the relationship between literacy proficiency and age.

FIGURE 3.7G

Literacy and age in United States

Relationship between prose literacy scores and age, with and without adjustment for level of education, 1994-1995

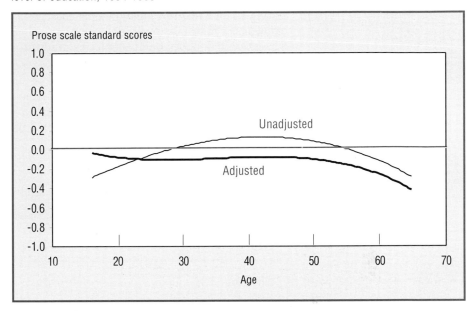

Conclusions drawn about literacy levels across countries and regions within countries should take account of the age distribution.

The strong relationship between literacy and age within each country means that conclusions drawn about literacy levels across regions within a country must take account of the age distribution. For example, in some Canadian provinces, notably New Brunswick and Quebec, a disproportionately large share of the adult population is above age 40, and many of these adults have relatively low levels of education. These two provinces, and any country with similar characteristics, would fare poorly in comparisons that do not take the age distribution into account.

Demographic considerations also have implications for the strategies employed to improve literacy scores. Ireland, for example, had a particularly young population in 1994; 18 per cent of its total population was aged 5-14, and 17.2 per cent was aged 15-24. Australia and New Zealand also have relatively young populations, with children and youth each comprising about 15 per cent of the total populations. The economic success of these countries will depend heavily on their ability to provide employment opportunities for their young people. In contrast, the 5-14 cohort comprises only 11 per cent of Germany's total population, and the 15-24 cohort only 11.8 per cent (OECD, 1996*b*). In that country, then, a somewhat higher priority might be placed on improving the skills of older workers.

Generally, because the literacy skills of youth are on average higher than the skills of adults aged 45-65 in most countries, the average levels of literacy in the workforce should increase as the youth cohort replaces workers in the older cohort over the next 10 years. However, only about 3 per cent of the workforce is replaced annually in most countries, so it is unlikely that the "rejuvenation" effect by itself will be sufficient to meet the generally increasing demands for highly skilled workers in OECD countries. This point is elaborated in Chapter 4.

3.3 Literacy Skills and Socio-economic Status

The level of literacy performance of a nation's youth is an indicator of the success of families, schools and communities in producing tomorrow's literate society.

The literacy level of a society's youth, and the extent of disparities in literacy skills among youth with differing individual characteristics and family backgrounds, are indicators of how investments of material, social and cultural resources made during the past few decades have been translated into skills and competencies in the generation now coming into adulthood: they denote the success of families, schools and communities in producing a literate society. These indicators are also indices of the pool of economic and social capital available to sustain the labour market over the next few decades. To the extent that there is a relationship between education and physical well-being, they may also foretell the future health of a society.

FIGURE 3.8A

Socio-economic gradients for document literacy scores

Relationship between document literacy scores and level of education of respondents' parents, for young adults aged 16-25, 1994-1995

Countries vary substantially in their stock of literacy skills, even after account is taken of parents' levels of education. Countries with high scores tend to have shallow gradients.

The gradient lines show the effect on literacy of each additional year of parents' education within a country. The length of the line covers the middle 90 per cent of the range of parental years of education. The effect size is the difference between the mean and the score divided by the standard deviation of the sample. In this chart, countries differ in the steepness of the gradient (in countries with steep gradients each additional year of parents' education has a greater effect than in the countries where the gradient is not as steep).

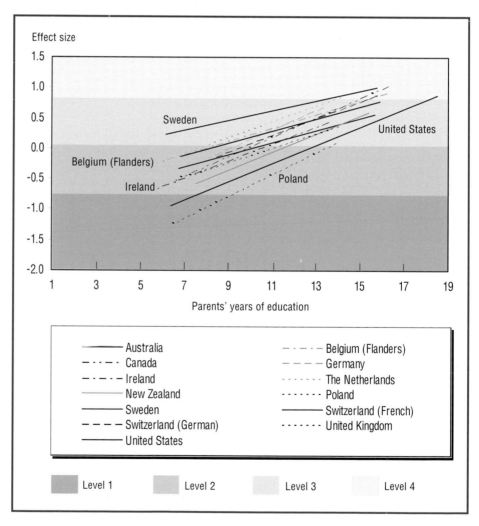

Source: International Adult Literacy Survey, 1994-1995.

FIGURE 3.8B

Socio-economic gradients for document literacy scores

Relationship between document literacy scores and level of education of respondents' parents, for the entire adult population aged 26-65, 1994-1995

In many countries – though not in all – the gradients are less steep for younger than older adults. Thus, parental education tends to have a stronger effect on the document literacy performance of older than younger adults.

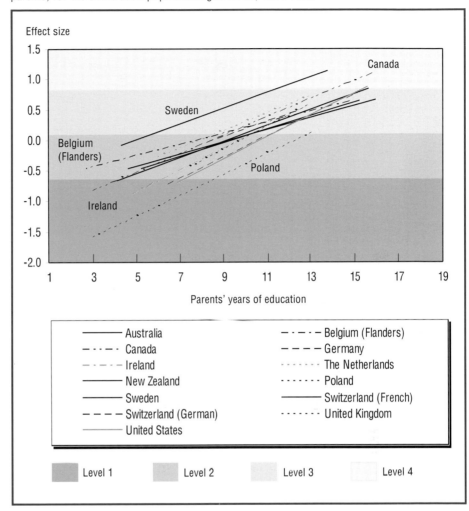

Source: International Adult Literacy Survey, 1994-1995.

Figure 3.8a displays the relationship between the document literacy scores for youth (aged 16-25) and their parents' levels of initial educational attainment for each country studied. Figures 3.8b and 3.8c show the gradients (see Box 3B) for adults aged 26-65, both for the total and the employed population aged 26-65.

Box 3B   What do Gradients Show?

Gradients are indicators of the extent of inequalities among racial, ethnic or socio-economic groups, or between men and women. They are being used increasingly in the fields of economics, education and population health to characterise the quality of life of a society. The levels of education of an individual's parents are commonly used in conjunction with measures of family income and socio-economic status, but data for these variables were not available for all of the countries studied.

FIGURE 3.8C

Socio-economic gradients for document literacy scores

Relationship between document literacy scores and level of education of respondents'
parents, for the employed population aged 26-65, 1994-1995

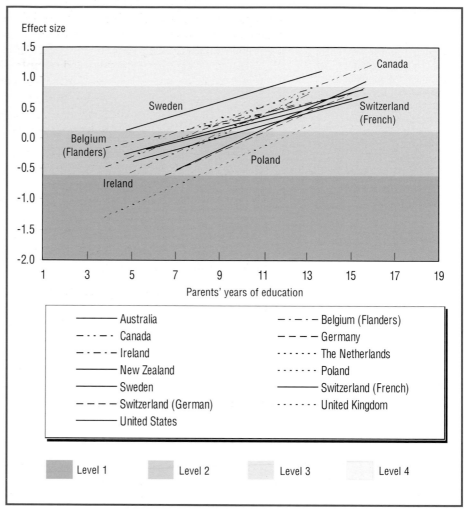

Source: International Adult Literacy Survey, 1994-1995.

Countries differ in the relationship between parental education and literacy
skill, as Figures 3.8a-c show. In Belgium (Flanders), Canada and the United States,
the relationship is stronger than in Sweden or the United Kingdom, where the
gradients are shallower. In the first three countries, schools seem less able to
transform or ameliorate the differences students bring to school with them and so
tend to reproduce rather than ameliorate skill and socio-economic inequalities.

The gradients for older adults (see Figure 3.8b) are steeper in most countries
than those for younger adults (see Figure 3.8a). Only in Germany, Belgium
(Flanders) and the United States is the relationship between parents' education and
skill stronger for the younger population. It may be that schools are increasingly
more able to provide skills equitably, so that an individual's abilities now depend
less on his or her parents and more on education. It may also be that the process of
skill gain and loss during the later adult years is itself related to literacy practices
that are a result of parental influence.

Two findings revealed by this analysis are particularly striking. First, countries vary substantially in their literacy skills, even after account is taken of parents' levels of education. Youth in Poland and the United States, for example, whose parents had both completed twelve years of education on average, scored approximately 40 per cent of a standard deviation lower than comparable youth in Canada and Germany. This is a very large difference: on average, youth increase their literacy scores on this test by about 12 to 13 per cent of a standard deviation for each additional year they remain in school. Thus, in Poland or the United States, the literacy scores of youth who had completed two years of post-secondary schooling were similar to those of Canadian or German youth who had completed the 11th grade. However, youth in Canada and Germany lag behind Sweden by nearly the same amount – about one-third of a standard deviation, the equivalent of literacy gain associated with roughly three years of additional schooling.

The second striking feature of these findings is that countries with high literacy scores tend to have shallow gradients.[1] In Sweden, for example, youth whose parents had completed only the 8th grade scored, on average, 13 per cent of a standard deviation above the international average; whereas in the United States, the country with the greatest inequalities, youth with similar family backgrounds scored 60 per cent of a standard deviation below the international mean. In contrast, the variation among countries is relatively small for youth whose parents had both completed tertiary-level studies.[2]

An analysis based on the pooled data set, for which the data sets for all countries were combined, showed no statistically significant differences between men and women in the average literacy scores. Poland and Germany were the exceptions: in Germany, men scored about 12 per cent of a standard deviation higher than women, and in Poland women outperformed men by about 16 per cent of a standard deviation. For Canada, there was a significant gender-parental education interaction, indicating that the parental education gradients for women were somewhat steeper than for men.[3]

Inequalities appear at an early age

The results presented in Figures 3.8a-c suggest that the literacy skills of youth who are completing their formal schooling are on average comparable to, or even higher than, the skills of adults who completed their schooling in the 1970s or 1980s. At the same time as the IALS was conducted, a first wave of data were collected for Canada's National Longitudinal Study of Children and Youth, the first major study of its kind in that country. The study entailed detailed interviews with the parents of a representative sample of over 22 000 children. During the interviews, children who were aged 4 or 5 were administered the Peabody Picture Vocabulary Test (PPVT), a measure of early literacy skills and a relatively good predictor of later school success. Analyses of these data indicate that inequalities are apparent at ages 4 and 5, and that performance is especially closely linked with mothers' education and whether the child was being reared in a single- or two-parent family (Willms, 1996; see also Härnqvist, 1989).

An important aspect of the findings is that at ages 4 and 5 there were significant differences among Canada's ten provinces in average levels of literacy scores, and yet socio-economic inequalities were similar across the provinces. Data

The results indicate that the literacy skills of youth are on average comparable to, or in some instances higher than, the skills of adults who completed their schooling in the 1970s or 1980s. Employers would do well to make good use of the skills young people possess.

---

[1]   The correlation between levels and gradients in this analysis was -0.79.

[2]   It is unlikely that the observed relationships stemmed from so-called ceiling effects on the test. In every country, there was a relatively small proportion of respondents scoring at level 5 – the top level on the literacy test.

[3]   A slope of 0.12 for women compared with 0.08 for men.

from the Third International Mathematics and Science Study, which were also collected in 1994-1995, indicate that by the time children reach 8th grade, there are significant differences among the provinces with regard to their socio-economic status inequalities (Willms, 1997*a* and *b*). Analyses of the IALS data for youth aged 16-25 reveal large inter-provincial differences in socio-economic inequalities for all three literacy domains. The pattern is similar to that of the international inequalities shown previously in Figure 3.8a: the variation among provinces in literacy scores is small for youth from advantaged backgrounds, whereas it is large for youth from relatively disadvantaged backgrounds.

These findings suggest that differences in the literacy profiles of societies are apparent already in the pre-school period, and that they increase during the years of formal schooling. Societies that are rich in human capital, as gauged by the literacy levels of their youth, achieve this wealth by enabling children from less advantaged backgrounds to achieve relatively high levels of literacy. An important structural feature of a schooling system, which likely contributes to the relationship between literacy skills and social background, concerns the manner in which students are assigned to schools, classrooms and instructional groups. Research studies conducted in the Netherlands (van den Eeden, 1994), the United Kingdom (Kerckhoff, 1986; Willms, 1986) and the United States (Gamoran and Berends, 1987; Rumberger and Willms, 1992) have found that when students from less advantaged backgrounds are segregated, they are less likely to attain high levels of literacy. Teachers in segregated classrooms and schools find it difficult to establish an atmosphere conducive to learning; there is generally less support from parents; there tend to be more discipline problems; and teacher morale is difficult to sustain. Moreover, establishing a positive learning climate depends on having a nucleus of able students who have high expectations and are motivated to learn.

Most school systems assign children on a "catchment" basis, and between-school segregation to a large extent mirrors residential segregation. The geographical boundaries of these areas are, however, not necessarily drawn to achieve a comparable mix of students across schools. Also, certain school, district and national policies can contribute to segregation, such as the support of private schooling through tuition tax credits, the streaming or tracking of children into different academic programmes, the allocation of children into special education classes, and the placement into instructional groups within classrooms. Kerckhoff's (1993) study of the 1958 British birth cohort, *Diverging Pathways*, showed that ability grouping, streaming, and other structural features of the English school system constrained certain children's academic performance and had a cumulative and negative effect on their life chances. This finding echos the results of Swedish research studies conducted during the early 1960s, before and after schooling was made comprehensive in that country (Härnqvist, 1960; Husén and Boalt, 1968).

3.4 Factors that Strengthen Literacy during Adulthood

There are two lines of research that can help to explain why socio-economic status has such an important effect on key learning outcomes, and why it differs from country to country (Coleman, 1988). One emphasizes the independent actions of individuals. Parents make independent decisions to achieve what they perceive to be best for their family – what economists call "maximising utility". Higher levels of literacy skill will result because parents with more economic and social capital do things differently: on average, they are likely to talk more with their children, read to them more often, buy them educational games – generally provide them with a richer environment – than parents with fewer resources. They are also more likely to participate in activities at their child's school. The skill levels that are developed

Establishing a nucleus of able students who have high expectations and are highly motivated to succeed is an essential ingredient in creating "positive" learning environments.

during the period of formal schooling are then strengthened during adulthood by the literacy practices individuals engage in at home and at work.

The other line of research, more in the sociologist's domain, stresses the importance of the social context in shaping, constraining, and redirecting individuals' actions. For example, one would expect adults' engagement in literacy practices to depend on the norms of their workplace and immediate community, and the social support available to them. Socio-economic inequalities will persist if those with poorer skills have less exposure to high literacy contexts than those with superior skills, or if there are differences in opportunities to participate in adult education and training.

Socio-economic inequalities will persist if those with poorer skills have less exposure to high literacy contexts than those with superior skills.

Literacy practices at home

The IALS respondents were asked a number of questions pertaining to the cultural and literacy-related activities (see Box 3C) they engage in as part of their daily lives, including reading newspapers or magazines, reading books, writing letters, and watching television. Figure 3.9 shows the distribution of scores for each country on an index of literacy engagement at home, which is a summary measure of participation in literacy-related activities. The plot shows that people who are more engaged in literacy activities at home have higher literacy scores. Literacy practices and literacy skill mutually reinforce each other. Wider and more frequent reading enhance skill and, in turn, growth in skill facilitates access to a wider variety of reading opportunities. Increased skill presumably makes reading more likable and, thus, an activity which an individual is more likely to pursue.

Box 3C Literacy Engagement at Home Index

The questions concerning literacy-related activities at home were used to construct scales indicating frequencies of engaging in particular activities. These scales were then averaged to construct an "engagement index" with values ranging from 0 to 5.

Figure 3.10a displays the relationship between respondents' levels of education and whether they engaged in book-reading at least once a week. Figure 3.10b presents similar findings pertaining to whether they write a letter (or anything else that is more than one page in length) at least once per month. Figure 3.10c, finally, shows the relationship between levels of education and the average number of hours spent per day watching television.

Within each country, the pattern is the same: those with higher levels of education are, on average, more often engaged in reading books and writing letters. The amount of television watched is negatively related to the respondents' level of education. Results of a more detailed analysis of data indicated that respondents' prose literacy scores are positively related to their daily reading practices, and negatively related to the amount of television they watch, even after taking into account their age and level of education.

FIGURE 3.9

Literacy practices at home

Distribution of home engagement in literacy index scores by level of prose literacy, 1994-1995

People who are more engaged in literacy activities at home have higher literacy scores. There is a wide range of engagement amongst people with very low literacy scores.

The literacy engagement scores are standardised to have a mean of zero and a standard deviation of one at the international level. Each box plot displays five statistics for a group. The left hand margin of the box denotes the 25th percentile of index scores, the right hand margin the 75th. The vertical line in the middle of the box denotes the median. The horizontal lines extend from the box 1.5 times the length of the box or to the minimum or the maximum, whichever is smaller.

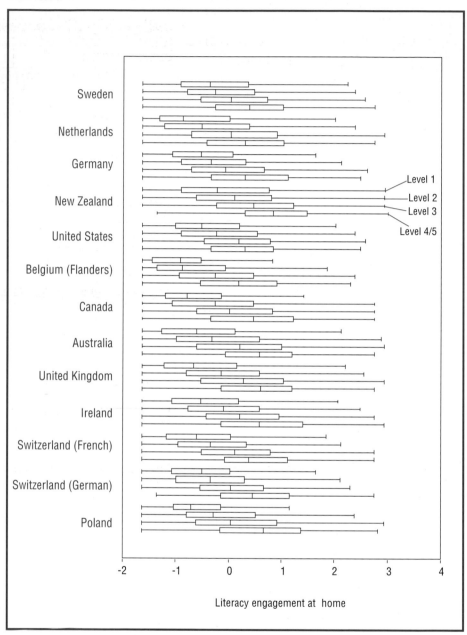

Countries are ranked in ascending order of their literacy engagement at home.

Note: Outlier data have been removed for producing this graph.

Source: International Adult Literacy Survey, 1994-1995.

FIGURE 3.10A

Reading and writing or television?

Percentage *reading a book* at least once a week, by level of education, 1994-1995

People with higher levels of education tend to spend more time reading. The frequency of engaging in reading tasks is related to literacy proficiency.

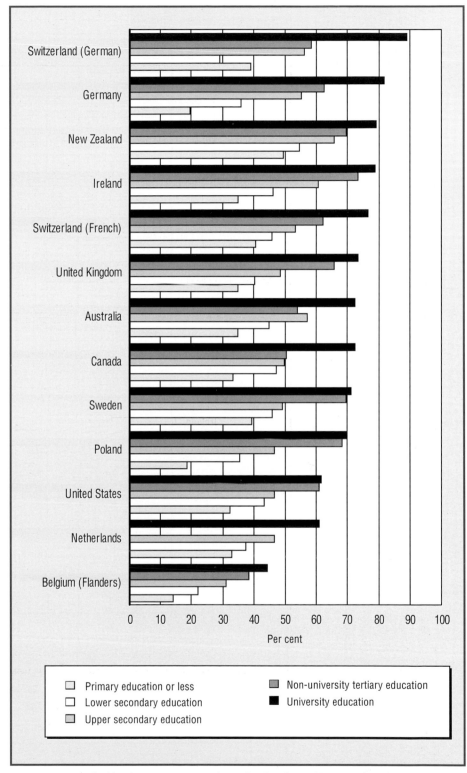

Countries are ranked by the percentage reading a book at least once a week in the university education category.

Source: International Adult Literacy Survey, 1994-1995.

FIGURE 3.10B

Reading and writing or television?

Percentage *writing a letter* at least once a month, by level of education, 1994-1995

More highly educated people tend to write more often than less educated persons. The frequency of writing at least once a month is comparatively high in Australia, Germany and Ireland, but less so in Belgium (Flanders) and the Netherlands.

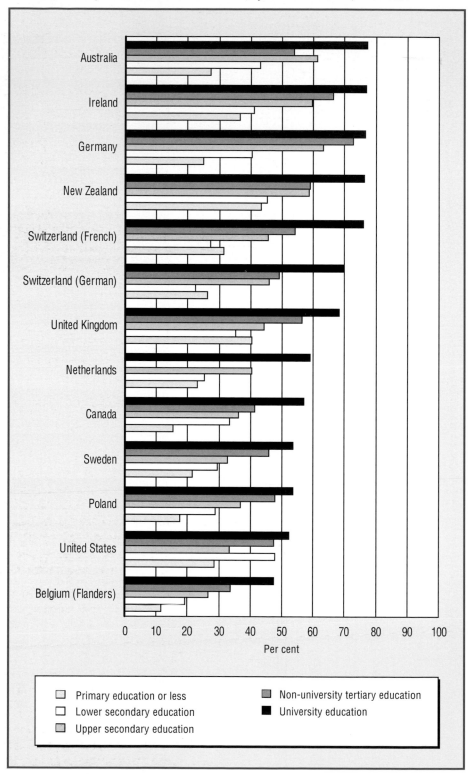

Countries are ranked by the percentage writing a letter at least once a month in the university education category.

Source: International Adult Literacy Survey, 1994-1995.

FIGURE 3.10C

Reading and writing or television?

Mean number of hours per day spent *watching television,* by level of education, 1994-1995

Television viewing is inversely related to educational attainment. Those with only a primary education or less watch the most, and those with a university degree the least. Adults in Germany, the United Kingdom and the United States appear to watch more television than adults in the other countries.

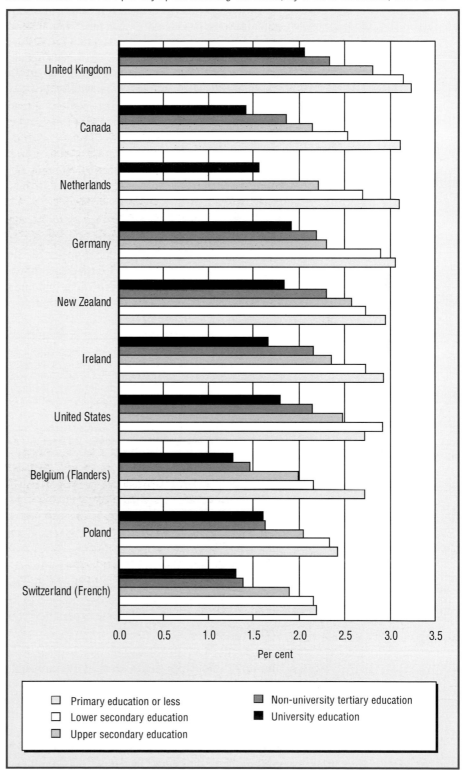

Countries are ranked by the number of hours per day spent watching television in the primary education category.

Source: International Adult Literacy Survey, 1994-1995.

Literacy practices at work

New theories of economic growth claim that production is not simply a function of capital and labour, but also a function of knowledge and ideas. They stress that "knowledge workers" at all levels of a firm or other organisation can enhance that organisation's productivity (Romer, 1993). If firms are to be competitive, they will require workers who have the requisite skills to contribute. In OECD countries, with the increased importance of the service sector and high-technology industries – and the disappearance of many relatively low-skilled manufacturing jobs – the new knowledge workers will need to have higher literacy skills. But firms also need to make the best use of the skills that workers already have. Employees may require further training that will enable them to make better use of their skills, and some firms may need to be structured in ways that provide greater opportunities for workers to contribute. An important question, therefore, is: To what extent are workers using their skills on the job? Are they being challenged in ways that make the best use of their range of skill and enable them to maintain and further develop those skills?

The respondents who were employed at the time of the survey were asked a series of questions about how often they engaged in literacy activities at work; the responses were used to construct an index of "literacy engagement at work" (see Box 3D). The activities included reading and writing letters, memos, reports and articles; filling out forms, bills, invoices and budgets; and calculating prices, costs and budgets. Figure 3.11 shows the distribution of scores on this index by level of education for each country.

Box 3D   Literacy Engagement at Work Index

Respondents were also asked a series of questions pertaining to the frequency with which they engaged in nine literacy tasks at work – reading magazines or journals; manuals or reference books; diagrams or schematics; reports or articles; reading or writing letters or memos; bills, invoices or budgets; writing reports or articles; estimates or technical specifications; and calculating prices, costs or budgets. For each task, a scale was constructed that indicates the number of times per week the respondent engaged in the task, assuming a five-day work week. The scores were then averaged within each category to provide an "engagement index" that ranges 0 to 5. The data analysis was restricted to those aged 16-65 who were working full-time.

A person's engagement in literacy activities at work is influenced not only by his or her effort and motivation but also, and especially, by the demands posed by the job. Employers therefore play a key role in sustaining and developing literacy skills.

A person's engagement in literacy activities at work is affected not only by his or her own effort and motivation, but also by the demands of the job. Within every country there is a wide range of literacy scores at every level of education (see Chapter 1). This suggests that the "fit" between literacy engagement and level of education is imperfect. Figure 3.11 shows that there are many workers with a low level of education who are heavily engaged in literacy activities, and conversely, there are many workers with some experience of tertiary education whose skills are underutilised.

Figure 3.11 also shows that the average level of literacy engagement at work and its relationship to the level of educational attainment varies substantially among countries. In Germany, for example, the extent of engagement is uniformly high for workers at all levels of education, and there is a relatively weak relationship between engagement and level of educational attainment. This is not the case for most other countries. In Sweden, for example, the level of engagement is about average, and there is a fairly strong relationship between engagement and level of education. In Belgium (Flanders), Canada, Ireland, the Netherlands, and the United States, engagement in literacy activities at work is low for workers who have not undertaken any post-secondary education. But workers who have had some experience of tertiary education have levels of engagement comparable to those of workers in Germany.

The fit between literacy engagement and level of educational attainment is not particularly strong: there are a number of workers with less than completed upper secondary education who are heavily engaged in literacy activities, and conversely, there are many workers with at least some tertiary education whose skills are underutilised.

The literacy engagement scores are standardised to have a mean of zero and a standard deviation of one at the international level. Each box plot displays five statistics for a group. The left hand margin of the box denotes the 25th percentile of index scores, the right hand margin the 75th.

FIGURE 3.11

Literacy practices at work

Index scores for engagement in literacy activities at work by level of educational attainment, 1994-1995

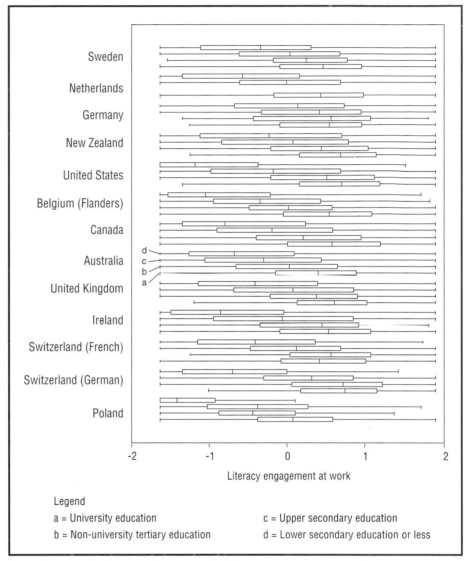

Countries are ranked in ascending order of their literacy engagement at work.

Note: Outlier data have been removed for producing this graph.

Source: International Adult Literacy Survey, 1994-1995.

Levels of literacy engagement also vary across sectors of the labour market. Figure 3.12 shows the distribution of index scores for six industrial groups, for Germany and the United States. In agriculture and mining, the median level of engagement is relatively low in both countries. However, even in this sector, there is considerable variation among workers. The majority of workers in the construction and transportation group, both in Germany and the United States, have levels of engagement that are close to the international average. Workers in personal services have somewhat higher levels than the construction and transportation group, and workers in financial services have by far the highest engagement level. The distributions of literacy skill scores for personal and financial services are dissimilar in Germany and the United States.

Levels of literacy engagement vary among sectors of employment, but there is large variation among workers within sectors. The largest differences between the United States and Germany are for the manufacturing, and trade and hospitality sectors.

The literacy engagement scores are standardised to have a mean of zero and a standard deviation of one.

FIGURE 3.12

Literacy practices and sectors of the labour market

Index scores for engagement in literacy activities at work by industrial groups for Germany and the United States, 1994-1995

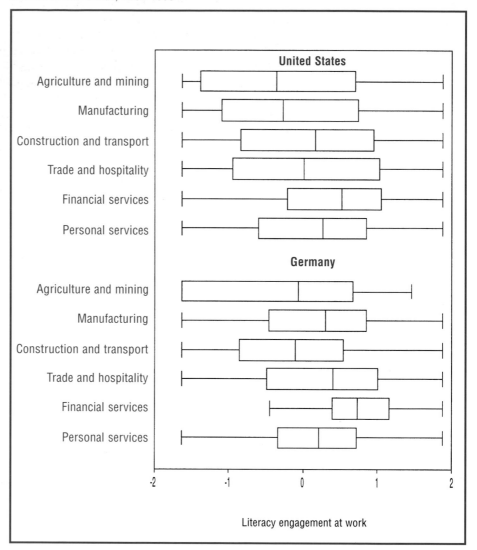

Industrial groups are ranked in ascending order of the mean engagement scores for the United States.

Note: Outlier data have been removed for producing this graph.

Source: International Adult Literacy Survey, 1994-1995.

   The largest differences between countries are for the manufacturing and trade or hospitality sectors. In the United States, the majority of workers in this category fall below the international mean on the engagement index, whereas in Germany the majority of workers score above the mean. Given the role which level of engagement in literacy at work is thought to play in the maintenance and growth of literacy skill in adulthood, the existence of these differences is cause for concern.

3.5 Conclusions

Raising a country's literacy profile requires a change in its culture. Underpinning this argument are four conclusions derived from the theory and analyses presented in this chapter. First, literacy development begins at birth. This is evident from several studies in child development, and the results presented here show that there is a strong relationship between the literacy scores of young children and those of youth and young adults. Second, better-educated parents are more likely to raise children with higher levels of literacy. Analyses of mother-child interactions have shown that a child's language development depends heavily on the quantity and quality of language to which a child is exposed. The close relationship between literacy and parents' educational background is evident throughout the years of compulsory schooling, and extends into adulthood. Third, a person's ultimate level of literacy is not fully determined during early childhood, or even at the end of formal schooling. Although the early periods are important, a person's experiences and social and economic environment during adulthood can dramatically affect their literacy skills. People can improve their skills, but skills can also deteriorate if they are not used. Fourth, countries that have high mean levels of literacy have small differences in performance between social groups. People from advantaged backgrounds tend more or less to do equally well in every country studied. What differentiates countries in their literacy levels is the performance of people from less advantaged backgrounds.

The results evidently stress the need for implementing a comprehensive strategy for developing literacy skills that is supported by a wide range of partners.

These conclusions imply that low levels of literacy are not solely the result of inadequate support from families, low-quality schooling, a lack of workplace programmes, or any other single factor. By implication, they stress the need for a comprehensive strategy for developing literacy that requires support from governments, employers and social partners, local communities and families. The first step is to create a framework of understanding that literacy is important to economic productivity, to health and well-being, and to social cohesion in a modern society; that literacy is everyone's concern; and that reducing inequalities in opportunity is the key to achieving high literacy scores. Perhaps the biggest policy challenge is achieving effective partnerships across a number of policy domains.

The immediate question for governments and employers is how they can best invest their limited resources to achieve these aims. Should they place more resources on targeted programmes for particular groups – e.g., adults with low levels of literacy? Or should a greater share of resources be spent on more universal programmes, such as the media campaigns that have been used with some success to discourage youth from smoking and to encourage increased physical activity among adults? Should more money be spent on general infrastructure, such as assistance to libraries or the development of telecommunication systems that could deliver instruction more efficiently? Will these investments enable adults with low levels of literacy to be less dependent on public assistance, and help them better manage their health-care? The data furnished by this study cannot answer these questions directly, as those answers depend on the particular economic and social context of each country. However, the findings from this survey, alongside other research, provide some guidance on how best to invest resources.

First, there are interventions that could bring a "three-to-one" or "two-to-one" return, compared with other kinds of investments. For example, a literacy programme that emphasized parent training could potentially have three benefits: better care and literacy development for the participants' children; improved literacy for the participants, possibly leading to greater self-sufficiency; and, in the longer term, reduced health care and other social costs for both the participants and their children. Similarly, a literacy programme for older adults that emphasized health and fitness could have a two-fold return.

Second, employers have an essential role to play in developing literacy. The results show that youth and young adults in every country have relatively high literacy skills. Hence, the social partners will need to work with government to develop innovative strategies that will reduce youth unemployment, lest valuable skills atrophy. The findings suggest that employers' efforts to enhance productivity might be channelled in two directions: improving the literacy abilities of less-literate workers, and enabling workers to make the best use of the skills they do have. Many employers might be willing to invest in further education and training, but they are unclear about what kind of training to invest in, and the ways in which it will be cost-effective. Governments could help by setting recommended levels of employer-sponsored education and training, and by providing the infrastructure necessary to deliver high-quality instruction. They also need to pay special attention to the needs of small businesses.

Third, in many countries there is a need for a concerted effort to be made to reduce inequalities between social groups. In several countries, the majority of respondents whose scores were at the lowest literacy level were receiving social assistance. A primary link between literacy and socio-economic status is the effect of segregating low-status groups from mainstream society. This segregation limits access to certain labour markets and to the best schools for some children (London and Flanagan, 1976). The effects of residential segregation can be either reduced or exacerbated by government policy and workplace practices that determine where educational and training programmes are located, and who has access to them. Employers, policy-makers, educators, and other community leaders need to become aware of those structural features of the education system and labour-market that lead to steep skill differences between social groups, and take steps to ensure that children and workers from differing backgrounds have equal opportunities for high-quality schooling and training. They also need to ensure that there are a number of different avenues for youth and adults to recover from inadequate educational experiences.

A strong research infrastructure is important because this will provide the empirical knowledge base needed for informed decision-making.

Finally, investments in research are the foundation for action. A strong research infrastructure is critical to making decisions based on empirical evidence. Greater use could be made of international data sets assembled by the OECD and its partners in examining the determinants of literacy within countries. However, there is also a need for research that is "close to the ground", that examines the link between literacy training in schools and adult education programmes, that determines the needs of employers, that assesses the cost-efficiency of different kinds of training programmes, or that produces fine-grained measures of literacy for assessing the progress of adults struggling to become more literate (Tuijnman *et al.*, 1997). This kind of research could enlighten investment decisions and contribute to the success of public policy development and individual decisions.

References

COLEMAN, J.S. (1988), "Social capital in the creation of human capital", *American Journal of Sociology,* Vol. 94, pp. S95-S120.

COURTS, P. (1991), *Literacy and Empowerment*, Bergin and Garvey, New York.

DEUTSCH, M., DEUTSCH, C., JORDAN, T., and GRALLO, R. (1983), *The IDS Program: An Experiment in Early and Sustained Enrichment*, Lawrence Erlbaum Associates, Princeton, New Jersey.

FOOT, D.K. and STOFFMAN, D. (1996), *Boom, Bust and Echo: How to Profit from the Coming Demographic Shift*, Mcfarlane, Walter and Ross, Toronto.

GAMORAN, A. and BERENDS, M. (1987), "The effects of stratification in secondary schools: Synthesis of survey and ethnographic research", *Review of Educational Research*, Vol. 57, pp. 415-435.

GLENN, N.D. (1997), *Cohort Analysis,* Sage Publications, Beverley Hills, CA.

GRAY, J. (1989), "Multi-level models: Issues and problems emerging from their recent application in British studies of school effectiveness", in D.R. Bock (Ed.), *Multi-level Analyses of Educational Data,* University of Chicago Press, Chicago, MA, pp. 127-145.

HÄRNQVIST, K. (1960), *Individuella differenser och skoldifferentiering*, SOU 1960:13, Fritzes, Stockholm.

HÄRNQVIST, K. (1989), *Background, Education and Work as Predictors of Adult Skills*, Department of Education and Educational Research, University of Göteborg, Göteborg.

HO-SUI CHU, E. and WILLMS, J.D. (1996), "The effects of parental involvement on eighth grade achievement", *Sociology of Education*, Vol. 69, pp. 126-141.

HRDC Bulletin (1996), "Linking home environment and child development", *HRDC Applied Research Bulletin*, Human Resources Development Canada, Vol. 3(1), pp. 4-5.

HUSÉN, T. and BOALT, G.S. (1968), *Educational Research and Educational Change: The Case of Sweden*, John Wiley and Sons, New York.

HUSÉN, T. and TUIJNMAN, A.C. (1991), "The contribution of formal schooling to the increase in intellectual capital", *Educational Researcher*, Vol. 20 (7), pp. 17-25.

HUTTENLOCHER, J., HAIGHT, W., BRYK, A., SELTZER, M., and LYONS, T. (1991), "Early vocabulary growth: Relation to language input and gender", *Developmental Psychology*, Vol. 27(2), pp. 236-248.

KERCKHOFF, A.C. (1986), "Effects of ability grouping in British secondary schools", *American Sociological Review*, Vol. 51, pp. 842-858.

KERCKHOFF, A.C. (1993), *Diverging Pathways: Social Structure and Career Deflections,* Cambridge University Press, Cambridge.

LEVENSTEIN, P., O'HARA, J., and MADDEN, J. (1983*)*, "The mother-child home program of the verbal interaction project", in Consortium for Longitudinal Studies, *As the Twig Is Bent*, Lawrence Erlbaum Associates, New Jersey, pp. 237-264.

LONDON, B., and FLANAGAN, W.G. (Eds.) (1976*)*, *Comparative Urban Ecology: A Summary of the Field*, John Wiley and Sons, New York.

LUTHGART, E., ROEDERS, P.J.B., BOSKER, R.J., and BOS, K.T. (1989), *Effektieve schoolkenmerken in het voortgezet onderwijs: Een literatuuroverzicht*, RION, University of Groningen, Groningen.

OECD (1996*a*), *What Works in Innovation: Parents as Partners in Schooling*, Centre for Educational Research and Innovation, Paris.

OECD (1996*b*), *Education at a Glance: OECD Indicators*, Paris.

RAFFE, D. and WILLMS, J.D. (1989), "Schooling the discouraged worker: Local labour-market effects on educational participation", *Sociology*, Vol. 23(4), pp. 559-581.

ROMER, P. (1993), "Ideas and Things", *The Economist*, pp. 70-72, September 11-17.

RUBENSON, K. and WILLMS, J.D. (1993), "Human Resources Development in British Columbia: An Analysis of the 1992 Adult Education and Training Survey", Mimeo, Statistics Canada, Ottawa.

RUMBERGER, R. and WILLMS, J.D. (1992), "The impact of racial and ethnic segregation on the achievement gap in California high schools", *Educational Evaluation and Policy Analysis*, Vol. 14(4), pp. 377-396.

SCARR, S. and WEISBERG, R.A. (1978), "The influence of family background on intellectual attainment", *American Sociological Review*, Vol. 43, pp. 674-692.

SCHWEINHART, L.J., BARNES, H.V., and WEIKART, D.P. (1993*)*, *Significant Benefits: The High/Scope Perry Preschool Study through Age 27*, Monographs of the High/Scope Educational Research Foundation, Vol. 10.

SPODEK, B. and SARACHO, O. (1993), *Language and Literacy in Early Childhood Education*, Teachers College Press, New York.

TUIJNMAN, A.C., KIRSCH, I.S., and WAGNER, D.A. (1997), *Adult Basic Skills: Advances in Measurement and Policy Analysis*, Hampton Press, Creskil, New Jersey.

van den EEDEN, P. (1994), "Educational selectivity from the multilevel perspective", Unpublished manuscript, Department of Social Research Methodology, Vrije Universiteit van Amsterdam, Amsterdam.

WENGLINSKY, H. (1997), *When Money Matters*, Educational Testing Service, Princeton, New Jersey.

WILLMS, J.D. (1986), "Social class segregation and its relationship to pupils' examination results in Scotland", *American Sociological Review*, Vol. 51, pp. 224-241.

WILLMS, J.D. (1992), *Monitoring School Performance: Guide for Educators*, The Falmer Press, Lewis.

WILLMS, J.D. (1996), "Indicators of mathematics achievement in Canadian elementary schools", in *Growing Up in Canada: National Longitudinal Survey of Children and Youth*, Human Resources Development Canada and Statistics Canada, Ottawa, pp. 69-82.

WILLMS, J.D. (1997*a*), *Literacy Skills of Canadian Youth,* Statistics Canada and Human Resources Development Canada, Ottawa.

WILLMS, J.D. (1997*b*), "Literacy skills and social class gradients", *Policy Options*, Vol. 18(6), pp. 22-26.

WILLMS, J.D. and JACOBSEN, S. (1990), "Growth in mathematics skills during the intermediate years: Sex differences and school effects", *International Journal of Educational Research,* Vol. 14, pp. 157-174.

Chapter 4

Adults' Readiness to Learn

4.1 Introduction

At a meeting of the OECD Education Committee at Ministerial level held in 1996, a decision was taken to make lifelong learning for all a priority for Member countries over the next five-year period (OECD, 1996). This decision brings the question of adults' readiness to engage actively in learning to the forefront of the policy agenda.

Today that question is discussed in the context of a new economic imperative that emphasises the importance of highly developed human capital and technological innovation. Together these facilitate economic restructuring and, ultimately, can lead to increased productivity. The neoclassical view of innovation and technological change is now being challenged by an evolutionary view, in which economic development is seen more as a learning process – as indeed are technological, organisational and institutional change (Hommen, 1997). Lundvall (1991) uses the phrase "learning by interacting" when describing how product innovations occur through interaction with, and feedback from, customers and suppliers. The learning perspective also features prominently in theories of industrial restructuring and flexible specialisation. Nonaka (1994) argues that the traditional focus on the input-process-output sequence results in a static view of organisations that does not accord due importance to what the organisation produces in terms of created information and knowledge.

Understanding what influences adults' readiness to learn is a prerequisite for designing cohesive policy strategies for lifelong learning.

The economic imperative, although dominant, is not the sole force driving the interest in lifelong learning. In the Eastern European countries, there is a struggle to build a new system after the collapse of the old order. Learning is a necessity in the search for a new identity, establishment of democratic institutions, and re-creation of society. Giddens (1994) notes that in the post-traditional order, individuals have to engage with the wider world if they are to survive: "Information produced by specialists (including scientific knowledge) can no longer be wholly confined to specific groups, but becomes routinely interpreted and acted on by lay individuals in the course of their everyday actions" (Giddens, 1994, p. 7).

Countries may agree on the importance of lifelong learning for all, but achieving that goal is difficult. A prerequisite for a cohesive strategy is understanding what influences adults' readiness to engage in learning, and understanding why large groups are excluded from the emerging learning society. Unfortunately, the general conclusion reached by Johnstone and Rivera (1965, p. 231), in their comprehensive study, is as true today as it was then: "One of the most persistent findings emerging from the inquiry is that a great disparity exists in the involvement in continuing education of segments of the population situated at different levels of the social hierarchy".

In that quote, "continuing education" refers to organised forms of education for adults. In contrast, today's discussion on lifelong learning covers more ground: the emphasis now is on the nature and structure of everyday experiences (Dohmen, 1996, p. 46), and their consequences for a person's learning processes, ways of thinking, and competencies. The challenges facing people today can create possibilities, not only for limited forms of learning geared to producing set, specific behaviour, but also for investigative learning that promotes new ways of thinking and acting. This broader perspective on lifelong learning is shared across the OECD: "Ministers agreed to focus on how to make learning a process extending from early age through retirement, and occurring in schools, the workplace and many other settings" (OECD, 1996, p. 3).

That process thus involves both time and context. The time element is clear from the term, "lifelong". It is no longer possible to adhere to a "front-end" perspective on schooling; education and adults' readiness to learn must be considered in a life-span context. The other aspect – "life-wide learning" – shifts the focus from organised forms of education to the total learning experiences of the individual. Thus it becomes particularly important to observe the relationship between everyday learning and participation in organised education and training. For example, does everyday learning increase or decrease the knowledge gaps between social groups? The previous chapter gave part of the answer to that question. As described in Figures 3.9 and 3.11, everyday learning in the form of reading or writing activity at work and outside work is unevenly distributed, and varies with educational attainment and socio-economic status. Those who obtained a good education initially further strengthen their capacity to read and write by engaging in a multitude of activities, both at work and elsewhere, that involve these skills. Those with a low level of initial schooling tend not to engage in such activity to the same extent.

While recognising the value of this broader interpretation of lifelong learning, this chapter will focus, in the main, on participation in organised adult education and training, and the barriers faced by those who are underserved at present.

4.2 Readiness to Learn and Literacy

In many OECD countries, participation in adult education and training[1] is becoming a common activity rather than an exception (Figure 4.1). The countries surveyed can roughly be divided into two major groups and two extreme cases.[2] The majority of the countries have a participation rate in education and training of around 40 per cent for the twelve months preceding the survey. Ireland and Belgium (Flanders) make up a second group, with rates in the low 20s. Sweden is the outlier at the high end with a participation rate of just over 50 per cent; the other outlier is Poland, with 14 per cent. Thus, in each country, there are large groups outside the emerging learning society, and these are often those most in need of skill improvement.

Everyday learning in the form of reading or writing activity at work and in daily life is unevenly distributed in the population.

---

[1]   In the data analyses, "adults" range in age from 16 to 65. Full-time students under 25 who were not in the labour force and classified themselves as "student" are excluded.

[2]   Germany is not included in the analyses presented in this chapter because the questions asked in that country's background questionnaire concern continuing vocational training rather than adult education defined more broadly. The German data are not comparable with the estimates obtained for the other countries as a result.

FIGURE 4.1

Literacy and adult education participation

Per cent of population aged 16-65 participating in adult education and training during the year preceding the interview, by document literacy level, 1994-1995

It is the more literate who mostly engage in adult education and training.

The figure shows the variation in participation rates for adults with low and high levels of literacy skills.

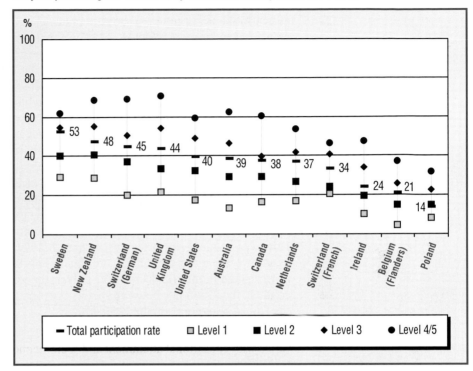

Countries are ranked by the overall participation rate.

Source: International Adult Literacy Survey, 1994-1995.

Figure 4.1 shows that rates of participation in adult education and training augment gradually with increasing levels of literacy skill. The level of inequality – although large everywhere – is comparatively small in Sweden and French-speaking Switzerland. The disparity is attributable to many factors but has its roots in what can be called "the long arm of the family".

Readiness to learn and the "long arm" of the family

As shown in the previous chapter, there exists a strong link between an individual's level of proficiency and the literate culture of the family in which the person grew up. While the roots are established during childhood, readiness for learning is further fostered in the education system. The social and cultural factors that are behind the relationship between early literacy and family background also link the distribution of educational attainment and reading and writing habits across different socio-economic groups. The influence of the family is further extended through the way in which educational credentials, to a large extent, determine entry into the labour market and subsequent life career (Chapter 2). Two key issues are:

● A realistic policy on lifelong learning for all should take into account that, at present, not all adults are ready to make use of existing opportunities for education and training; and

● A restrictive literacy environment during childhood is not necessarily connected with negative school experience. Longitudinal studies show that social background is a better predictor of readiness to engage in adult education or training than experiences of schooling (Rubenson, 1975; Hammarström, 1996). Thus, non-participation has less to do with bad memories of time at school and more with having been socialised into thinking that school "is not for me".

The long arm of the family is also apparent in the relationship between educational attainment and adults' readiness to engage in organised forms of education and training. Figure 4.2 shows that participation in adult education and training increases with the level of education initially received: the higher the level, the more likely a person is to participate. In the United States, for example, only 10 per cent of those with a primary education or less participate, compared with 64 per cent among those with a university education. The equivalent rates for Ireland are 9 and 51 per cent. Participation rates among those with a brief initial schooling are comparatively high in Sweden and the United Kingdom. Thus, organised adult learning is not for all, but for the already well educated. Figure 4.2 also indicates a marked difference between those with completed upper secondary education and those without. There is also a clear distinction between those who went on to tertiary education and those who did not. In Canada, for example, the participation rate jumps from 34 per cent among those with a full cycle of secondary education to 52 per cent among those with a non-university tertiary education. However, in most countries, differences between those with a university and a non-university tertiary education are small. This is especially true of countries with a strong and highly respected non-university sector, such as in Switzerland. In contrast, the difference between sectors is pronounced in Australia, New Zealand, the United Kingdom and the United States.

FIGURE 4.2

Participation predicted by educational attainment

Per cent of population aged 16-65 participating in adult education and training during the year preceding the interview, by level of educational attainment, 1994-1995

Most organised adult learning is for those who are well-educated already.

The figure shows the variation in participation rates for adults with different levels of schooling.

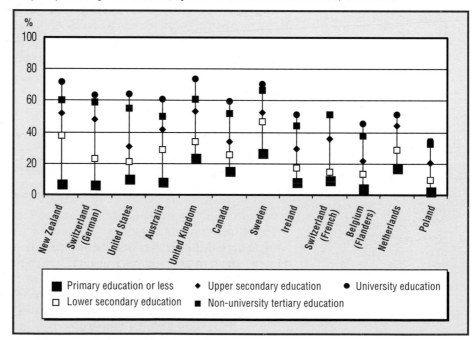

Countries are ranked according to the difference between those with the lowest and the highest level of educational attainment.

Source: International Adult Literacy Survey, 1994-1995.

FIGURE 4.3

Likelihood of participation by educational attainment

Adjusted odds ratios showing the likelihood of adults aged 16-65 receiving adult education and training during the year preceding the interview, by level of educational attainment, 1994-1995

People with a university degree in Switzerland (German) are 24 times more likely to receive adult education compared with those with a primary education.

The odds ratios are adjusted for age and gender. They show the chances of each group participating, relative to those with a primary education (for whom the likelihood is set at 1).

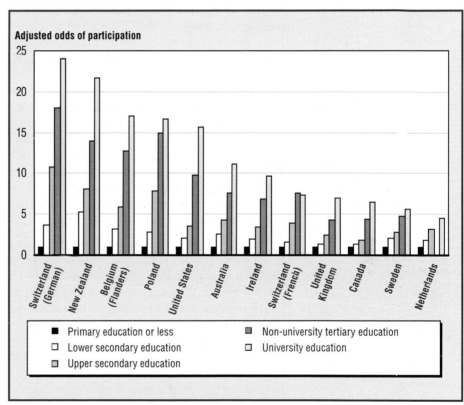

Countries are ranked according to the difference in the odds.

Source: International Adult Literacy Survey, 1994-1995.

Figure 4.3 presents results of an analysis of the relationship between educational attainment and participation in adult education using logistic regression. This method makes it possible to obtain comparable estimates even though the actual participation rates vary between countries. The results indicate that the long arm of the family – as reflected in the relationship between social background, educational attainment and participation in adult education – is noticeable in all countries, albeit more so in some than in others. The likelihood of a Swiss-German with a university degree participating in some form of adult education or training is 24 times that of a Swiss-German with primary school as highest credential. In New

Zealand it is 22 times and in the United States 16 times. These countries have relatively high overall participation rates, whereas the opposite is true of Poland and Belgium (Flanders) where those with a brief initial education are 17 times as likely not to participate.

In some countries the difference is less pronounced. In the Netherlands those with a very brief initial education are "only" 5 times as likely not to receive training as those with a university education. In Sweden it is 6 times, French-speaking Switzerland, the United Kingdom and Canada 7 times. In Sweden, the high level of participation and somewhat lower level of inequality might be explained by the country's long history of adult education. Other important factors are a large publicly funded voluntary sector and funding earmarked for recruiting groups with low readiness to participate. This involves funds for outreach activities at work and in the community, and study assistance for courses of a long and brief duration. In the Netherlands there has been an attempt in recent years to strengthen the adult education sector and to find new ways of combining public and private initiatives, with the committed involvement of employers and the social partners. Thus the data suggest that public policy can be somewhat effective in reducing inequality in participation amongst those with different schooling backgrounds.

4.3 Readiness to Learn across the Life-span

In most countries, the rate of participation in organised learning activities declines sharply for older adults.

Readiness to participate in organised forms of learning varies across the life-span. Figure 4.4 shows that in most countries the participation rate declines steadily with an increase in age. Only Sweden and, to a lesser extent, German-speaking Switzerland, New Zealand and the United States have a high rate of participation among 56-65-year-olds, with rates close to or exceeding 25 per cent. A sharp decline occurs after age 55 in all countries surveyed. The high overall participation rate in Sweden is influenced by the high enrolment among those 46 and older. For older Swedes, the access to publicly supported study circles organised by volunteer associations plays an important role.

Naturally, even when full-time students are excluded, the duration of study is by far the longest for young adults, those aged 25 and under (Figure 4.5). After this period of foundation learning follows a decline – at first sharp and then gradual – in the time and effort invested in organised learning activities. This decline may reflect a lack of incentives to prolong formal education. Those aged 36 and over are instead attracted to courses of a briefer duration, related either to work or general interest. In terms of total time devoted to studies, participants in Canada and Ireland take longer courses than those in the other countries. Study intensity as measured by duration is, among 26-35-year-olds, the highest in New Zealand, followed by Ireland and the Netherlands. Countries with low overall participation rates tend to have lower intensity as measured by duration – Ireland excepted.

FIGURE 4.4

Adult education participation and age

Per cent of population aged 16-65 participating in adult education and training during the year preceding the interview, by 10-year age intervals, 1994-1995

In most countries the participation rate declines steadily with an increase in age. A sharp decline in participation occurs after age 55 in all countries.

The figure shows the participation rate for each age group.

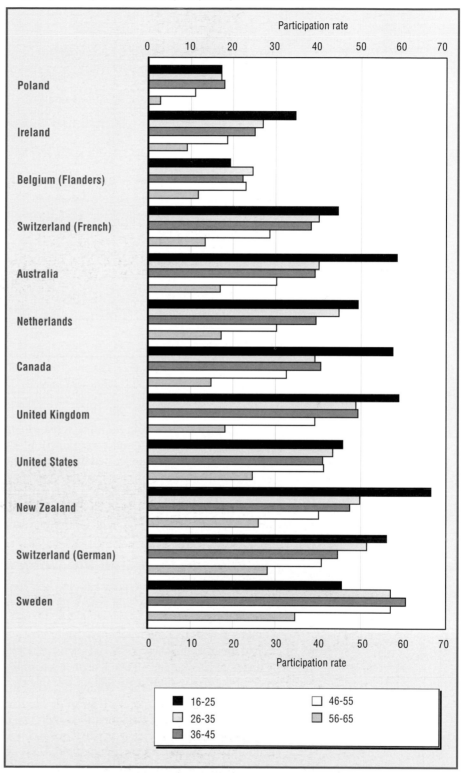

Countries are ranked by the average rate of participation for those aged 46-65.

Source: International Adult Literacy Survey, 1994-1995.

FIGURE 4.5

Duration of studies by age

Mean hours of study by age groups, participants aged 26-35 and 46-55, 1994-1995

**Training duration declines
sharply with increasing age
in most countries.**

The figure shows the mean
number of hours studied by
those taking part in adult
education and training
courses during the year
preceding the survey.

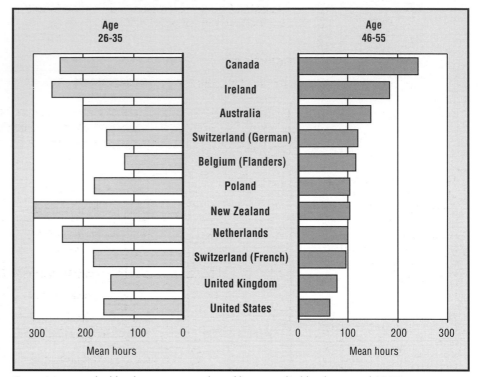

Countries are ranked by the average number of hours studied by those aged 46-55.

Source: International Adult Literacy Survey, 1994-1995.

Gender differences in total participation are quite small in most countries. However, an analysis of employer-sponsored training indicates that women are more disadvantaged than suggested by these overall comparisons.[3] Men take a much larger share of total employer-sponsored course provision than women in Australia, Belgium (Flanders), Ireland, the Netherlands, Switzerland (French- and German-speaking) and the United Kingdom. In contrast, women have a larger share of non-employer sponsored training in all countries surveyed (see Table 4.6 in Annex C).

Readiness to learn and the "long arm" of the job

The evidence on adults' everyday learning behaviours confirms an influence perhaps best characterised as "the long arm of the job": the increased importance of adult education and training as investment. The increase in employer-supported learning activities signals a dramatic change that has radically altered the landscape of adult education since the early 1980s (Rubenson, 1996; Skaalvik and Engesbak, 1996; Bélanger and Tuijnman, 1997). The increase in job-related adult education explains much of the rise in total participation rates since that time.

Figure 4.6 shows that close to or over half of the participants in adult education and training, in all countries, attend an employer-supported activity. The role of employers in training is particularly important in Sweden and the United Kingdom. Employers are comparatively less committed to training in Canada,

---

[3] For a more detailed analysis of the relationships between educational attainment, age, gender and participation, see Leuven (1997).

Ireland and Switzerland. While employer-sponsored education reaches a large number of people, the learning activities tend to be of briefer duration compared with non-employer-supported educational activities. This is especially true in countries with high numbers of younger adults in part-time education, as in Australia, Canada, New Zealand, Switzerland (German) and the United Kingdom (see Table 4.4 in Annex C).

FIGURE 4.6

Extent of employer-sponsored education and training

Share of employer-sponsored courses in total adult education and training provision, for the employed and general adult population aged 16-65, 1994-1995

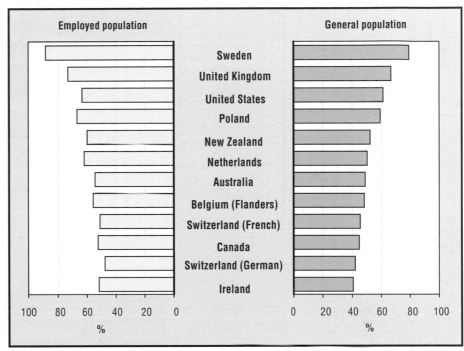

Countries are ranked by the share of employer-sponsored training in total provision for the general population aged 16-65.

Source: International Adult Literacy Survey, 1994-1995.

More than, or close to half, of all participants attend courses sponsored by employers. The contribution of employers is particularly important in Sweden and the United Kingdom.

The figure shows, for each country, the share of employer-sponsored adult education and training for the employed and total population.

In all countries, women benefit less often than men do from employer support for their education; they must to a larger extent than men rely on alternate sources – mainly, as illustrated in Figure 4.7, self-financing. In part, this gender imbalance relates to differences in labour force participation rates, but there is still a difference among the employed. In the Netherlands, a larger proportion of employed men than women receive employer support; on the other hand, the latter are supported for a longer period than the former. In Ireland as well, women on average receive training of a longer duration than men. However, the opposite case is more common in the other countries.

The data in Figure 4.7 thus confirm that work is a key factor in explaining adult education participation. In French- and German-speaking Switzerland participation is to a large extent self-financed, although employers also play an important role. In Canada and New Zealand a substantial proportion of female participants obtained subsidies from government sources, which is not the case in most other countries. Governments play a modest role in financing in Poland and the United States, where less than 5 per cent of men obtained such support.

FIGURE 4.7

Sources of financial support for adult education and training

A.   Per cent of men participating in adult education and training who receive financial support from various sources, for the general population aged 16-65, 1994-1995

Employers are the main source of funding for men...

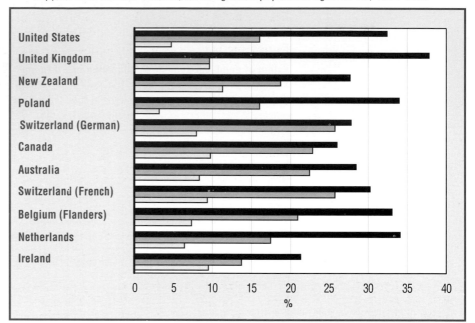

...but with the exception of the United Kingdom and the United States, self-financing is most common for women.

The figure shows the contribution individuals, governments and employers make towards the financing of adult education and training.

B.   Per cent of women participating in adult education and training who receive financial support from various sources, for the general population aged 16-65, 1994-1995

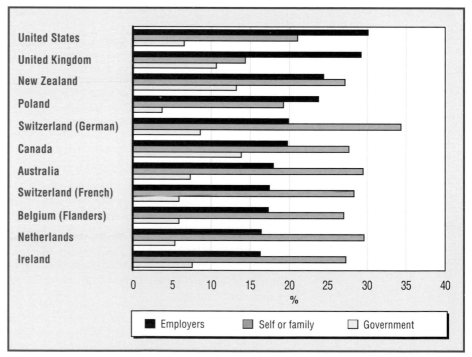

Countries are ranked by the share of employers in the financing of studies for women.

Source: International Adult Literacy Survey, 1994-1995.

Figure 4.8 shows that the strong influence of the world of work is also evident in the reasons why people chose to engage in education or training. Participants who are supported by their employer almost invariably mention job-related reasons. A large proportion of participants not sponsored by their employer nonetheless report that they participate for reasons linked to job and career. This is particularly the case in the English-speaking countries and Poland, whereas the reasons are more diverse in the Netherlands and both French- and German-speaking Switzerland. Surprising is the way in which job-related reasons predominate among those aged 46-55 and, in the cases of Canada and the United States, for those aged 56-65 (Rubenson, 1997). In fact, only 14 per cent of older adults in the United States take part in organised learning activities for reasons not related to their job.

FIGURE 4.8

Reasons given for participation in adult education and training

Per cent of non-employer-sponsored and employer-sponsored courses taken for job-related reasons, adults aged 16-65, 1994-1995

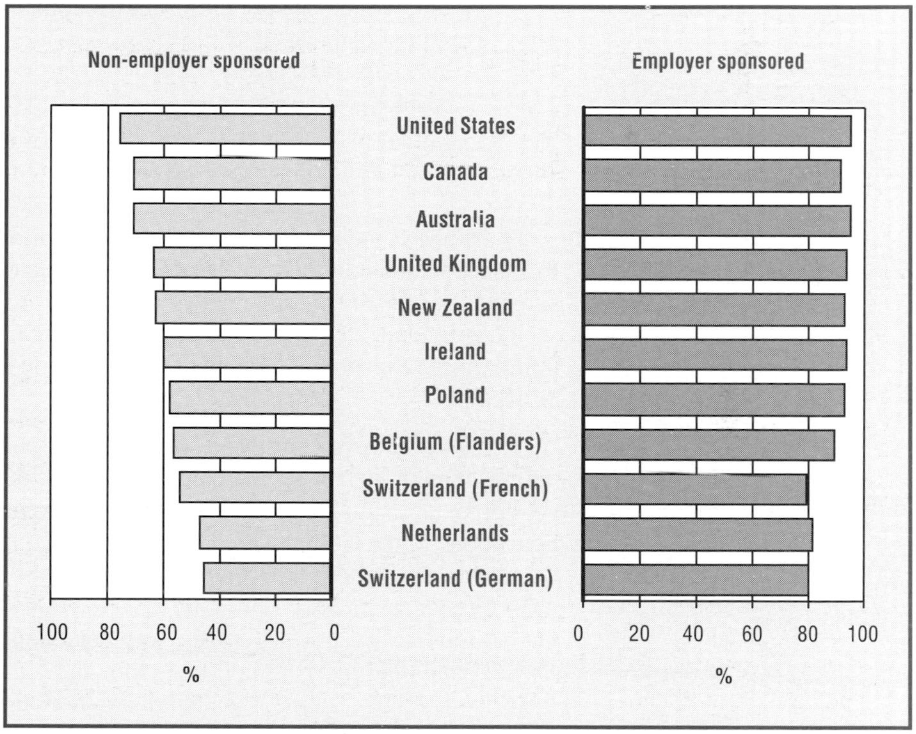

Countries are ranked by the share of non-employer-sponsored learning activities undertaken for job-related reasons.

Source: International Adult Literacy Survey, 1994-1995.

The strong influence of the world of work is also evident in the reasons for which people say they engage in adult education and training. Nearly all activities supported by employers are undertaken for job-related reasons. Much of the adult education financed from other sources is also related to job and career.

The figure shows the share in the total number of courses taken for job-related reasons.

Because adult education is strongly linked to work, policy strategies promoting lifelong learning *for all* must recognise the centrality of employers. It is also important to consider how the work setting frames the nature and quality of everyday learning. Further, the data analyses show that the likelihood of a worker receiving some support for education and training from the employer is related to firm size, nature of job and sector of employment. Demand for literacy skills at work is another contributing factor. Additional findings based on the IALS data include:

- The high degree of formalisation of adult education and training in large firms compared with small and medium-sized firms is reflected in higher training rates in the former. The differences in training rates are particularly large in Australia and the United Kingdom, where those working in firms with more than 500 employees are seven times as likely to receive support as those working in firms with fewer than 20 employees (see Table 4.9 in Annex C).

- As noted in the study, *Enterprise Training in Australia*, due to their restricted internal labour markets, small firms are less willing to fund the costs of developing portable skills than larger firms. Their training demands are also different from those of larger companies. This needs to be taken into account in reforms of vocational education and training policies (Australian National Training Authority, 1996).

- There is a clear relationship between occupation and employer support for adult education and training. In all countries, professionals, technicians and in some cases also managers benefit the most, whereas those in elementary occupations receive the least. In the United Kingdom, 62 per cent of professionals receive some support, compared with 18 per cent of blue-collar workers. Even after controlling for differences in industry, size of company and engagement in literacy activities at work, the former are as likely to receive support towards education and training from their employer than the latter (see Table 4.10). In contrast, clerks in Ireland, Poland and the United States do relatively well, compared with both blue-collar workers and services workers in other countries.

Firm size, industry and occupation are indicators of work environments which influence training decisions. However, these factors do not reveal the nature of the job and associated training needs. It is therefore of interest to note the extent to which individuals feel that work tasks encourage them to use their literacy skills – comparing the responses of those who do and do not receive employer support for education.[4]

Figure 4.9 reveals a strong connection between employer support for training and the level of literacy required on the job. The more demands are made on the use of literacy skills the more likely it is that employers will invest in workers' further education. In the United Kingdom, close to two in three workers in jobs requiring extensive use of literacy receive employer support for education and training but only 13 per cent of those with jobs that required little use of literacy skills receive such support. Even after controlling for occupation, firm size and industry, Switzerland (German), United Kingdom and United States workers who employ their literacy skills extensively at work are more than 6 times as likely to participate in employer-supported training than workers who use their skills minimally (Figure 4.9). The chances of obtaining employer support for training are somewhat more equally distributed in Australia, Ireland, New Zealand, Poland and Sweden.

There is a strong relationship between employer support for training and the level of literacy required on the job.

---

[4]   See Chapter 3 for a description of the index used to describe literacy engagement at work.

FIGURE 4.9

Likelihood of participation by literacy engagement at work

Adjusted odds of receiving employer-sponsored adult education and training by the level of literacy engagement at work, employed adults aged 16-65, 1994-1995

The higher the demand for literacy skills at work, the more likely an employer will invest in adult education and training.

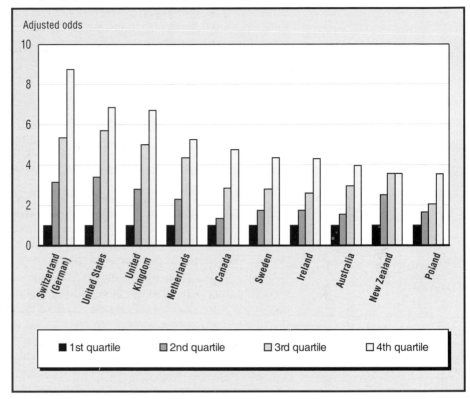

The literacy engagement at work index is constructed using frequencies of nine literacy tasks – reading magazines or journals; manuals or reference books; diagrams or schematics; reports or articles; reading or writing letters or memos; bills, invoices or budgets; writing reports or articles; estimates or technical specifications; and calculating prices, costs or budgets. The 1st quartile represents workers who use workplace literacy skills the least; the 4th quartile represents workers who use them the most.

The odds ratios are adjusted for industry, full- or part-time work, firm size and occupational status. They show the chances of each group participating, relative to those with low literacy use at work (1st quartile), whose likelihood is set at 1.

Countries are ranked according to the difference in the odds.

Note: Data for this figure are given in Table 4.11 in Annex C.

Source: International Adult Literacy Survey, 1994-1995.

These findings shift the discussion about the design of strategies for lifelong learning for all from a narrow supply question to a demand issue. Both the employer's willingness to support an individual's learning activities and that person's own incentive for investing in learning are strongly influenced by the opportunity to use literacy skills at work. Persons not in the labour force or in undemanding jobs are clearly up against a barrier with regard to both engagement in learning and their readiness for it. This, in combination with the fact that even publicly funded adult education is increasingly relevant to work and tied in with employer support, is the reality in which a strategy for realising lifelong learning for all must be grounded.

Rather than costs or lack of time, it is probably the differences in anticipated benefits that explain why some people participate in adult education while others do not.

Policy developers should also take note of new findings concerning barriers to participation.[5] As part of the survey people were asked whether there had been some education or training they wanted to take for either work or non-work related reasons but, for some reason or other, did not pursue. Those responding in the affirmative were then given a list of reasons for not having participated. Results show stable patterns across countries (Rubenson, 1997). It was more common to state situational barriers than institutional ones, particularly for non-work related education. With respect to individual barriers, a general lack of time was by far the major reason for not starting a course one needed or wanted to take. Around 60 per cent of respondents in Canada, the Netherlands, and the United States gave this as the main reason. It was less common to refer to a specific situation, like being too busy at work or family responsibility. With regard to the latter, the gender inequalities in family responsibilities are evident. Between 10 and 15 per cent of women mention family responsibilities as a reason for not engaging in adult learning. In most countries, the comparable figure for men is about 3 per cent. Among institutional barriers, lack of money was by far the most prevalent. Lack of employer support was mentioned infrequently.

"Lack of time" is ultimately a subjective answer. Granted, time is not an endless resource – but people have to make choices. Some people, because of work and family, may have little opportunity to choose at all. Nonetheless, for many people, "lack of time" amounts to a statement of the value they ascribe to a given activity – in this case, education and training – and to the expected outcome of engaging in such an activity. It is striking that participants and non-participants mentioned situational barriers such as "lack of time" to roughly the same extent – in the case of participants, these were given as the reason for not having taken other courses they were "interested in". Further, participants referred to institutional barriers slightly more often than non-participants. Similarly, Jonsson and Gähler (1995) found that situational barriers (handicaps, young children, working hours, etc.) were shared equally between those who participated in adult education and those who did not. The authors therefore concluded that, instead of barriers having to do with cost or lack of time, it is probably differences in expected rewards that explain why some choose to participate while others do not (Jonsson and Gähler, 1995, p. 38). It would appear, therefore, that the major barriers to improved readiness to engage in lifelong learning concern the long arms of job and family.

---

[5]   See Bélanger and Tuijnman (1997) for additional findings on barriers to adult education participation.

4.4 Conclusions

The data analyses contained in this chapter offer a few clear messages regarding adults' readiness and opportunities to participate in learning:

- Parents' education and the respondents' own experience of schooling strongly govern later readiness to engage in learning;

- In order to succeed in improving adults' readiness to learn, policy-makers must recognise the crucial influence of the workplace;

- When it comes to strengthening literacy skills, everyday learning is not a compensation for organised forms of adult education, because participation in adult education and everyday learning are interrelated;

- Policy does matter. The evidence suggests that co-ordinated policy can have an impact on the quantity and equitable distribution of adult education and training opportunities.

All countries investigated face major challenges in extending lifelong learning to the least qualified. With literacy skills becoming increasingly important in recruitment and screening practices, low-skill adults, young as well as old, are most at risk of exclusion. But the evidence shows that these people seldom participate in adult education and training and spend little time on everyday reading either at or outside work. Moreover, these groups often also find themselves in circumstances that do not stimulate a readiness to engage in learning.

Lifelong learning for all can be achieved only in a literate society.

Lifelong learning *for all* can only be achieved in a society that actively engages and makes demands on the literacy skills of all its citizens. This is conditional on work life organised in ways that promote learning. Accordingly, approaches to developing strategies for lifelong learning need to be broad, and build on the efforts of different constituencies. Obviously, no one formula would work everywhere; each country must, according to its structures, history and culture, find the most appropriate approach to a co-ordinated strategy for promoting lifelong learning for all.

Lifelong learning is not solely the responsibility of government and the public sector; employers have a major role to play. The majority of people engaging in adult education in the survey countries say they do so for work-related reasons. Even though a strategy for lifelong learning for all must take account of what seems to motivate an individual to learn, this does not imply that all adult education involves vocational training. On the contrary, those with limited literacy skills are in need of a broad and general education – one that will better equip them for engagement in work and daily life. Employers invest heavily in education and training, but the learning efforts tend to be of a brief duration and are less often directed to those with insufficient literacy skills. It is, therefore, necessary to search for approaches that can be effective in promoting general skill upgrading while strengthening the connections with the world of work.

The Ministers' policy statement on lifelong learning for all (OECD, 1996) confirms that adult learning can no longer be treated as a marginal activity. Instead, it must become a central element in a range of policies targeting lifelong learning. Having demonstrated the impact of work and the family – and their influence on everyday learning and on participation in organised education and training – this chapter concludes that countries must find new approaches to stimulating adults' readiness to learn. Literacy is the key to such readiness.

References

AUSTRALIAN NATIONAL TRAINING AUTHORITY (1996), *Enterprise Training in Australia*, Australian National Training Authority, Melbourne.

BÉLANGER, P. and TUIJNMAN, A.C. (Eds.) (1997), *New Patterns of Adult Learning: A Six-Country Comparative Study*, Pergamon Press, Oxford.

DOHMEN, G. (1996), *Lifelong Learning: Guidelines for a Modern Education Policy*, Federal Ministry of Education, Science, Research and Technology, Bonn.

GIDDENS, A. (1994), *Beyond Left and Right*, Stanford University Press, Stanford, CA.

HAMMARSTRÖM, M. (1996), *Varför inte högskolan?*, Acta Universitatis Gothoburgensis, Göteborg.

HOMMEN, L. (1997), "The British Columbia Labour Force Development Board delivering consensus", in R. Haddow (Ed.), *The Emergence of Labor Force Development Boards in Canada*, Toronto University Press, Toronto.

HOSMER, D.W. and LEMESHOW, S. (1989), *Applied Logistic Regression*, John Wiley and Sons, New York.

JOHNSTONE, J. and RIVERA, R. (1965), *Volunteers for Learning*, Aldine Hawthorne, New York.

JONSSON, J. and GÄHLER, M. (1995), *Folkbildning och vuxenstudier. Rekrytering, omfattning, erfarenheter*, SOU 1995:141, Fritzes, Stockholm.

LEUVEN, E. (1997), "Gender differences in work-related adult education and training", in P. Bélanger and A.C. Tuijnman (Eds.), *New Patterns of Adult Learning: A Six-Country Comparative Study*, Pergamon Press, Oxford.

LUNDVALL, B.-A. (1991), " Explaining inter-firm co-operation and innovation: The limits of the transaction cost approach", in G. Grahber (ed.), *The Embedded Firm: On the Socio-economics of Industrial Networks*, Mansell, London.

NONAKA, I. (1994), "A dynamic theory of organizational knowledge creation", *Organizational Science*, Vol. 5(1), pp. 15-37.

OECD (1996), *Lifelong Learning for All*, Paris.

RUBENSON, K. (1975), *Rekrytering till vuxenutbildning*, Acta Universitatis Gothoburgensis, Göteborg.

RUBENSON, K. (1996), "Studieförbundens roll i vuxenutbildningen", Chapter in SOU 1996:154, Fritzes, Stockholm.

RUBENSON, K. (1997), "Barriers to adult education participation revisited", in P. Bélanger and A.C. Tuijnman (Eds.), *New Patterns of Adult Learning: A Six-Country Comparative Study*, Pergamon Press, Oxford.

SKAALVIK, E.M. and ENGESBAK, H. (1996), "Selvrealisering og kompetanseutvikling. Rekruttering til voksenopplaering i et tjugearsperspektiv", in S. Tosse (Ed.), *Fra lov - til Reform*, NVI, Trondheim.

Policy Conclusions

On the whole, the IALS findings suggest that literacy acquisition and population skill profiles are sensitive to policy intervention. Perhaps one of the most striking examples is the effect of selective immigration policy on Canada's literacy scores. While the family reunification and refugee aspects of the policy have added notably to that country's population with level 1 scores, the large number of highly literate immigrants admitted to Canada as a result of its preference for independent immigrants and professionals has actually raised the Canadian overall mean scores.

With this example in mind, it is worth considering the wide array of public policy domains which are literacy-sensitive. Sometimes indirectly – rather than by design – policy can influence literacy acquisition and use. An example is the potential impact of introducing library user fees on the borrowing of reading materials: such fees could act as an impediment to the exercise of literacy skills. The IALS findings lend support for the creation of literacy- and learning-rich environments in the home, at work, and in the community. Even tax policies can have an effect on literacy through, for example the taxation (or exemption from taxation) of reading materials.

While literacy can be affected, directly or indirectly, by decisions taken on other policy fronts, it can also be a factor in the development of good policy in other domains. For instance, the survey findings underline the importance of literacy for the economic success of individuals and, in aggregate, for countries. Obviously, then, there are implications for human resources, labour market, employment and education and training policies which governments, the private sector, communities and non-governmental organisations need to identify.

Literacy also has social policy implications. One example relates to the administration of justice: the majority of the prison population in the United States is at level 1 on the literacy scale. This suggests a role for literacy in crime prevention and the rehabilitation of offenders. Low literacy is likely to have health policy implications as well. A limited ability to read will circumscribe access to nutritional and other health-related information.

The point is that literacy affects policy, or is affected by policy, across a broad number of issues that have literacy dimensions: justice and health are but two examples, others include youth and seniors; language and culture; social welfare; rural development; migration; and disadvantaged groups.

Due to its multifaceted nature and the multiple policy domains implicated, a national, regional or local literacy policy cannot be effective if it deals with one dimension only. The low literacy levels of 25 to 50 per cent or more of the populations in the 12 countries surveyed for this report are a pressing reality. But literacy issues require more than just appropriate literacy policies, important though they be. The development, enhancement and maintenance of literacy skills must also be seen as an integral concern in the design of other public policies. Only if social, economic and education policies converge in their attention to literacy issues will countries be able to develop true cultures of lifelong learning *for all*.

Annex A

Definitions of Literacy Performance on Three Scales

This annex explains how the literacy proficiency scores can be interpreted.

The performance results for the 1994-1995 International Adult Literacy Survey (IALS) were reported on three scales – prose, document and quantitative – rather than on a single scale. Each scale ranges from 0 to 500. Scale scores have, in turn, been grouped into five empirically determined literacy levels. As shown in the Introduction, each of these levels implies an ability to cope with a particular subset of reading tasks. This annex explains in more detail how the proficiency scores can be interpreted, by describing the scales and the kinds of tasks that were used in the test, and the literacy levels that have been adopted.[1]

While the literacy scales make it possible to compare the prose, document and quantitative skills of different populations and to study the relationships between literacy skills and various factors, the scale scores by themselves carry little or no meaning. In other words, whereas most people have a practical understanding of what it means when the temperature outside reaches 10°C, it is not intuitively clear what it means when a particular group is at 287 on the prose scale, or 250 on the document scale, or at level 2 on the quantitative scale.

One way to gain some understanding about what it means to perform at a given point along a literacy scale is to identify a set of variables that can be shown to underlie performance on these tasks. Collectively, these variables provide a framework for understanding what is being measured in a particular assessment, and what knowledge and skills are being demonstrated by various levels of proficiency.

Sample tasks are presented to illustrate the types of task demands that characterise the five levels on each scale.

Toward this end, the text below begins by describing how the literacy scale scores were defined. Detailed descriptions of the prose, document and quantitative scales are then provided, along with definitions of the five levels. Sample tasks are presented to illustrate the types of materials and task demands that characterise the levels.

---

[1]   This text is partially reprinted from Chapter 2 in *Literacy, Economy and Society* (OECD and Statistics Canada, 1995).

Defining the Literacy Levels

The Item Response Theory (IRT) scaling procedures that were used in the IALS constitute a statistical solution to the challenge of establishing one or more scales for a set of tasks with an ordering of difficulty that is essentially the same for everyone.[2] First, the difficulty of tasks is ranked on the scale according to how well respondents actually perform them. Next, individuals are assigned scores according to how well they perform on a number of tasks of varying difficulty.

Individuals estimated to have a particular scale score will perform tasks at that point on the scale with an 80 per cent probability of a correct response.

The scale point assigned to each task is the point at which individuals with that proficiency score have a given probability of responding correctly. In this survey, an 80 per cent probability of correct response was the criterion used. This means that individuals estimated to have a particular scale score will perform tasks at that point on the scale with an 80 per cent probability of a correct response. It also means they will have a greater than 80 per cent chance of performing tasks that are lower on the scale. It does not mean, however, that individuals with given proficiencies can never succeed at tasks with higher difficulty values; they may do so some of the time. It does suggest that their probability of success is "relatively" low – i.e. the more difficult the task relative to their proficiency, the lower the likelihood of a correct response.

An analogy might help clarify this point. The relationship between task difficulty and individual proficiency is much like the high jump event in track and field, in which an athlete tries to jump over a bar that is placed at increasing heights. Each high jumper has a height at which he or she is proficient – that is, the jumper can clear the bar at that height with a high probability of success, and can clear the bar at lower heights almost every time. When the bar is higher than the athlete's level of proficiency, however, it is expected that the athlete will be unable to clear the bar consistently.

Once the literacy tasks are placed along each of the scales using the criterion of 80 per cent, it is possible to see to what extent the interactions among various task characteristics capture the placement of tasks along the scales. Analyses of the task characteristics which include the materials being read and the type of questions asked about these materials reveal that ordered sets of information-processing skills appear to be called into play to successfully perform the various tasks displayed along each scale (Kirsch and Mosenthal, 1993).

To capture this order, each scale is divided into five levels reflecting the empirically determined progression of information-processing skills and strategies. While some of the tasks were at the low end of a scale and some at the very high end, most had values in the 200-to-400 range. It is important to recognise that these levels were selected not as a result of any inherent statistical property of the scales, but rather as the result of shifts in the skills and strategies required to succeed at various tasks along the scales, ranging from simple to complex.

The remainder of this annex describes each scale in terms of the nature of task demands at each of the five levels. Sample tasks are presented and the factors contributing to their difficulty discussed. The aim is to facilitate interpretation of the results and data analyses presented in the main body of the report.

---

[2] The reader is referred to Murray, Kirsch and Jenkins (1997) for a complete description of the scaling procedures used in this assessment.

Interpreting the Literacy Levels

Prose literacy

The ability to understand and use information contained in various kinds of text is an important aspect of literacy. The study therefore included an array of prose selections, including text from newspapers, magazines and brochures. The material varied in length, density of text, content, and the use of structural or organisational aids such as headings, bullets and special typefaces. All prose samples were reprinted in their entirety with the original layout and typography unchanged.

The tasks require the respondents to use three types of information-processing skills: locating, integrating and generating.

Each prose selection was accompanied by one or more questions asking the reader to perform specific tasks. These tasks represent three major aspects of information-processing: *locating*, *integrating* and *generating*. Locating tasks require the reader to find information in the text based on conditions or features specified in the question or directive. The match may be literal or synonymous, or the reader may need to make an inference in order to perform successfully. Integrating tasks ask the reader to pull together two or more pieces of information in the text. The information could be found in a single paragraph, or in different paragraphs or sections. With the generating tasks, readers must produce a written response by processing information from the text and by making text-based inferences or drawing on their own background knowledge.

In all, the prose literacy scale includes 34 tasks with difficulty values ranging from 188 to 377. These tasks are distributed by level as follows: Level 1, 5 tasks; Level 2, 9 tasks; Level 3, 14 tasks; Level 4, 5 tasks; and Level 5, 1 task. It is important to remember that the tasks requiring the reader to locate, integrate and generate information extend over a range of difficulty as a result of combining other variables, including:

- the number of categories or features of information the reader must process;
- the extent to which information given in the question or directive is obviously related to the information contained in the text;
- the amount and location of information in the text that shares some of the features with the information being requested and thus appears relevant, but that in fact does not fully answer the question (these are called "distractors");
- the length and density of the text.

The five levels of prose literacy are defined as follows.

Prose level 1   **Score range: 0 to 225**

Most of the tasks at this level require the reader to locate one piece of information in the text that is identical to or synonymous with the information given in the directive. If a plausible incorrect answer is present in the text, it tends not to be near the correct information.

Typically the match between the task and the text is literal, although sometimes a low-level inference may be necessary. The text is usually brief or has organisational aids such as paragraph headings or italics that suggest where the reader can find the specified information. Generally, the target word or phrase appears only once in the text.

The easiest task in level 1 (difficulty value of 188) directs respondents to look at a medicine label to determine the "maximum number of days you should take this medicine". The label contains only one reference to number of days and this information is located under the heading "DOSAGE". The reader must go to this part of the label and locate the phrase "not longer than 7 days".

MEDCO ASPIRIN   *500*

INDICATIONS: Headaches, muscle pains, rheumatic pains, toothaches, earaches. RELIEVES COMMON COLD SYMPTOMS.

DOSAGE: ORAL. 1 or 2 tablets every 6 hours, preferably accompanied by food, for not longer than 7 days. Store in a cool, dry place.

CAUTION: Do not use for gastritis or peptic ulcer. Do not use if taking anticoagulant drugs. Do not use for serious liver illness or bronchial asthma. If taken in large doses and for an extended period, may cause harm to kidneys. Before using this medication for chicken pox or influenza in children, consult with a doctor about Reyes Syndrome, a rare but serious illness. During lactation and pregnancy, consult with a doctor before using this product, especially in the last trimester of pregnancy. If symptoms persist, or in case of an accidental overdose, consult a doctor. Keep out of reach of children.

INGREDIENTS: Each tablet contains
500 mg acetylsalicicylic acid.
Excipient c.b.p.   1 tablet.
Reg. No. 88246

Made in Canada by STERLING PRODUCTS, INC.
1600 Industrial Blvd., Montreal, Quebec H9J 3P1

Reprinted by permission

Prose level 2   *Score range: 226 to 275*

Tasks at this level generally require the reader to locate one or more pieces of information in the text, but several distractors may be present, or low-level inferences may be required. Tasks at this level also begin to ask readers to integrate two or more pieces of information, or to compare and contrast information.

As with level 1, most of the tasks at level 2 ask the reader to locate information. However, more varied demands are made in terms of the number of responses the question requires, or in terms of the distracting information that may be present. For example, a task based on an article about the impatiens plant asks the reader to determine what happens when the plant is exposed to temperatures of 14°C or lower. A sentence under the section "*General care*" states that "When the plant is exposed to temperatures of 12-14°C, it loses its leaves and won't bloom anymore." This task received a difficulty value of 230, just in the level 2 range.

What made this task somewhat more difficult than those identified at level 1 is that the previous sentence in the text contains information about the requirements of the impatiens plant in various temperatures. This information could have distracted some readers, making the task slightly more difficult.

IMPATIENS

Like many other cultured plants, impatiens plants have a long history behind them. One of the older varieties was sure to be found on grandmother's windowsill. Nowadays, the hybrids are used in many ways in the house and garden.

Origin: The ancestors of the impatiens, *Impatiens sultani* and *Impatiens holstii*, are probably still to be found in the mountain forests of tropical East Africa and on the islands off the coast, mainly Zanzibar. The cultivated European plant received the name *Impatiens walleriana*.

Appearance: It is a herbaceous bushy plant with a height of 30 to 40 cm. The thick, fleshy stems are branched and very juicy, which means, because of the tropical origin, that the plant is sensitive to cold. The light green or white speckled leaves are pointed, elliptical, and slightly indented on the edges. The smooth leaf surfaces and the stems indicate a great need of water.

Bloom: The flowers, which come in all shades of red, appear plentifully all year long, except for the darkest months. They grow from "suckers" (in the stem's "armpit").

Assortment: Some are compact and low-growing types, about 20 to 25 cm. high, suitable for growing in pots. A variety of hybrids can be grown in pots, window boxes, or flower beds. Older varieties with taller stems add dramatic colour to flower beds.

General care: In summer, a place in the shade without direct sunlight is best; in fall and spring, half-shade is best. When placed in a bright spot during winter, the plant requires temperatures of at least 20°C; in a darker spot, a temperature of 15°C will do. When the plant is exposed to temperatures of 12-14°C, it loses its leaves and won't bloom anymore. In wet ground, the stems will rot.

Watering: The warmer and lighter the plant's location, the more water it needs. Always use water without a lot of minerals. It is not known for sure whether or not the plant needs humid air. In any case, do not spray water directly onto the leaves, which causes stains.

Feeding: Feed weekly during the growing period from March to September.

Repotting: If necessary, repot in the spring or in the summer in light soil with humus (prepacked potting soil). It is better to throw the old plants away and start cultivating new ones.

Propagating: Slip or use seeds. Seeds will germinate in ten days.

Diseases: In summer, too much sun makes the plant woody. If the air is too dry, small white flies or aphids may appear.

A similar task involving the same text asks the reader to identify "what the smooth leaf and stem suggest about the plant". The second paragraph of the article is labelled "*Appearance*" and contains a sentence that states, ". . . stems are branched and very juicy, which means, because of the tropical origin, that the plant is sensitive to cold." This sentence distracted some readers from the last sentence in that same paragraph: "The smooth leaf surfaces and the stems indicate a great need of water." This task received a difficulty value of 254, placing it in the middle of level 2.

Prose level 3   *Score range: 276 to 325*

Tasks at this level generally direct readers to locate information that requires low-level inferences or that meets specified conditions. Sometimes the reader is required to identify several pieces of information that are located in different sentences or paragraphs rather than in a single sentence. Readers may also be asked to integrate or to compare and contrast information across paragraphs or sections of text.

PROPER FRAME FIT

RIDER MUST BE ABLE TO STRADDLE BICYCLE WITH AT LEAST 2 cm CLEARANCE ABOVE THE HORIZONTAL BAR WHEN STANDING.

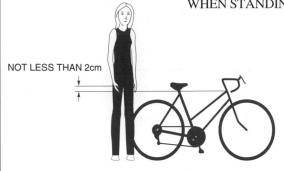

NOT LESS THAN 2cm

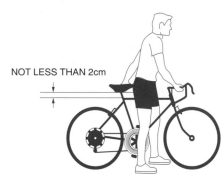

NOT LESS THAN 2cm

NOTE: Measurement for a female should be determined using a men's model as a basis.

PROPER SIZE OF BICYCLE	
FRAME SIZE	LEG LENGTH OF RIDER
430mm	660mm-760mm
460mm	690mm-790mm
480mm	710mm-790mm
530mm	760mm-840mm
560mm	790mm-860mm
580mm	810mm-890mm
635mm	860mm-940mm

OWNER'S RESPONSIBILITY

1. **Bicycle Selection and Purchase:** Make sure this bicycle fits the intended rider. Bicycles come in a variety of sizes. Personal adjustment of seat and handlebars is necessary to assure maximum safety and comfort. Bicycles come with a wide variety of equipment and accessories . . . make sure the rider can operate them.

2. **Assembly:** Carefully follow all assembly instructions. Make sure that all nuts, bolts and screws are securely tightened.

3. **Fitting the Bicycle:** To ride safely and comfortably, the bicycle must fit the rider. Check the seat position, adjusting it up or down so that with the sole of rider's foot on the pedal in its lowest position the rider's knee is slightly bent.

Note: Specific charts illustrated at left detail the proper method of determining the correct frame size.

The manufacturer is not responsible for failure, injury, or damage caused by improper completion of assembly or improper maintenance after shipment.

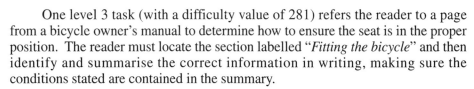

One level 3 task (with a difficulty value of 281) refers the reader to a page from a bicycle owner's manual to determine how to ensure the seat is in the proper position. The reader must locate the section labelled "*Fitting the bicycle*" and then identify and summarise the correct information in writing, making sure the conditions stated are contained in the summary.

A second level 3 task, receiving a difficulty value of 310, directs the reader to look at a set of four film reviews to determine which review was least favourable. Some reviews rate films using points or some graphic such as stars; these reviews contain no such indicators. The reader needs to glance at the text of each review to compare what is said in order to judge which film received the worst rating.

Another level 3 question involves an article about cotton diapers. Here readers are asked to write three reasons why the author prefers to use cotton diapers over disposable ones. This task is relatively difficult (318) because of several variables. First, the reader has to provide several answers requiring text-based inferences. Nowhere in the text does the author say, "I prefer cotton diapers because ...". These inferences are made somewhat more difficult because the type of information requested is a "reason" rather than something more concrete such as a date or person. And finally, the text contains information that may distract the reader.

Prose level 4   *Score range: 326 to 375*

These tasks require readers to perform multiple-feature matching or to provide several responses where the requested information must be identified through text-based inferences. Tasks at this level may also require the reader to integrate or contrast pieces of information, sometimes presented in relatively lengthy texts. Typically, these texts contain more distracting information, and the information requested is more abstract.

Finding similarities between texts is easier than locating differences.

One task falling within level 4 (338) directs readers to use the information from a pamphlet about hiring interviews to "write in your own words one difference between the panel interview and the group interview". Here readers are presented with brief descriptions of each type of interview; then, rather than merely locating a fact about each or identifying a similarity, they need to integrate what they have read to infer a characteristic on which the two types of interviews differ. Experience from other large-scale assessments reveals that tasks in which readers are asked to contrast information are more difficult, on average, than tasks in which they are asked to find similarities.

The Hiring Interview

Preinterview

Try to learn more about the business. What products does it manufacture or services does it provide? What methods or procedures does it use? This information can be found in trade directories, chamber of commerce or industrial directories, or at your local employment office.

Find out more about the position. Would you replace someone or is the position newly created? In which departments or shops would you work? Collective agreements describing various standardized positions and duties are available at most local employment offices. You can also contact the appropriate trade union.

The Interview

Ask questions about the position and the business. Answer clearly and accurately all questions put to you. Bring along a note pad as well as your work and training documents.

The Most Common Types of Interview

One-on-one: Self explanatory.

Panel: A number of people ask you questions and then compare notes on your application.

Group: After hearing a presentation with other applicants on the position and duties, you take part in a group discussion.

Postinterview

Note the key points discussed. Compare questions that caused you difficulty with those that allowed you to highlight your strong points. Such a review will help you prepare for future interviews. If you wish, you can talk about it with the placement officer or career counsellor at your local employment office.

Prose level 5   *Score range: 376 to 500*

*Tasks at this level typically require the reader to search for information in dense text that
contains a number of plausible distractors. Some require readers to make high-level
inferences or to use specialised knowledge.*

There is one level 5 task in this assessment, with a difficulty value of 377.
Readers are required to look at an announcement from a personnel department and
"list two ways in which CIEM (an employee support initiative within a company)
helps people who will lose their jobs because of a departmental reorganisation."
Responding correctly requires readers to search through this text to locate the
embedded sentence "CIEM acts as a mediator for employees who are threatened
with dismissal resulting from reorganisation, and assists with finding new positions
when necessary." This task is difficult because the announcement is organised
around information that is different from what is being requested in the question.
Thus, while the correct information is located in a single sentence, this information
is embedded under a list of headings describing CIEM's activities for employees
looking for other work. This list of headings serves as an excellent set of distractors
for the reader who does not search for or locate the phrase containing the
conditional information stated in the directive – that is, those who lose their jobs
because of a departmental reorganisation.

Document literacy

*Document literacy skills
become increasingly
important in knowledge-
oriented economies and
societies.*

Adults often encounter materials such as schedules, charts, graphs, tables, maps and
forms at home, at work, or when travelling in their communities. The knowledge
and skills needed to process information contained in these documents is therefore
an important aspect of literacy in a modern society. Success in processing
documents appears to depend at least in part on the ability to locate information in
a variety of displays, and to use this information in a number of ways. Sometimes
procedural knowledge may be required to transfer information from one source to
another, as is necessary in completing applications or order forms.

Thirty-four tasks are ordered along the IALS document literacy scale from
182 to 408, as the result of responses of adults from each of the participating
countries. These tasks are distributed as follows: Level 1, 6 tasks; Level 2 , 12
tasks; Level 3, 13 tasks; Level 4, 2 tasks; and Level 5, 1 task. By examining tasks
associated with these proficiency levels, characteristics that are likely to make
particular document tasks more or less difficult can be identified. There are
basically four types of questions associated with document tasks: *locating, cycling,
integrating* and *generating*. Locating tasks require the reader to match one or more
features of information stated in the question to either identical or synonymous
information given in the document. Cycling tasks require the reader to locate and
match one or more features of information, but differ from locating tasks in that they
require the reader to engage in a series of feature matches to satisfy conditions given
in the question. The integrating tasks typically require the reader to compare and
contrast information in adjacent parts of the document. In the generating tasks,
readers must produce a written response by processing information found in the
document and by making text-based inferences or drawing on their own background
knowledge.

Centre on Internal and External Mobility

What is CIEM?

CIEM stands for Centre on Internal and External Mobility, an initiative of the personnel department. A number of workers of this department work in CIEM, together with members from other departments and outside career consultants.
CIEM is available to help employees in their search for another job inside or outside the Canco Manufacturing Company.

What does CIEM do?

CIEM supports employees who are seriously considering other work through the following activities:

- **Job Data Bank**

After an interview with the employee, information is entered into a data bank that tracks job seekers and job openings at Canco and at other manufacturing companies.

- **Guidance**

The employee's potential is explored through career counselling discussions.

- **Courses**

Courses are being organized (in collaboration with the department for information and training) that will deal with job search and career planning.

- **Career Change Projects**

CIEM supports and coordinates projects to help employees prepare for new careers and new perspectives.

- **Mediation**

CIEM acts as a mediator for employees who are threatened with dismissal resulting from reorganization, and assists with finding new positions when necessary.

How much does CIEM cost?

Payment is determined in consultation with the department where you work. A number of services of CIEM are free. You may also be asked to pay, either in money or in time.

How does CIEM work?

CIEM assists employees who are seriously considering another job within or outside the company.
That process begins by submitting an application. A discussion with a personnel counsellor can also be useful. It is obvious that you should talk with the counsellor first about your wishes and the internal possibilities regarding your career. The counsellor is familiar with your abilities and with developments within your unit.
Contact with CIEM in any case is made via the personnel counsellor. He or she handles the application for you, after which you are invited to a discussion with a CIEM representative.

For more information

The personnel department can give you more information.

As with the prose tasks, each type of question extends over a range of difficulty as a result of combining other variables:

- the number of categories or features of information in the question the reader must process or match;

- the number of categories or features of information in the document that seem plausible or correct because they share some but not all of the information with the correct answer;

- the extent to which the information asked for in the question is clearly related to the information stated in the document;

- the structure and content of the document.

A more detailed discussion of the five levels of document literacy follows.

Document level 1   *Score range: 0 to 225*

Most of the tasks at this level require the reader to locate a single piece of information based on a literal match. Distracting information, if present, is typically located away from the correct answer. Some tasks may direct the reader to enter personal information onto a form.

One document task at this level (with a difficulty value of 188) directs the reader to identify from a chart the percentage of teachers from Greece who are women. The chart displays the percentages of women teachers from various countries. Only one number appears on the chart for each country.

FEW DUTCH WOMEN AT THE BLACKBOARD

There is a low percentage of women teachers in the Netherlands compared to other countries. In most of the other countries, the majority of teachers are women. However, if we include the figures for inspectors and school principals, the proportion shrinks considerably and women are in a minority everywhere.

Percentage of women teachers (kindergarten, elementary, and secondary).

A similar task involves a chart from a newspaper showing the expected amounts of radioactive waste by country. This task, which has a difficulty value of 218, directs the reader to identify the country that is projected to have the smallest amount of waste by the year 2000. Again, there is only one percentage associated with each country; however, the reader must first identify the percentage associated with the smallest amount of waste, and then match it to the country.

Document level 2   *Score range: 226 to 275*

Document tasks at this level are a bit more varied. While some still require the reader to match a single feature, more distracting information may be present or the match may require a low-level inference. Some tasks at this level may require the reader to enter information onto a form or to cycle through information in a document.

One level 2 task on the document scale (242) directs the reader to look at a chart to identify the year in which the fewest people in the Netherlands were injured by fireworks. Part of what perhaps makes this task somewhat more difficult than those in level 1 is that two charts are presented instead of just one. One, labelled "Fireworks in the Netherlands", depicts years and numbers representing funds spent in millions of Canadian dollars, whereas the other, "Victims of fireworks", uses a line to show numbers of people treated in hospitals. It is worth noting that in a second version of the assessment this label was changed to read "number injured."

Several other tasks falling within level 2 direct the reader to use information given to complete a form. In one case they are asked to fill out an order form to purchase tickets to see a play on a particular day and at a particular time. In another, readers are asked to complete the availability section of an employment application based on information provided that included: the total number of hours they are willing to work, the hours they are available, how they heard about the job, and the availability of transportation.

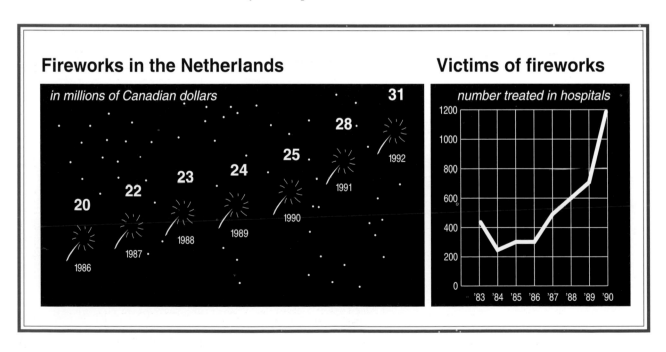

Document level 3   *Score range: 276 to 325*

Tasks at this level are varied. Some require the reader to make literal or synonymous matches, but usually the reader must take conditional information into account or match on the basis of multiple features of information. Some require the reader to integrate information from one or more displays of information. Others ask the reader to cycle through a document to provide multiple responses.

One task falling around the middle of level 3 in difficulty (with a value of 295) involves the fireworks charts shown earlier (see *Document level 2*). This task directs the reader to write a brief description of the relationship between sales and injuries based on the information shown in the two graphs. A second task, falling at high end of level 3 (321), involves the use of a quick copy printing requisition form that might be found in the workplace. The task asks the reader to state whether or not the quick copy centre would make 300 copies of a statement that is 105 pages long. In responding to this directive, the reader must determine whether conditions stated in the question meet those provided in the requisition form.

QUICK COPY Printing Requisition   FILL IN ALL INFORMATION REQUESTED

GUIDELINES: This requisition may be used to order materials to be printed BLACK INK only, and in the quantities that are listed at the right.

■ SINGLE SHEET PRINTED 1 OR 2 SIDES — 2000 copies maximum
■ MORE THAN ONE SHEET UP TO 100 PAGES — 400 copies maximum
     OVER 100 PAGES — 200 copies maximum

1. PROJECT TO BE CHARGED

2. TODAY'S DATE

3. TITLE OR DESCRIPTION _____

4. DATE DELIVERY REQUIRED _____

5.   DO NOT MARK IN SHADED BOXES

X   **=**

NUMBER OF ORIGINALS   NUMBER OF COPIES TO BE PRINTED   TOTAL NUMBER OF IMPRESSIONS

6. NUMBER OF SIDES TO BE PRINTED (Check one box.)   1 ☐ One side   2 [☐ BOTH sides

7. COLOR OF PAPER (Fill in only if NOT white.) _____

8. SIZE OF PAPER (Fill in only if NOT 8¹/₂ x 11) _____

9. Check any that apply:
   ☐ COLLATE

   BINDING: ☐ One staple at upper left
            ☐ Two staples in left margin
            ☐ BIND-FAST ☐ Black
                        ☐ Brown
            ☐ 3-hole punch

   ☐ Other instructions _____
   _____
   _____
   _____

AUTHORIZATION AND DELIVERY

10. Project Director (print name) _____

11. Requisitioner (print your own name and phone no.) _____
                                        extension

12. Check one:
    ☐ Requisitioner will PICK UP completed job.   MAIL STOP

    ☐ Mail completed   ROOM NO.
      job to: _____
              Print name, room number, and mail stop

13. **KEEP PINK COPY at least 3 months.** When requesting information, you must refer to the requisition number printed here.

140468
QUICK COPY REGISTRATION NUMBER

D1320-03116 • 000000 • 000000

One of the two tasks falling within this level (341) asks the reader to look at two pie charts showing oil use for 1970 and 1989. The question directs the reader to summarise how the percentages of oil used for different purposes changed over the specified period. Here the reader must cycle through the two charts, comparing and contrasting the percentages for each of the four stated purposes, and then generate a statement that captures these changes.

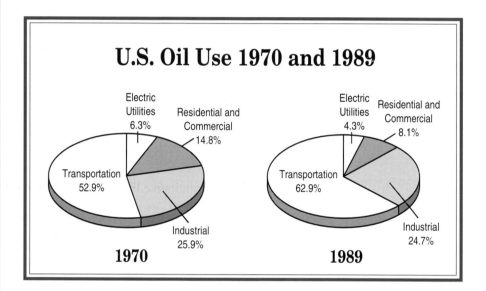

Comparing ratings for clock radios is not an easy task.

The only level 5 task in this international assessment (with a difficulty value of 408) involves a page taken from a consumer magazine rating clock radios. The reader is asked for the average advertised price for the "basic" clock radio receiving the highest overall score. This task requires readers to process two types of conditional information. First, they need to identify the clock radio receiving the highest overall score while distinguishing among the three types reviewed: "full-featured", "basic" and those "with cassette player". Second, they need to locate a price. In making this final match, they need to notice that two are given: the suggested retail price, followed by the average advertised price.

The same document is used for a second and considerably easier task that falls at the low end of level 4 (327). The reader is asked "which full-featured radio is rated the highest on performance". Again, it is necessary to find the correct category of clock radio, but the reader needs to process fewer conditions. All that is required is to distinguish between the rating for "Overall Score" and that for "Performance." It is possible that some adults note the distractor ("Overall Score") rather than the criterion specified in the question, "Performance". Another factor that likely contributes to this task's difficulty is that "Overall Score" is given a numerical value while the other features are rated by a symbol. Also, some adults may find the correct category ("Performance") but select the first radio listed, assuming it performed best. The text accompanying the table indicates that the radios are rated within a category by an overall score; it is easy to imagine that some people may have equated overall score with overall performance.

Quantitative literacy

Since adults are frequently required to perform arithmetic operations in everyday life, the ability to perform quantitative tasks is another important aspect of literacy. These skills may at first seem to differ fundamentally from those associated with prose and document literacy, and therefore to extend the concept of literacy beyond its traditional limits. Experience in North America with large-scale assessments of adults indicates that the processing of printed information plays an important role in affecting the difficulty of tasks along the quantitative scale (Montigny *et al.*, 1991; Kirsh *et al.*, 1993).

Being able to deal with numbers and basic mathematical operations is an essential skill.

In general, it appears that many individuals can perform single arithmetic operations when both the numbers and operations are made explicit. However, when the numbers to be used must be located in and extracted from different types of documents that contain other similar but irrelevant information, when the operations to be used must be inferred from printed directions, and when multiple operations must be performed, the tasks become increasingly difficult.

The IALS quantitative literacy scale contains 33 tasks ranging from 229 to 408 in difficulty. These tasks are distributed as follows: Level 1, 1 task; Level 2, 9 tasks; Level 3, 16 tasks; Level 4, 5 tasks; and Level 5, 2 tasks. The difficulty of these tasks – and therefore, their placement along the scale – appears to be a function of several factors including:

- the particular arithmetic operation the task requires;
- the number of operations needed to perform the task successfully;
- the extent to which the numbers are embedded in printed materials;
- the extent to which an inference must be made to identify the type of operation to be performed.

RATINGS

Better ←————————→ Worse

Clock radios

Listed by types; within types, listed in order of overall score. Differences in score of 4 points or less were not deemed significant.

1 Brand and model. If you can't find a model, call the company. Phone numbers are listed on page 736.

2 Price. The manufacturer's suggested or approximate retail price, followed by the average advertised price.

3 Dimensions. To the nearest centimetre.

4 Overall score. A composite, encompassing all our tests and judgments. A "perfect" radio would have earned 100 points.

5 Convenience. This composite judgment reflects such things as the legibility of the display, the ease of tuning the radio and setting the alarm, and the presence or absence of useful features.

6 Performance. An overall judgment reflecting performance in our tests of: sensitivity and selectivity; tuning ease; capture ratio, the ability to bring in the stronger of two stations on the same frequency; image rejection, the ability to ignore signals from just above the band, resistance to interference from signals bouncing off aircraft and such.

7 Sensitivity. How well each radio received a station with little interference.

8 Selectivity. How well each radio received clearly a weak station next to a strong one on the dial.

9 Tone quality. Based mainly on computer analysis of the speaker's output and on listening tests, using music from CDs. No model produced high-fidelity sound.

10 Reversible time-setting. This useful feature makes setting clock and alarm times easy. If you overshoot the desired setting, you simply back up.

11 Dual alarm. Lets you set two separate wake-up times.

1 Brand and model	2 Price	3 Dimensions, HxWxD, cm.	4 Overall Score	5 Convenience	6 Performance	7 Sensitivity	8 Selectivity	9 Tone quality	10 Reversible time setting	11 Dual alarm	Warranty, months	Advantages	Disadvantages	Comments
Full-featured clock radios														
RCA RP-3690	$50/$40	8x25x18	86	◉	◓	◓	◒	◉	✔	✔	12	A,B,D,H,J,L,O,T,U		A
Sony ICF-C303	50/45	5x20x15	84	◉	◓	◉	○	◒	✔	✔	12	C,E,F,I,N,T		C
Panasonic RC-X220	50/45	10x28x13	82	◒	◓	◓	◓	○	✔	✔	12	A,G,K,M,O,S,T,U	b,c	A
Realistic 272	50/30	5x28x15	79	◒	◓	◓	◓	◓	✔	✔	3	A,G,H,K,O,T		D
Magnavox AJ3900	65/—	15x38x13	78	○	◉	◓	◉	◒	—	✔	3	D,G,K,M,O,R,T	b,g	B
Emerson AK2745	39/20	8x28x15	70	○	◓	◓	◒	◒	✔	✔	3	G,O	g	K
Soundesign 3753	20/20	8x23x13	62	○	◓	●	○	○	✔	✔	3	J,Q	d,h	J
Basic clock radios														
Realistic 263	28/18	10x20x10	74	○	◓	◓	○	◒	—	—	3	A,D,H,O,P,U	h	—
Soundesign 3622	12/10	5x20x13	68	◒	◓	◉	◒	◒	—	—	3	U	d	L
Panasonic RC-6064	18/15	5x20x13	67	◒	◒	◉	○	○	—	—	12	—	b,c	
General Electric 7-4612	13/10	5x20x13	66	◒	○	◉	◒	○	—	—	12	A,D	a,g	—
Lloyds CR001	20/15	5x18x13	64	◒	○	◉	◒	◒	—	—	3	U	—	—
Sony ICF-C240	15/13	5x18x15	63	◒	◒	○	◒	◒	—	—	12	—	f,g	—
Emerson AK2720	19/10	5x20x13	61	◒	○	◒	●	●	—	—	3	O,T	e	K
Gran Prix D507	15/10	5x18x10	54	◒	●	○	●	●	—	—	3	—	d	—
Clock radios with cassette player														
General Electric 7-4965	60/50	10x30x15	85	◓	◓	◓	◓	◓	✔	✔	12	A,D,G,H,K,O,S,T	—	B,E
Panasonic RC-X250	[1]	10x33x13	76	◓	◓	◓	◓	◓	✔	✔	12	A,G,K,O,R,U	b,c	A,H
Sony ICF-CS650	75/65	15x28x15	74	○	◓	◉	○	◒	✔	✔	12	G,R,T,U	c,f,i	A,F,H
Soundesign 3844MGY	40/30	13x30x13	62	○	●	●	●	◒	—	—	3	G,K,J,S,U		F,G,I,M

[1] Discontinued. Replaced by **RC-X260**, $79 list and $60 average advertised sale price.

Features in Common

All: • Permit snooze time of about 8 min. • Retain time settings during short power failures.
Except as noted, all have: • Battery backup for clock and alarm memory. • Red display digits 1 cm. high. • Sleep-time radio play for up to 60 min. before automatic shutoff. • Switch to reset alarm.

Keys to Advantages

A–Alarm works despite power failure.
B–Shows actual time plus up to 2 alarm times.
C–Twin alarms settable for 2 different stations.
D–Tone alarm has adjustable volume control.
E–Memory needs no battery.
F–Digital tuner with presettable stations.
G–Tuner can receive in stereo.
H–Battery-strength indicator.
I–Illuminated tuning dial.
J–Illuminated tuning pointer.

K–Earphone jack.
L–Nap timer.
M–Audio input for tape deck or CD player.
N–Display can show date and time.
O–Display has high/low brightness switch.
P–Display has larger digits than most.
Q–Night light—adjusts for room light.
R–Bass-boost tone control.
S–Treble-cut tone control.
T–Better than most in tuning ease.
U–Better than most in image rejection.

Key to Disadvantages

a–Possible to reset time by accident.
b–Controls for time-setting or dimmer inconveniently located on radio's bottom or rear.
c–Display dimmer than most in brightly lit room.
d–Radio volume must be turned completely down for alarm buzzer to sound.
e–Lacks alarm buzzer; radio is sole alarm.

f–Lacks indication alarm is set.
g–Lacks alarm-reset button.
h–Time-setting lacks fast reverse.
i–No slow forward, fast reverse for time setting.

Key to Comments

A–Display shows green digits.
B–Display shows blue digits.
C–Display uses LCD (liquid crystal) digits.
D–Terminals for external antenna.
E–3-position graphic equalizer.
F–Cassette player lacks Record function.
G–Cassette player lacks Rewind function.
H–Model permits wake-up to cassette play.
I–Cassette-deck flutter worse than most.
J–Warranty repairs cost $3 for handling.
K–Warranty repairs cost $3.50 for handling.
L–Warranty repairs cost $6 for handling.
M–Warranty repairs cost $10 for handling.

The five levels of quantitative literacy are described in detail below.

> *Quantitative level 1*   *Score range: 0 to 225*
>
> *Although no quantitative tasks used in the assessment fall below the score value of 225, experience suggests that such tasks would require the reader to perform a single, relatively simple operation (usually addition) for which either the numbers are clearly noted in the given document and the operation is stipulated, or the numbers are provided and the operation does not require the reader to find the numbers.*

The easiest quantitative task (225) directs the reader to complete an order form. The last line on this form says "Total with Handling". The line above it says "Handling Charge $2.00". The reader simply has to add the $2.00 to the $50.00 entered on a previous line to indicate the cost of the tickets. In this task, one of the numbers is stipulated; the operation is easily identified from the word "total"; and the operation does not require the reader to perform the "borrow" or "carry-over" function of addition. Moreover, the form itself features a simple column format, further facilitating the task for the reader.

> *Quantitative level 2*   *Score range: 226 to 275*
>
> *Tasks at this level typically require readers to perform a single arithmetic operation (frequently addition or subtraction), using numbers that are easily located in the text or document. The operation to be performed may be easily inferred from the wording of the question or the format of the material (for example, a bank deposit or order form).*

Substracting numbers appears to be more difficult than adding them up.

A typical level 2 task on the quantitative scale directs the reader to use a weather chart in a newspaper to determine how many degrees warmer today's high temperature is expected to be in Bangkok than in Seoul. Here the reader must cycle through the table to locate the two temperatures and then subtract one from the other to determine the difference. This task received a difficulty value of 255.

A similar but slightly more difficult task (268) requires the reader to use the chart about women in the teaching profession that is displayed in level 1 for the document scale. This task directs the reader to calculate the percentage of men in the teaching profession in Italy. Both this task and the one just mentioned involve calculating the difference between two numbers. In the former, however, both temperatures could be identified in the table from the newspaper. For the task involving male teachers in Italy, the reader needs to make the inference that the percentage is equal to 100 per cent minus the percentage of female teachers.

WEATHER

Europe

	Today High °C	Low °C	W	Tomorrow High °C	Low °C	W
Algarve	19	7	s	21	9	s
Amsterdam	11	6	pc	12	7	pc
Ankara	17	7	pc	19	8	pc
Athens	22	15	pc	23	14	pc
Barcelona	16	8	s	14	9	s
Belgrade	14	6	pc	10	1	c
Berlin	8	2	c	6	1	c
Brussels	11	6	pc	14	7	pc
Budapest	9	1	pc	9	2	c
Copenhagen	7	1	r	6	2	c
Costa del Sol	21	8	s	21	10	s
Dublin	10	6	pc	13	8	pc
Edinburgh	10	6	c	10	6	c
Florence	11	5	s	14	6	s
Frankfurt	12	6	pc	13	4	pc
Geneva	9	2	s	12	4	s
Helsinki	-1	-7	sf	-3	-10	pc
Istanbul	17	10	pc	15	9	sh
Las Palmas	26	18	s	27	18	pc
Lisbon	19	9	s	19	10	s
London	12	5	pc	13	7	pc
Madrid	17	3	s	18	4	s
Milan	9	3	s	13	6	s
Moscow	1	-3	r	-3	-11	sf
Munich	11	3	pc	12	6	pc
Nice	14	7	s	15	8	s
Oslo	4	-4	c	5	-2	c
Paris	12	6	pc	13	6	pc
Prague	11	1	pc	8	2	c
Reykjavik	4	2	r	6	-1	c
Rome	20	12	s	20	10	s
St. Petersburg	-1	-7	sf	-4	-12	pc
Stockholm	1	-5	sn	-2	-7	c
Strasbourg	12	5	pc	15	7	pc
Tallinn	-1	-7	sf	-4	-10	pc
Venice	10	3	s	11	4	s
Vienna	9	-1	pc	10	2	c
Warsaw	8	2	sh	6	1	c
Zurich	8	0	s	9	1	pc

Oceania

	Today High °C	Low °C	W	Tomorrow High °C	Low °C	W
Auckland	20	14	s	17	11	sh
Sydney	27	17	pc	25	16	pc

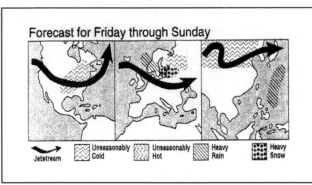

Forecast for Friday through Sunday

Legend: Jetstream — Unseasonably Cold — Unseasonably Hot — Heavy Rain — Heavy Snow

North America
Cold weather will engulf the Midwestern and Northeastern United States Friday and over the weekend. Although it will be cold in Chicago, Toronto and New York City, the weather is expected to be dry. Los Angeles will have some sunshine and seasonable temperatures each day.

Europe
Western and central Europe will have a spell of mild weather Friday into the weekend. London and Paris will have dry weather with some sunshine Friday into Sunday. Rain will continue to soak southwestern Norway. Snow will blanket the area from Minsk to Moscow.

Asia
Typhoon Elsie will probably stay to the east of the Philippines and south of Japan Friday and the weekend. Some rain is apt to fall in Seoul and there could even be a little ice or snow. Cold air will pour into Beijing and snow is a possibility. Hong Kong will start the weekend warm.

Middle East

	Today High °C	Low °C	W	Tomorrow High °C	Low °C	w
Beirut	28	19	pc	29	20	s
Cairo	29	20	pc	28	19	pc
Damascus	24	12	s	26	14	s
Jerusalem	27	15	s	26	14	s
Riyadh	34	13	s	32	13	s

Latin America

	Today High °C	Low °C	W	Tomorrow High °C	Low °C	w
Buenos Aires	23	11	pc	26	13	s
Caracas	29	20	s	31	18	s
Lima	23	17	c	23	16	c
Mexico City	23	11	sh	23	12	pc
Rio de Janiero	32	22	s	28	21	sh
Santiago	24	4	s	22	6	pc

Legend: s-sunny, pc-partly cloudy, c-cloudy, sh-showers, t-thunderstorms, r-rain, sf-snow flurries, sn-snow, i-ice, W-Weather. **All maps, forecasts and data provided by Accu-Weather, Inc. © 1992**

Asia

	Today High °C	Low °C	W	Tomorrow High °C	Low °C	W
Bangkok	32	22	pc	30	23	s
Beijing	11	0	s	8	2	pc
Hong Kong	30	23	s	29	22	pc
Manila	31	25	s	31	25	sh
New Delhi	31	13	s	32	16	s
Seoul	14	6	pc	14	4	pc
Shanghai	22	10	pc	24	12	s
Singapore	31	24	pc	28	23	sh
Taipei	26	21	pc	26	19	pc
Tokyo	18	9	pc	17	7	pc

Africa

	Today High °C	Low °C	W	Tomorrow High °C	Low °C	W
Algiers	27	14	s	26	13	s
Cape Town	20	11	sh	18	11	pc
Casablanca	20	14	c	21	11	pc
Harare	34	17	s	32	18	pc
Lagos	30	24	pc	29	24	pc
Nairobi	27	12	pc	26	13	pc
Tunis	27	17	pc	17	14	pc

North America

	Today High °C	Low °C	W	Tomorrow High °C	Low °C	W
Anchorage	0	-2	c	3	0	sh
Atlanta	14	4	pc	8	2	pc
Boston	15	4	c	8	-1	pc
Chicago	2	-5	c	-2	-8	pc
Denver	8	-3	pc	4	-6	sn
Detroit	4	-2	c	4	-5	pc
Honolulu	31	20	s	31	21	pc
Houston	15	3	pc	12	6	pc
Los Angeles	28	14	s	24	13	s
Miami	30	22	pc	29	21	pc
Minneapolis	-1	-8	c	1	-7	pc
Montreal	7	-2	sf	4	-3	c
Nassau	31	22	pc	28	21	sh
New York	14	4	r	10	2	pc
Phoenix	23	11	pc	22	8	s
San Fran.	20	11	pc	21	8	s
Seattle	11	6	pc	13	7	r
Toronto	6	-3	c	3	-3	c
Washington	14	6	r	11	4	pc

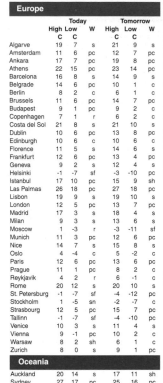

> *Quantitative level 3*   *Score range: 276 to 325*
>
> *Tasks at this level typically require the reader to perform a single operation. However, the operations become more varied – some multiplication and division tasks are included. Sometimes the reader needs to identify two or more numbers from various places in the document, and the numbers are frequently embedded in complex displays. While semantic relation terms such as "how many" or "calculate the difference" are often used, some of the tasks require the reader to make higher-order inferences to determine the appropriate operation.*

One task located at 302 on the quantitative scale directs the reader to look at two graphs containing information about consumers and producers of primary energy. The reader is asked to calculate how much more energy Canada produces than it consumes. Here the operation is not facilitated by the format of the document; the reader must locate the information using both bar graphs. Another task involving this document directs the reader to calculate the total amount of energy in quadrillion (10^{15}) BTU (British Thermal Unit) consumed by Canada, Mexico and the United States. This task, which falls at 300 on the scale, requires the reader to add three numbers. Presenting two graphs likely increases the difficulty; some respondents may perform the appropriate calculation for the three countries specified using the producer energy chart rather than the consumer energy chart.

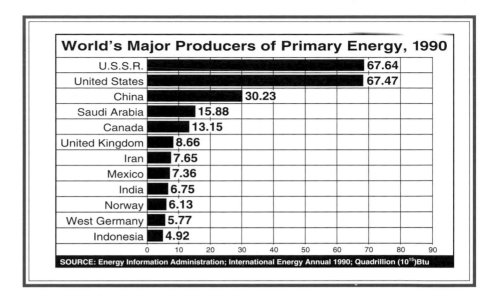

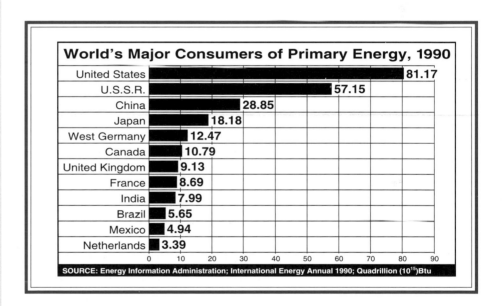

Another task at this level involves the fireworks chart shown previously for the document scale. The reader is asked to calculate how many more people were injured in 1989 than in 1988. What contributes to this task receiving a difficulty value of 293 is that one of the numbers is not given in the line graph; the reader needs to interpolate the number from information provided along the vertical axis.

A task located at 280 on the scale asks readers to look at a recipe for scrambled eggs with tomatoes. The recipe gives the ingredients for four servings: 3 tablespoons of oil, 1 garlic clove, 1 teaspoon of sugar, 500 grams of fresh red tomatoes and 6 eggs. They are then asked to determine the number of eggs they will need if they are using the recipe for six people. Here they must know how to calculate or determine the ratio needed. This task is somewhat easier than might be expected given others at the same level, perhaps because people are familiar with recipes and with manipulating them to fit a particular situation.

Another question using this recipe asks the reader to determine the amount of oil that would be needed if the recipe were being used for two people. This task received a value of 253 on the scale; a larger percentage of respondents found it easier to halve an ingredient than to increase one by 50 per cent. It is not clear why this is so. It may be that some of the respondents have an algorithm for responding to certain familiar tasks that does not require them to apply general arithmetic principles.

Quantitative level 4   *Score range: 326 to 375*

With one exception, the tasks at this level require the reader to perform a single arithmetic operation where typically either the quantities or the operation are not easily determined. That is, for most of the tasks at this level, the question or directive does not provide a semantic relation term such as "how many" or "calculate the difference" to help the reader.

One task at this level involves a compound interest table. It directs the reader to "calculate the total amount of money you will have if you invest $100 at a rate of 6 per cent for 10 years." This task received a difficulty value of 348, in part because many people treated this as a document rather than a quantitative task and simply looked up the amount of interest that would be earned. They likely forgot to add the interest to their $100 investment.

Compound Interest
Compounded Annually

Principal	Period	4%	5%	6%	7%	8%	9%	10%	12%	14%	16%
$100	1 day	0.011	0.014	0.016	0.019	0.022	0.025	0.027	0.033	0.038	0.044
	1 week	0.077	0.096	0.115	0.134	0.153	0.173	0.192	0.230	0.268	0.307
	6 mos	2.00	2.50	3.00	3.50	4.00	4.50	5.00	6.00	7.00	8.00
	1 year	4.00	5.00	6.00	7.00	8.00	9.00	10.00	12.00	14.00	16.00
	2 years	8.16	10.25	12.36	14.49	16.64	18.81	21.00	25.44	29.96	34.56
	3 years	12.49	15.76	19.10	22.50	25.97	29.50	33.10	40.49	48.15	56.09
	4 years	16.99	21.55	26.25	31.08	36.05	41.16	46.41	57.35	68.90	81.06
	5 years	21.67	27.63	33.82	40.26	46.93	53.86	61.05	76.23	92.54	110.03
	6 years	26.53	34.01	41.85	50.07	58.69	67.71	77.16	97.38	119.50	143.64
	7 years	31.59	40.71	50.36	60.58	71.38	82.80	94.87	121.07	150.23	182.62
	8 years	36.86	47.75	59.38	71.82	85.09	99.26	114.36	147.60	185.26	227.84
	9 years	42.33	55.13	68.95	83.85	99.90	117.19	135.79	177.31	225.19	280.30
	10 years	48.02	62.89	79.08	96.72	115.89	136.74	159.37	210.58	270.72	341.14
	12 years	60.10	79.59	101.22	125.22	151.82	181.27	213.84	289.60	381.79	493.60
	15 years	80.09	107.89	139.66	175.90	217.22	264.25	317.72	447.36	613.79	826.55
	20 years	119.11	165.33	220.71	286.97	366.10	460.44	572.75	864.63	1,274.35	1,846.08

Another task at this level requires respondents to read a newspaper article describing a research finding linking allergies to a particular genetic mutation. The question directs the reader to calculate the number of people studied who were found to have the mutant gene. To answer the question correctly, readers must know how to convert the phrase "64 per cent" to a decimal number and then multiply it by the number of patients studied (400). The text provides no clues on how to tackle this problem.

A third task involves a distance chart. Readers are asked to "calculate the total number of kilometres travelled in a trip from Guadalajara to Tecomán and then to Zamora". Here a semantic relation term is provided, but the format is difficult and the quantities are not easily identified. As a result, this task received a difficulty value of 335. In a level 3 task using the same chart, respondents are asked to determine how much less the distance from Guadalajara to Tecomán is than the distance from Guadalajara to Puerto Vallarta. In that task (308), the quantities are relatively easy to locate.

TABLE OF APPROXIMATE DISTANCES (in kilometres)

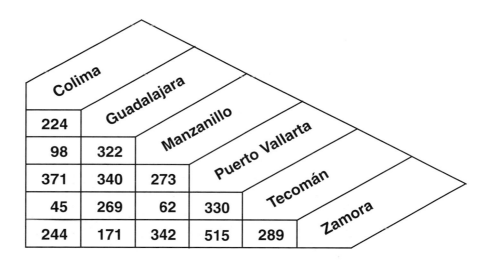

Colima	Guadalajara	Manzanillo	Puerto Vallarta	Tecomán	Zamora
224					
98	322				
371	340	273			
45	269	62	330		
244	171	342	515	289	

> *Quantitative level 5*   *Score range: 376 to 500*
>
> *These tasks require readers to perform multiple operations sequentially, and they must locate features of the problem embedded in the material or rely on background knowledge to determine the quantities or operations needed.*

One of the most difficult tasks on the quantitative scale (381) requires readers to look at a table providing nutritional analysis of food and then, using the information given, determine the percentage of calories in a Big Mac® that comes from total fat. To answer this question, readers must first recognise that the information about total fat provided is given in grams. In the question, they are told that a gram of fat has 9 calories. Therefore, they must convert the number of fat grams to calories. Then, they need to calculate this number of calories as a percentage of the total calories given for a Big Mac®. Only one other item on this scale received a higher score.

Estimating Literacy Performance across the Levels

The literacy levels not only provide a means for exploring the progression of information-processing demands across each of the scales, but also can be used to help explain how the proficiencies individuals demonstrate reflect the likelihood they will respond correctly to the broad range of tasks used in this assessment as well as to any task that has the same characteristics. In practical terms, this means that individuals performing at 250 on each scale are expected to be able to perform the average level 1 and 2 tasks with a high degree of proficiency – i.e. with an average probability of a correct response at 80 per cent or higher. It does not mean that they will not be able to perform tasks in levels 3 or higher. They would be expected to do so some of the time, but not consistently.

Nutritional Analysis

	Serving Size	Calories	Protein (g)	Carbohydrates (g)	Total Fat (g)	Saturated Fat (g)	Monounsaturated Fat (g)	Polyunsaturated Fat (g)	Cholesterol (mg)	Sodium (mg)
Sandwiches										
Hamburger	102 g	255	12	30	9	5	1	3	37	490
Cheeseburger	116 g	305	15	30	13	7	1	5	50	725
Quarter Pounder®	166 g	410	23	34	20	11	1	8	85	645
Quarter Pounder® w/Cheese	194 g	510	28	34	28	16	1	11	115	1110
McLean Deluxe™	206 g	320	22	35	10	5	1	4	60	670
McLean Deluxe™ w/Cheese	219 g	370	24	35	14	8	1	5	75	890
Big Mac®	215 g	500	25	42	26	16	1	9	100	890
Filet-O-Fish®	141 g	370	14	38	18	8	6	4	50	730
McChicken®	187 g	415	19	39	19	9	7	4	50	830
French Fries										
Small French Fries	68 g	220	3	26	12	8	1	2.5	0	110
Medium French Fries	97 g	320	4	36	17	12	1.5	3.5	0	150
Large French Fries	122 g	400	6	46	22	15	2	5	0	200
Salads										
Chef Salad	265 g	170	17	8	9	4	1	4	111	400
Garden Salad	189 g	50	4	6	2	1	0.4	0.6	65	70
Chunky Chicken Salad	255 g	150	25	7	4	2	1	1	78	230
Side Salad	106 g	30	2	4	1	0.5	0.2	0.3	33	35
Croutons	11 g	50	1	7	2	1.3	0.1	0.5	0	140
Bacon Bits	3 g	15	1	0	1	0.3	0.2	0.5	1	95

Soft Drinks

	Coca-Cola Classic®				diet Coke®				Sprite®			
	Small	Medium	Large	Jumbo	Small	Medium	Large	Jumbo	Small	Medium	Large	Jumbo
Calories	140	190	260	380	1	1	2	3	140	190	260	380
Carbohydrates (g)	38	50	70	101	0.3	0.4	0.5	0.6	36	48	66	96
Sodium (mg)	15	20	25	40	30	40	60	80	15	20	25	40

Level 3 is considered by experts as a suitable minimum for coping with the complex information produced in the knowledge society.

The three charts given in Tables A.1 to A.3 display the probability that individuals performing at selected points on each of the scales will give a correct response to tasks of varying difficulty. For example, a reader whose prose proficiency is 150 has less than a 50 per cent chance of giving a correct response to the level 1 tasks. Individuals whose proficiency score is 200, in contrast, have about an 80 per cent probability of responding correctly to these tasks.

In terms of task demands, it can be inferred that adults performing at 200 on the prose scale are likely to be able to locate a single piece of information in a brief text when there is no distracting information, or if plausible but incorrect information is present but located away from the correct answer. However, these individuals are likely to encounter far more difficulty with tasks in levels 2 through 5. For example, they would have only a 40 per cent chance of performing the average level 2 task correctly, an 18 per cent chance of success with tasks in level 3, and no more than a 7 per cent chance with tasks in levels 4 and 5.

In contrast, respondents demonstrating a proficiency of 300 on the prose scale have about an 80 per cent chance or higher of succeeding with tasks in levels 1, 2 and 3. This means that they demonstrate success with tasks that require them to make low-level inferences and with those that entail taking some conditional information into account. They can also integrate or compare and contrast information that is easily identified in the text. On the other hand, they are likely to encounter difficulty with tasks where they must make more sophisticated text-based inferences, or where they need to process more abstract types of information. These more difficult tasks may also require them to draw on less familiar or more specialised types of knowledge beyond that given in the text. On average, they have about a 50 per cent probability of performing level 4 tasks correctly; with level 5 tasks, their likelihood of responding correctly decreases to 40 per cent.

Similar kinds of interpretations can be made using the information presented for the document and quantitative literacy scales. For example, someone who is at 200 on the quantitative scale has, on average, a 67 per cent chance of responding correctly to level 1 tasks. His or her likelihood of responding correctly decreases to 47 per cent for level 2 tasks, 21 per cent for level 3 tasks, 6 per cent for level 4 tasks and a mere 2 per cent for level 5 tasks. Similarly, readers with a proficiency of 300 on the quantitative scale would have a probability of 92 per cent or higher of responding correctly to tasks in levels 1 and 2. Their average probability would decrease to 81 per cent for level 3 tasks, 57 per cent for level 4 and 20 per cent for level 5.

Estimating the Variability of Literacy Tasks Across the Participating Countries

One of the goals in conducting international surveys is to be able to compare populations on common scales. In this study, three literacy scales were used to compare both the distributions of literacy skills and the relationships between literacy skills and a variety of social, educational and labour market variables. Each literacy scale consisted of more than 30 literacy tasks which received item parameters that define the difficulty of the task and how well it discriminates among populations of adults. These parameters were determined on the basis of how adults within and across participating countries responded to each task.

TABLE A.1

Average probabilities of successful performance, prose scale

Prose level	Selected proficiency scores				
	150	200	250	300	350
	%				
1	48	81	95	99	100
2	14	40	76	94	99
3	6	18	46	78	93
4	2	7	21	50	80
5*	2	6	18	40	68

* Based on one task.

TABLE A.2

Average probabilities of successful performance, document scale

Document level	Selected proficiency scores				
	150	200	250	300	350
	%				
1	40	72	94	99	100
2	20	51	82	95	99
3	7	21	50	80	94
4	4	13	34	64	85
5*	< 1	1	3	13	41

* Based on one task.

TABLE A.3

Average probabilities of successful performance, quantitative scale

Quantitative level	Selected proficiency scores				
	150	200	250	300	350
	%				
1*	34	67	89	97	99
2	21	47	76	92	98
3	7	21	51	81	94
4	1	6	22	57	86
5	1	2	7	20	53

* Based on one task.

Under standard assumptions of Item Response Theory (IRT), item parameters are thought to be invariant among respondents and among countries as well as subgroups within countries. However, it has been discovered through performing large-scale assessments that this assumption is not always true. Yamamoto (1997) notes that some language/country populations do respond differently to a subset of literacy tasks. As described in the IALS Technical Report (Murray *et al.,* 1997), individual items were dropped from the assessment if at least seven of the original ten language or country populations were shown not to have the same item parameters – i.e. if the response data for a particular item proved to have a poor fit to the item parameters common to the rest of the language or country populations. In addition, if there were items in which only one, two or three countries varied, these countries were allowed to have unique parameters for that item. This resulted in a total of 13 items being dropped from the assessment, with 31 items getting a unique parameter for one language or country population, 16 for two language or country populations, and 6 for three language or country populations. Another way to look at this is that there were a total of 1 010 constraints (114 items minus the 13 dropped times 10 language samples). Of these, unique item parameters were required or allowed in 81 instances, meaning that 92 per cent of the constraints support a common scale across the ten original language or country populations.

These discrepancies were due largely to differences in translations among countries, or to differences in interpretation of scoring rubrics for individual items. The different performance on some items also reflected the variation in language and culture, although no obvious or specific reason could be identified. The fact that not all items had identical item parameters resulted in two types of variation. First, differences could influence the distribution of proficiency scores for a particular language or country group, if only slightly. Analyses indicated that the consequence of using a partially different set of item parameters on the proficiency distribution for a particular population was minimal. For any population, when the proficiency distribution was estimated based either on a set of items which included those common across countries as well as those unique to a given country, or on a set of items which were optimal for a different population, the means and standard deviations of estimated proficiencies differed by less than half of a standard error. Typically, standard errors of estimation ranged between 1 and 3 points on the 500-point scales depending on a particular language or country population.

The second type of variation which results from having a small set of items with unique parameters occurs in the placement of particular tasks along the scales according to their response probability of 80 per cent (RP80). At the beginning of this Annex, it was mentioned that a criterion of 80 per cent was used, meaning that tasks were placed along a scale based on the probability that someone with that level of proficiency would have an 80 per cent chance of getting that task and others like it correct. The fact that a small subset of tasks have unique parameters for particular country/language groups results in some tasks falling at different points along each scale. Since this Annex is about describing what it means to be at a particular point along each literacy scale and uses exemplar tasks to reflect on this meaning, it seems important to try to describe the extent of this variation.

To evaluate the variability of RP80s for each language or country population, the deviation of RP80s against the common RP80 was examined. It is important to note that no country received all common item parameters. That is, at least one item for each country received a unique set of parameters. However, at least seven of the original language or country populations received common parameters for each of the 101 items. In total, there are 15 language or country groups for which there are data to estimate this variation. Nine of the groups are from the first assessment and six are from the assessment just completed. There were a total of 101 literacy exercises, meaning that there could be as many as 1 515 deviations (101 times 15). The mean deviation among the RP80s was 4.7, with a standard deviation of 14.1. This means that the average variation among the RP80s for the literacy tasks was 4.7 points on a 500-point scale, or less than 10 per cent of the 50 points making up a particular literacy level. In addition, a small number of items had large deviations which made up a large percentage of this variation. Only 1 per cent of the actual deviations observed accounts for about 20 per cent of the average deviation. In other words, 99 per cent of the deviations have a mean of 3.6, or a 20 per cent reduction from the average of 4.7. Table A.4 shows the average deviation of RP80s by each of the 15 country or language groups; the average is seen to range from a low of 1.1 for the French-speaking Swiss to 7.6 for Australia.

TABLE A.4

Average deviation of RP80 values by country or language group

Australia	7.6	Northern Ireland	6.9
Belgium (Flanders)	5.8	Poland	5.4
Canada (English)	3.6	Sweden	5.2
Canada (French)	3.2	Switzerland (French)	1.1
Germany	5.3	Switzerland (German)	4.0
Ireland	4.5	Great Britain	5.2
Netherlands	3.4	United States	2.0
New Zealand	7.2		

Conclusion

One of the goals of large-scale surveys is to provide information that can help policy-makers during the decision-making process. Presenting that information in a way that will enhance understanding of what has been measured and the conclusions to be drawn from the data is important to reaching this goal. This Annex has offered a framework for understanding the consistency of task responses demonstrated by adults from a number of countries. The framework identifies a set of variables which have been shown to underlie successful performance on a broad array of literacy tasks. Collectively, they provide a means for moving away from interpreting survey results in terms of discrete tasks or a single number, and towards identifying levels of performance sufficiently generalised to have validity across assessments and groups.

The concept of test design is evolving. Frameworks such as the one presented here can assist in that evolution. No longer should testing stop at assigning a numerical value; it should assign meaning to that number. And, as concern ceases to centre on discrete behaviours or isolated observations and focus is more on providing a *meaningful* score, a higher level of measurement is reached (Messick, 1989).

References

KIRSCH, I.S. and MOSENTHAL, P. (1993), "Interpreting the IEA Reading Literacy Scales", in M. Binkley, K. Rust and M. Winglee (Eds.), *Methodological Issues in Comparative Educational Studies: The Case of the IEA Reading Literacy Study,* National Center for Education Statistics, United States Department of Education, Washington, DC.

KIRSCH, I.S., JUNGEBLUT, A., JENKINS, L. and KOLSTAD, A. (Eds.) (1993), *Adult Literacy in America: A First Look at the Results of the National Adult Literacy Survey,* National Center for Education Statistics, United States Department of Education, Washington, DC.

MESSICK, S. (1989), "Validity", in R. Linn (Ed.), *Educational Measurement*, 3rd edition, Macmillan, New York.

MONTIGNY, G., KELLY, K. and JONES, S. (1991), *Adult Literacy in Canada: Results of a National Study,* Minister of Industry, Science and Technology, Ottawa (Statistics Canada, Catalogue No. 89-525-XPE).

MURRAY, T.S., KIRSCH, I.S. and JENKINS, L. (Eds.) (1997), *Adult Literacy in OECD Countries: Technical Report on the First International Adult Literacy Survey,* United States Department of Education, Washington, DC.

YAMAMOTO, K. (1997), "Scaling and scale linking", in T.S. Murray, I.S. Kirsch, and L. Jenkins (Eds.), *Adult Literacy in OECD Countries: Technical Report on the First International Adult Literary Survey,* United States Department of Education, Washington, DC.

Annex B

Survey Administration, Response and Data Quality

Introduction

It was mentioned in the Introduction that the IALS had two primary objectives. The first was to develop an assessment instrument that would permit useful comparisons of literacy performance across languages and cultures. That achieved, the second aim was to perform such comparisons, describing the literacy skills of people from different countries; each country's skill profile would be obtained by conducting a sample survey of households representative of the entire adult population.

The skills test has provided literacy measures in a stable and reliable way across countries and languages.

The skills test used in the IALS demonstrated that a basis for literacy assessment across languages and cultures is possible. It provided literacy measures in a stable and reliable way across national and linguistic boundaries. The section below discusses the validity of the IALS testing framework.

As for the second aim, a third main section reviews the strength of the IALS literacy skill estimates through evaluation of the methodologies of the sample surveys conducted in each of the participating countries. Estimates from sample surveys are always subject to sampling error since data are obtained for only a portion of the population. Generally, sampling error can be easily controlled and measured in probability samples. However, sampling error does not include any additional error that may arise from the practical difficulties involved in conducting a survey. Measures used in the IALS to counter both types of error are discussed in the final section.

Framework Validity

The IALS framework is concerned mainly with measuring adult literacy skills, determined through tested proficiency levels; it uses reading materials drawn from real-world applications. The skill test measures adults' ability given their formal schooling and their application of reading practices and behaviours in daily life.

Extensive analyses of data were performed in order to determine whether the tests scored equivalently in each country.

The first step in obtaining literacy profiles is to assign scores to the tests that the respondents have completed. To ensure the correctness of the profiles, the scores must be properly assigned and be consistent across countries. Once the tests are scored and the literacy profiles calibrated, an analysis of the model parameters and the psychometric functioning of the tests can reveal whether the tests performed equivalently in each of the country and language groups.

Scoring of literacy tests

Regardless of its proven theoretical validity, testing technology is only as good as it is implemented. The first stage of hands-on intervention involved the scoring in each country of the IALS data; persons charged with that task had received intensive training in scoring responses to open-ended items using the IALS Scoring Manual. To further ensure accuracy, countries were monitored as to the quality of their scoring in two ways.

At least 20 per cent of all test booklets were rescored within each country.

First, within a country, at least 20 per cent of the tests were required to be rescored. The two sets of scores needed to match with at least 95 per cent accuracy before the next step of processing could begin. In fact, most of the intra-country scoring reliabilities were above 97 per cent (see Table B.1). Where errors occurred, a country was required to go back to the tests and rescore all the questions that were problematic and all the tests that belonged to a problem scorer.

Countries also had 10 per cent of their sample rescored by scorers in another country.

Second, an international rescore was performed: each country had 10 per cent of their sample rescored by the scorers in another participating country. For example, a sample of US test booklets was rescored by the persons who had scored Canadian English booklets, and vice versa. The main goal of the rescore was to verify that no country scored consistently differently from another. Inter-country score reliabilities were calculated by Statistics Canada, and then the results were evaluated by the Educational Testing Service (ETS) in Princeton, New Jersey. Again, strict accuracy was demanded: a 90 per cent correspondence was required before the scores were deemed acceptable. As was the case intra-country, all problem areas had to be rescored. Table B.1 shows the high level of score agreement between the participating countries.

TABLE B.1
Inter-country rescore reliability

Original country	Number of booklets rescored	Reliability; average per cent agreement	Rescored by
Australia	300	96	New Zealand
Belgium (Flanders)	300	94	Netherlands
Canada/English	158	97	United States
Canada/French	142	97	France
Germany	270	94	Switzerland
Ireland	300	97	United States
Netherlands	300	97	Netherlands*
New Zealand	300	98	Australia
Poland	300	99	Canada
Sweden	300	98	Sweden*
Switzerland/French	154	98	France
Switzerland/German	153	97	Germany
United Kingdom/Great Britain	300	97	Northern Ireland
United Kingdom/Northern Ireland	300	98	Great Britain
United States	315	97	Canada

* The Netherlands and Sweden carried out both inter- and intra-rescoring internally due to the lack of available language experts in Dutch and Swedish.

Source: International Adult Literacy Survey, 1994-1995.

Comparability of assessment tests across countries

Given the accuracy and consistency of the scoring, another condition crucial to the success of the project was that the test had to perform similarly in each country. The IALS test items – whether prose, document or quantitative – needed to pose the same level of difficulty regardless of the respondent's background or country of origin. The tests thus use a complex and sophisticated scaling technology, refined at the ETS. This scaling technology employs Item Response Theory (IRT) to estimate both item difficulty and proficiency; it has been used successfully in several international education assessments.

When more than three countries' response data for a particular item showed poor fit to the item parameters common to the rest of the countries, the item was dropped from the analyses. In all, 13 such items were dropped from the calibration. When data from one to three countries fit poorly with the common item parameters, unique item parameters were estimated only for countries displaying poor fit for the item. In some cases, poor fit could be explained by errors or ambiguities in the printed materials, but in other cases, no obvious reasons could be identified. Table B.2 shows the large number of common items by scale for the six countries or territories[1] participating in the second cycle of IALS (the results for countries in the first cycle are given in Murray, Kirsch and Jenkins, 1997). It should be noted that the tests had been formulated in such a way that literacy profiles could have been reliably constructed even if 40 per cent of the test items did not function consistently across countries.

TABLE B.2

Items common to country samples, by literacy scale

Scale	Dropped	Common items						Total number of items
		1	2	3	4	5	All 6	
Prose	5	0	2	2	9	6	15	39
Document	7	1	2	3	6	2	20	41
Quantitative	1	0	0	3	4	6	20	34
Total	**13**	**1**	**4**	**8**	**19**	**14**	**55**	**114**

Evaluating the literacy test at an item-by-item level is one way to detect a systematic bias against one particular country; another is evaluation at test level.

The test as a whole can be evaluated by comparing its empirical characteristic curves with its theoretical curves. Figures B.1a-c show the difference between the average empirical proportion correct and the expected proportions correct for the items in a given proficiency scale for each sample. A two-step estimation was made for each point on the scale. First, the proportions of correct responses were calculated for each sample whose proficiency values were in the selected range; secondly, the proportions correct were then averaged for all items on the scale. Next, the theoretical proportion correct was calculated based on the estimated item parameters, and averaged for all items on the scale. This procedure was repeated for each country. Although some figures show deviations in the test characteristic curves at the low end (below 200) of the proficiency range, the number of individuals performing in these ranges is very small and therefore stable estimates cannot be obtained. Test characteristic curves should thus be compared only in that portion of the proficiency range where most of the population scores.

---

[1]   In the United Kingdom separate samples were used for Great Britain and Northern Ireland.

If the test characteristic curves had deviated systematically for a country, this would have been evidence that the test was biased for that country. However, the absolute values of deviation for the primary range of scales (between 200 and 350) are negligible. Shown in Figures B.1a-c are the test characteristics curves for Australia, Belgium (Flanders), United Kingdom (Great Britain), Ireland, New Zealand and United Kingdom (Northern Ireland).

Methodology

Sample surveys are used to draw conclusions about a population. In order to ensure that the conclusions drawn from sample surveys are correct, the methodology employed should be of sound design. In order to ensure that the sample designs employed for the surveys were of high quality, the participating countries were provided with guidelines covering the survey instruments, sample design and estimation, and interviewer training and procedures.

The figures show that the test performed similarly for the countries. No systematic bias appears to be present in the data.

FIGURE B.1A

Prose scale test characteristics, deviation by country or territory, observed minus predicted proportion correct

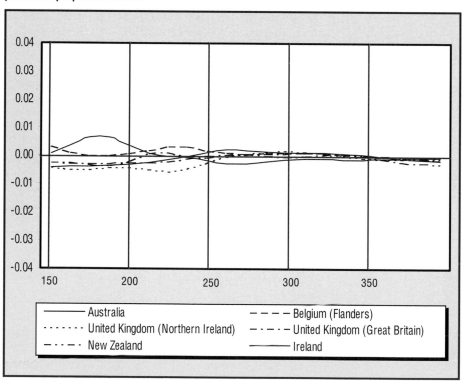

Source: Educational Testing Service.

FIGURE B.1B

Document scale test characteristics, deviation by country or territory, observed minus predicted proportion correct

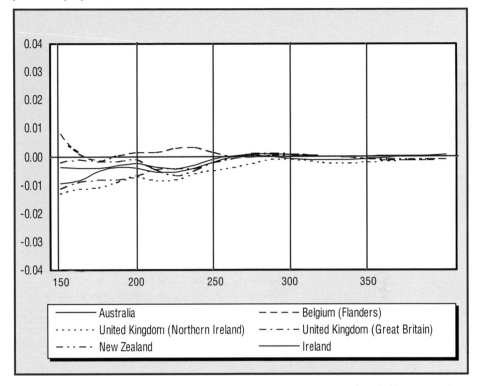

FIGURE B.1C

Quantitative scale test characteristics, deviation by country or territory, observed minus predicted proportion correct

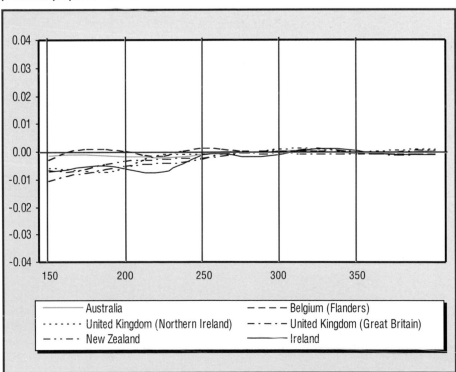

Achieving representative samples

Each country was required to employ a sample that would be representative of its civilian, non-institutionalised population aged 16-65. Table B.3 shows the high rate of coverage achieved by the countries.

TABLE B.3

Survey coverage and exclusions

Country	Coverage (per cent)	Exclusions
Australia	98	Members of the permanent armed forces, non-Australian diplomats, all persons in special dwellings, all persons in remote and sparsely settled areas
Belgium (Flanders)[1]	99	Residents of institutions and the Brussels region
Canada	98	Residents of institutions, persons living on Indian reserves, members of the armed forces, residents of the Yukon and Northwest Territories
Germany	98	Residents of institutions
Ireland	100	None
Netherlands	99	Residents of institutions
New Zealand	99	Residents of institutions; offshore islands, onshore islands, waterways and inlets
Poland	99	Persons residing in Poland for less than three months
Sweden	98	Persons living in institutions (including those doing their military service), persons living abroad during the survey period
Switzerland	89	Persons in Italian and Rhaeto-Romanic regions, persons in institutions, persons without telephones
United Kingdom	97	Residents of institutions; the Scottish Highlands and islands north of the Caledonian Canal
United States	97	Members of the armed forces on active duty, those who reside outside the United States, those with no fixed household address

[1] The Belgium IALS-sample is representative of the "Flemish Region", excluding Brussels. Therefore, the name Flanders is used throughout this publication, rather than the more conventional "Flemish Community".

The sample selected was required to provide results for at least 1 000 respondents – the size necessary to produce reliable literacy population profiles. The tests were to be conducted in the official language(s) of the country. In Canada, respondents were given a choice of English or French; in Switzerland, samples drawn from French-speaking and German-speaking cantons were required to respond in those respective languages (Italian- and Rhaeto-Romanic-speaking regions were excluded; these areas are being surveyed as part of the Second International Adult Literacy Survey). When respondents could not speak the designated language, attempts were made to complete the questionnaire establishing their background to allow imputation of their literacy level and reduce the possibility of obtaining distorted results.

Several countries sampled older adults too.

Countries were free to sample older adults too, and several did so. Canada, Sweden and Switzerland sampled persons at least 16 years of age but with no upper limit, while the Netherlands sampled persons aged 16-74, and Australia sampled those aged 15-74.

TABLE B.4

Test language, target population size and number of respondents

Country	Test language	Population aged 16-65	Survey respondents aged 16-65
Australia	English	11 900 000	8 204
Belgium (Flanders)	Dutch	4 500 000	2 261
Canada	English	13 700 000	3 130
	French	4 800 000	1 370
Germany	German	53 800 000	2 062
Ireland	English	2 200 000	2 423
Netherlands	Dutch	10 500 000	2 837
New Zealand	English	2 100 000	4 223
Poland	Polish	24 500 000	3 000
Sweden	Swedish	5 400 000	2 645
Switzerland	French	1 000 000	1 435
	German	3 000 000	1 393
United Kingdom	English	37 000 000	6 718
United States	English	161 100 000	3 053

Sample Size and Selection

Every country had to employ an appropriate probability sample.

Each country was responsible for designing its own sample; the one guideline was that they select a probability sample representative of their population aged 16-65. No uniform sampling plan was imposed due to differences in the data sources, collection practices and resources available in each of the participating countries. The designs used can be summarised as follows.

Australia: Sample selection in Australia was carried out using the same probability framework that is used for the Monthly Population Survey, an important large-scale household survey. This was a multi-stage area design where the first stage of sampling selects census collection districts, the second stage dwellings and the final stage one person per household. The total number of respondents was 9 302 persons.

Belgium (Flanders): The designated area of Flanders was divided into statistical sectors, from which 200 were selected with probability proportional to size. Then, 40 persons were chosen from a complete list of persons for each of these selected sectors. Finally, in order to get an equal distribution of persons by education level, the chosen persons were then selected into the final sample based on their level of education. Those people who were not sampled due to their education level were given a short questionnaire but these results were not included as part of the sample. This explains, in part, the relatively low response rate. The resulting number of respondents in the final sample was 2 261 persons.

Canada: Two samples were combined. The main IALS sample was a sub-sample of the May 1994 Canadian Labour Force Survey (LFS) file using probability sampling at all stages. The sub-sample of 6 427 LFS respondents was stratified, with an oversample of certain target groups of policy interest. ("Oversampling" is the inclusion in a sample of more randomly selected households than are necessary for the required number of completed interviews, to ensure a sufficient number of responses.) The sample resulted in 4 703 responses to the IALS. The other was a three-stage probability sample of Francophones from the province of Ontario selected from the 1991 census. This sample resulted in 1 044 interviews.

Germany: The country used a master sample of sampling points, with the selection of addresses being made using the random route method. At each of the 525 sampling points, a single random route of addresses was followed, and along each route eight addresses were selected. In each household one person was selected for the interview using the Kish method. The sample comprised 4 033 addresses, of which 997 did not belong to the target population; 2 100 interviews were conducted.

Ireland: Probability sampling was used at each of three stages of selection. At the first stage of sampling, district electoral divisions were selected by stratum, where strata were defined in terms of population size and urban/rural type. Within each selected division, electoral registers were used to select a household. One adult per household was then selected randomly according to their date of birth. The Irish sample yielded 2 423 respondents.

Netherlands: The Dutch approach was to use two-stage systematic sampling. In the first stage, postal codes were selected; in the second, one address was chosen from each selected postal code. The person to be interviewed in each sampled household was determined randomly according to their date of birth. Three thousand responses were obtained.

New Zealand: The initial sampling frame was a list of geographical regions ("meshblocks"). The country was stratified by region and population size, and meshblocks were selected within strata with probability proportional to size. Households were then randomly selected within the meshblock. Finally, a Kish sampling grid was used to select one person per household. A total of 4 223 responses were obtained.

Poland: The country used a stratified, multi-stage design employing probability sampling at the various stages. The sample was selected from the Polish National Register of Citizens, a register that covers all persons living permanently (longer than three months) in Poland. Data were collected for 3 000 persons.

Sweden: A stratified, self-weighting master sample was used. The sample was drawn from a national register of individuals. The data collection resulted in 3 038 interviews.

Switzerland: The target population was divided into two strata, corresponding to German- and French-speaking regions. Household telephone numbers were selected, and in each household the first member by alphabetical order of first name was selected. A complementary sample was selected in the canton of Geneva, using the same methods as the principal sample. Interviews were conducted with 2 843 persons, of whom 1 399 were German speaking and 1 444 French speaking.

United Kingdom: Two samples were selected – one for Great Britain and the other for Northern Ireland. In Great Britain, the post code address file (PAF) was used to select the initial sample of addresses by postal code sectors. At each of the 35 addresses contained within each grouping, the Kish method was used to select one adult. In Northern Ireland, a list of all private addresses was used to select an initial systematic sample of 7 000. At each of these addresses, one person was selected using the Kish method. The United Kingdom had a total sample of 6 718 respondents: 3 811 from Great Britain and 2 907 from Northern Ireland.

United States: The sample was selected from housing units undergoing their final Current Population Survey interviews in March-June 1994. A probability sample of 4 901 persons was selected using a disproportionate stratified design, with strata formed by race/ethnicity and education. This allocation was designed to provide an efficient linkage of the IALS survey to the earlier National Adult Literacy Survey (NALS). A sample of 3 053 respondents was achieved.

All 12 countries used probability sampling for most of the stages of their sample designs; in fact, ten used it in all stages.

Two countries – Switzerland and Germany – used a non-probability sampling method in one stage of their multi-stage designs. Switzerland selected one household member using an alphabetic sort. Germany used the "random walk" method for selecting households for their sample. This non-probability method is often used with area frames because of practical constraints – namely the cost associated with enumerating every household within a geographic area, necessary for a probability sample. With non-probability sampling, there is no information about the properties of the resulting estimates. This is not to say that the quality is better or worse than that of a probability sample; rather, the degree of quality is unknown. This issue is examined in greater detail in Murray *et al.* (1997).

Data Collection

The IALS was conducted in homes by experienced interviewers who administered the literacy tasks in a neutral manner. Respondents were first asked a series of questions to obtain background and demographic information on educational attainment, literacy practices at work and at home, labour force information, adult education participation and literacy self-assessment. Once the Background Questionnaire was completed, the interviewer presented a booklet containing six simple tasks. If the respondent failed to complete at least two of these correctly, the interview was ended. Respondents who completed two or more tasks correctly were given a much larger variety of tasks, drawn from a pool of 114 items, in a separate booklet.

Six easy questions were used at the beginning of test administration to identify persons with very weak skills, for whom taking the full test would have been difficult and possibly embarassing. Such people were assigned level 1 scores.

Response rates

The IALS survey consists of three parts:

a) the Background Questionnaire, for demographic information about the respondent;

b) the Core Tasks Booklet, which screens out respondents with very low levels of literacy; and

c) the Main Tasks Booklet, used to calibrate literacy levels.

The definition of an IALS respondent is a person who has fully or partially completed the Background Questionnaire. With this information, as well as the reason why the Tasks Booklet was not completed, it was possible to impute a literacy score (given a sufficient number of complete responses). Thus, the IALS data collection procedures stressed that at least the Background Questionnaire should be completed for every person sampled. Given the length of the IALS interview as well as the fact that part of the interview is administered as a test, some countries had lower-than-average response rates. Table B.5 summarises the response rates by country.

TABLE B.5

IALS response rates by country

Country	Ages	Number of respondents	Response rate (per cent)
Australia	15-74	9 302	96
Belgium (Flanders)[1]	16-65	2 261	36
Canada	16+	5 660	69
Germany	16-65	2 062	69
Ireland	16-65	2 423	60
Netherlands	16-74	3 090	45
New Zealand	16-65	4 223	74
Poland	16-65	3 000	75[2]
Sweden	16+	3 038	60
Switzerland	16+	3 000	55
United Kingdom	16-65	6 718	63
United States	16-65	3 053	60

[1] In Flanders, the sample design did not allow for replacement. See sampling information.

[2] Poland's response rate includes only the first wave of sampled persons, before interviewer follow-up.

The IALS took several precautions to minimise bias resulting from non-response.

The reason that low response rates are of concern in any survey is that bias might exist in the resulting estimates. The IALS took several precautions against non-response bias. Interviewers were instructed to return several times to non-responding households in order to obtain as many responses as possible. In addition, all countries' sample designs included some oversampling. Finally, the IALS sampling guidelines included an adjustment during the weighting procedure to help correct for non-response bias.

This correction, known as post-stratification, adjusts the population weights so that they match known population counts, e.g. by age group or education level. All countries post-stratified their data to such counts. The underlying assumption behind this compensation for non-response is that the respondents and non-respondents have the same literacy profile for the characteristic for which the adjustment is made. Table B.6 shows the non-response adjustments that were used in each country.

The country with the lowest response rate, Belgium (Flanders) had 6 167 records that were in-scope; 2 261 were response records (36.4 per cent) and 3 952 were non-response. The response rates by demographic characteristic were as shown in Table B.7. Any major difference between the total response rate and the response rate by characteristic would have been indicative of non-response bias.

TABLE B.6

Post-stratification variables used to correct for non-response bias

Country	Benchmark variables
Australia	Age, sex, region
Belgium (Flanders)	Age, sex, education
Canada	Province, economic region, census metropolitan area, age, sex, in-school youth, out-of-school youth, unemployment insurance recipients, social assistance recipients
Germany	Number of household members aged 16-65, age, sex, citizenship
Ireland	Area, sex, age
Netherlands	Region, age, sex, education
New Zealand	Sex, age, household size, urban/rural
Poland	Region, urban/rural, age
Sweden	Region, education, age, sex
Switzerland	Number of household members aged 16-65, total number of persons in the household, level of education, size of community, age, sex
United Kingdom	Education, age, sex
United States	Education

TABLE B.7

Response rates by characteristic for Belgium (Flanders)

Characteristic	Sample size	Rate of response (per cent)
Total	**2 261**	**36.7**
Gender		
Male	1 066	34.6
Female	1 180	37.9
Age		
16-24	720	52.3
25-44	890	32.3
45-65	651	31.3
Area		
Rural	640	29.7
Urban	1 621	40.0

There are some differences in response rates between rural and urban dwellers as well as between age groups. However, the post-stratification, which was done by sex, age and region, will help to correct these discrepancies. Table B.8 shows a comparison of the education distribution in Belgium (Flanders) compared to the distribution for Belgium given in the publication, *Education at a Glance: OECD Indicators*, for persons aged 25-64. The comparison shows that the IALS and the OECD education level estimates match, considering that the OECD data also cover the French Community and the Brussels region.

A detailed analysis of the potential for non-response bias was conducted for the first-wave countries.

TABLE B.8

Comparison of education distribution estimates based on IALS and OECD sources, Belgium, 1994

Educational attainment	IALS weighted distribution (per cent)	OECD distribution (per cent)
Primary and lower secondary	42	51
Upper secondary	33	27
Non-university tertiary	15	12
University	10	10

Finally, an analysis was conducted to study the potential for non-response bias in the IALS. First, the characteristics of the non-respondents were studied to determine if one group in particular was not responding to the survey. This issue is of concern when such a group is defined by a characteristic that is strongly correlated to literacy level. The weights before and after the post-stratification adjustment were also compared. This analysis of the weights would show the amount of bias present before the post-stratification adjustment was carried out. Associated with this part of the analysis was an evaluation of the post-stratification model. Further, the amount of bias that would have had to be present to alter the IALS estimates significantly was calculated.

The results show that the small levels of bias that may be present are not sufficient to alter any of the main IALS findings. Exhaustive non-response bias analyses can be found in Murray *et al.* (1997).

Reference

MURRAY, T.S., KIRSCH, I.S. and JENKINS, L. (Eds.) (1997), *Adult Literacy in OECD Countries: Technical Report on the International Adult Literacy Survey*, National Center for Education Statistics, United States Department of Education, Washington, DC.

Annex C

Data Values for the Figures

This annex presents data tables showing the numeric values used for the production of the figures featured in the text.

The values in parentheses are the standard errors of the estimates. Standard jack-knife procedures have been used for the calculation of these errors, which should be seen as indicators of the probable range of error, given that other methods might produce slightly different results. For information about the reliability and comparability of data values not derived from IALS the reader is referred to the original sources.

All IALS estimates based on less than 30 cases are flagged with an asterisk (*). In all such cases the estimates are considered to be unreliable, even though the standard errors might be small. In certain cases, countries did not include all of the common questions in their background questionnaire, or asked them in ways that differed from the standard format. Such cases are noted by a dash (—). The symbol x is used to indicate that a particular data value is not available.

TABLE 1.1

Mean scores and scores at the 5th, 25th, 75th and 95th percentiles on a scale with range 0-500 points, prose, document and quantitative literacy scales, 1994-1995

	A: Prose				
	5th percentile	25th percentile	Mean		75th percentile	95th percentile
Australia	145.1	245.8	274.2	(1.0)	315.7	359.0
Belgium (Flanders)	161.0	240.3	271.8	(3.9)	308.8	353.6
Canada	144.5	242.6	278.8	(3.2)	321.7	363.4
Germany	199.6	245.0	275.9	(1.0)	308.0	350.2
Ireland	159.6	230.6	265.7	(3.3)	307.4	352.3
Netherlands	202.8	257.7	282.7	(0.8)	312.7	349.0
New Zealand	164.8	240.7	275.2	(1.3)	315.3	362.9
Poland	115.3	194.4	229.5	(1.1)	272.3	318.1
Sweden	214.0	271.2	301.3	(0.8)	335.1	381.1
Switzerland (French)	150.8	240.6	264.8	(1.7)	302.6	336.9
Switzerland (German)	150.3	238.2	263.3	(1.4)	299.2	341.0
United Kingdom	151.2	233.0	266.7	(1.8)	311.0	353.2
United States	136.7	236.7	273.7	(1.6)	320.0	368.1

	B: Document				
	5th percentile	25th percentile	Mean		75th percentile	95th percentile
Australia	143.7	245.9	273.3	(1.0)	314.1	357.9
Belgium (Flanders)	170.4	251.2	278.2	(3.2)	314.2	353.6
Canada	133.9	243.3	279.3	(3.0)	326.1	377.4
Germany	207.2	256.1	285.1	(1.0)	317.8	361.1
Ireland	146.7	225.3	259.3	(3.2)	300.6	345.3
Netherlands	202.4	260.1	286.9	(0.9)	319.0	355.6
New Zealand	153.8	233.8	269.1	(1.3)	312.0	360.5
Poland	85.2	181.1	223.9	(1.8)	274.3	330.2
Sweden	218.6	275.9	305.6	(0.9)	341.4	386.8
Switzerland (French)	153.8	246.9	274.1	(1.7)	313.5	353.6
Switzerland (German)	117.1	241.2	269.7	(2.0)	313.2	360.1
United Kingdom	143.3	230.2	267.5	(1.9)	314.4	363.6
United States	125.4	230.1	267.9	(1.7)	315.7	368.0

	C: Quantitative				
	5th percentile	25th percentile	Mean		75th percentile	95th percentile
Australia	149.5	246.0	275.9	(1.0)	316.6	359.9
Belgium (Flanders)	158.4	249.9	282.0	(3.8)	322.6	369.3
Canada	155.1	246.8	281.0	(3.8)	323.0	375.6
Germany	217.8	265.0	293.3	(1.1)	323.7	366.5
Ireland	146.2	226.4	264.6	(3.2)	308.8	360.7
Netherlands	200.9	260.8	287.7	(1.0)	319.5	359.4
New Zealand	154.1	236.6	270.7	(1.3)	312.7	360.0
Poland	97.6	192.9	234.9	(1.7)	286.2	334.9
Sweden	215.9	275.5	305.9	(1.0)	341.9	390.7
Switzerland (French)	145.7	257.7	280.1	(1.7)	319.6	356.7
Switzerland (German)	146.1	252.1	278.9	(1.8)	318.4	357.2
United Kingdom	141.5	230.5	267.2	(1.9)	314.1	362.0
United States	138.3	236.9	275.2	(1.7)	322.5	376.3

Source: International Adult Literacy Survey, 1994-1995.

TABLE 1.2

Percentage of adult population aged 16-65 at each prose, document and quantitativo literacy level, 1994-1995

	A: Prose							
	Level 1		Level 2		Level 3		Level 4/5	
Australia	17.0	(0.5)	27.1	(0.6)	36.9	(0.5)	18.9	(0.5)
Belgium (Flanders)	18.4	(1.5)	28.2	(2.1)	39.0	(2.4)	14.3	(1.2)
Canada	16.6	(1.6)	25.6	(1.8)	35.1	(2.4)	22.7	(2.3)
Germany	14.4	(0.9)	34.2	(1.0)	38.0	(1.3)	13.4	(1.0)
Ireland	22.6	(1.4)	29.8	(1.6)	34.1	(1.2)	13.5	(1.4)
Netherlands	10.5	(0.6)	30.1	(0.9)	44.1	(1.0)	15.3	(0.6)
New Zealand	18.4	(0.9)	27.3	(1.0)	35.0	(0.8)	19.2	(0.7)
Poland	42.6	(0.9)	34.5	(0.9)	19.8	(0.7)	3.1	(0.3)
Sweden	7.5	(0.5)	20.3	(0.6)	39.7	(0.9)	32.4	(0.5)
Switzerland (French)	17.6	(1.3)	33.7	(1.6)	38.6	(1.8)	10.0	(0.7)
Switzerland (German)	19.3	(1.0)	35.7	(1.6)	36.1	(1.3)	8.9	(1.0)
United Kingdom	21.8	(1.0)	30.3	(1.2)	31.3	(1.1)	16.6	(0.7)
United States	20.7	(0.8)	25.9	(1.1)	32.4	(1.2)	21.1	(1.2)

	B: Document							
	Level 1		Level 2		Level 3		Level 4/5	
Australia	17.0	(0.5)	27.8	(0.7)	37.7	(0.7)	17.4	(0.6)
Belgium (Flanders)	15.3	(1.7)	24.2	(2.8)	43.2	(4.1)	17.2	(0.9)
Canada	18.2	(1.9)	24.7	(1.5)	32.1	(1.8)	25.1	(1.3)
Germany	9.0	(0.7)	32.7	(1.2)	39.5	(1.0)	18.9	(1.0)
Ireland	25.3	(1.7)	31.7	(1.2)	31.5	(1.3)	11.5	(1.2)
Netherlands	10.1	(0.7)	25.7	(0.8)	44.2	(0.9)	20.0	(0.8)
New Zealand	21.4	(0.9)	29.2	(1.1)	31.9	(0.8)	17.6	(0.7)
Poland	45.4	(1.3)	30.7	(1.0)	18.0	(0.7)	5.8	(0.3)
Sweden	6.2	(0.4)	18.9	(0.7)	39.4	(0.8)	35.5	(0.6)
Switzerland (French)	16.2	(1.3)	28.8	(1.4)	38.9	(1.3)	16.0	(1.1)
Switzerland (German)	18.1	(1.0)	29.1	(1.5)	36.6	(0.8)	16.1	(1.0)
United Kingdom	23.3	(1.0)	27.1	(1.0)	30.5	(1.0)	19.1	(1.0)
United States	23.7	(0.8)	25.9	(1.1)	31.4	(0.9)	19.0	(1.0)

	C: Quantitative							
	Level 1		Level 2		Level 3		Level 4/5	
Australia	16.8	(0.5)	26.5	(0.6)	37.7	(0.7)	19.1	(0.6)
Belgium (Flanders)	16.7	(1.8)	23.0	(1.7)	37.8	(2.0)	22.6	(1.3)
Canada	16.9	(1.8)	26.1	(2.5)	34.8	(2.1)	22.2	(1.8)
Germany	6.7	(0.4)	26.6	(1.2)	43.2	(0.8)	23.5	(0.9)
Ireland	24.8	(1.5)	28.3	(0.8)	30.7	(1.0)	16.2	(1.6)
Netherlands	10.3	(0.7)	25.5	(0.9)	44.3	(1.0)	19.9	(0.8)
New Zealand	20.4	(1.0)	28.9	(1.1)	33.4	(0.8)	17.2	(0.8)
Poland	39.1	(1.1)	30.1	(1.2)	23.9	(0.6)	6.8	(0.5)
Sweden	6.6	(0.4)	18.6	(0.6)	39.0	(0.9)	35.8	(0.7)
Switzerland (French)	12.9	(0.9)	24.5	(1.4)	42.2	(1.6)	20.4	(1.0)
Switzerland (German)	14.2	(1.0)	26.2	(1.3)	40.7	(1.5)	19.0	(1.3)
United Kingdom	23.2	(0.9)	27.8	(1.0)	30.4	(0.9)	18.6	(1.0)
United States	21.0	(0.7)	25.3	(1.1)	31.3	(0.8)	22.5	(1.0)

Source: International Adult Literacy Survey, 1994-1995.

TABLE 1.3

Percentage of population aged 25-64 with upper secondary education, by age group, 1994

	Age group				
	25-34	35-44	45-54	55-64	Total 25-64
Australia	54	54	47	41	50
Belgium	65	54	43	28	49
Canada	82	79	70	53	74
Germany	90	88	84	72	84
Ireland	61	47	35	27	45
Netherlands	69	64	54	44	60
New Zealand	62	60	56	45	57
Poland	88	82	68	47	74
Sweden	85	78	69	52	72
Switzerland	89	84	79	73	82
United Kingdom	86	78	69	57	74
United States	86	89	85	76	85

Source: OECD, *Education at a Glance: OECD Indicators*, 1996.

TABLE 1.4

Mean prose, document and quantitative scores on a scale with range 0-500 points, by level of educational attainment, persons aged 16-65, 1994-1995

	A: Prose					
	With less than upper secondary education		Completed upper secondary education		With some tertiary-level education	
Australia	250.6	(1.6)	280.0	(1.3)	310.4	(1.4)
Belgium (Flanders)	242.5	(6.9)	281.0	(2.1)	312.3	(1.7)
Canada	233.4	(4.6)	283.8	(3.8)	314.8	(5.3)
Germany	265.6	(1.4)	283.8	(2.2)	310.1	(2.6)
Ireland	238.8	(2.8)	288.2	(2.7)	308.3	(2.6)
Netherlands	257.5	(1.2)	297.0	(1.3)	312.1	(1.4)
New Zealand	252.1	(2.3)	290.6	(1.9)	307.3	(1.5)
Poland	210.5	(1.2)	252.7	(1.6)	277.3	(2.3)
Sweden	275.4	(2.1)	302.3	(1.2)	329.1	(1.7)
Switzerland (French)	228.1	(4.3)	274.1	(2.0)	298.3	(2.7)
Switzerland (German)	227.3	(5.0)	273.4	(1.8)	288.9	(2.4)
United Kingdom	247.9	(2.2)	281.9	(2.7)	309.5	(1.8)
United States	207.1	(3.5)	270.7	(2.8)	308.4	(2.5)

	B: Document					
	With less than upper secondary education		Completed upper secondary education		With some tertiary-level education	
Australia	248.5	(1.5)	281.9	(1.3)	308.0	(1.2)
Belgium (Flanders)	250.9	(5.3)	288.6	(2.1)	313.3	(1.5)
Canada	227.1	(5.7)	288.0	(5.3)	318.4	(4.9)
Germany	276.1	(1.1)	295.4	(2.2)	314.5	(1.6)
Ireland	231.5	(2.6)	280.5	(2.9)	303.5	(3.3)
Netherlands	262.6	(1.5)	302.3	(1.4)	311.2	(1.6)
New Zealand	244.5	(2.3)	287.3	(2.0)	302.1	(1.5)
Poland	201.5	(1.7)	251.5	(2.0)	275.6	(3.9)
Sweden	280.6	(2.4)	308.3	(1.0)	331.2	(2.0)
Switzerland (French)	235.0	(4.1)	283.4	(2.2)	312.5	(2.7)
Switzerland (German)	230.6	(6.2)	283.2	(2.1)	300.4	(2.7)
United Kingdom	247.4	(2.4)	285.5	(3.1)	311.8	(1.9)
United States	199.9	(4.6)	266.1	(2.3)	302.5	(2.4)

TABLE 1.4 (concluded)

Mean prose, document and quantitative scores on a scale with range 0-500 points, by level of educational attainment, persons aged 16-65, 1994-1995

	C: Quantitative					
	With less than upper secondary education		Completed upper secondary education		With some tertiary-level education	
Australia	250.0	(1.5)	284.7	(1.2)	311.9	(1.3)
Belgium (Flanders)	251.7	(7.0)	291.3	(2.3)	324.2	(2.0)
Canada	233.7	(4.5)	285.6	(5.6)	320.5	(6.0)
Germany	285.2	(1.6)	300.2	(2.4)	321.0	(2.4)
Ireland	236.8	(2.6)	285.6	(3.1)	310.5	(3.2)
Netherlands	263.7	(1.6)	300.2	(1.5)	316.2	(2.0)
New Zealand	246.9	(2.3)	287.8	(2.0)	302.9	(1.6)
Poland	213.2	(1.7)	263.2	(1.8)	285.8	(3.2)
Sweden	282.3	(2.1)	307.4	(1.1)	331.7	(2.0)
Switzerland (French)	243.8	(3.8)	293.0	(1.9)	311.7	(3.1)
Switzerland (German)	245.4	(6.4)	289.7	(1.7)	305.3	(2.4)
United Kingdom	246.4	(2.4)	285.0	(2.8)	314.6	(1.8)
United States	208.4	(4.8)	270.1	(2.3)	311.8	(2.5)

Source: International Adult Literacy Survey, 1994-1995.

TABLE 1.5

Proportion of adults aged 16-65 who have not completed upper secondary education, but who nevertheless score at levels 3 and 4/5 on the document scale, 1994-1995

	Proportion at levels 3 and 4/5	
Australia	37.6	(0.8)
Belgium (Flanders)	40.2	(8.3)
Canada	27.3	(2.7)
Germany	50.6	(1.1)
Ireland	23.0	(1.7)
Netherlands	42.3	(1.2)
New Zealand	30.3	(1.3)
Poland	14.0	(0.7)
Sweden	59.3	(2.3)
Switzerland (French)	20.6	(2.8)
Switzerland (German)	24.6	(3.7)
United Kingdom	36.7	(1.2)
United States	17.1	(1.9)

Source: International Adult Literacy Survey, 1994-1995.

TABLE 1.6

Proportion of persons aged 16-25 and 46-55 who are at each document literacy level, 1994-1995

	Age	Level 1		Level 2		Level 3		Level 4/5	
Australia	16-25	9.7	(0.7)	28.4	(1.5)	42.6	(1.8)	19.2	(1.4)
	46-55	23.6	(1.2)	27.5	(1.4)	34.3	(1.9)	14.5	(1.1)
Belgium (Flanders)	16-25	5.8	(5.2)	17.8	(12.5)	51.4	(18.2)	25.0	(2.5)
	46-55	20.5	(3.1)	27.8	(2.5)	41.5	(2.9)	10.3	(1.6)
Canada	16-25	10.4	(1.3)	22.3	(3.6)	36.4	(2.1)	31.0	(4.7)
	46-55	23.0	(4.7)	31.0	(3.4)	23.6	(6.8)	22.4	(10.7)
Germany	16-25	5.2 *	(1.4)	29.0	(3.5)	43.0	(4.9)	22.8	(3.7)
	46-55	7.4 *	(1.3)	35.0	(4.3)	43.1	(3.4)	14.5	(2.5)
Ireland	16-25	17.0	(1.6)	32.9	(2.1)	36.9	(2.3)	13.2	(1.8)
	46-55	36.1	(3.6)	29.8	(2.2)	24.8	(1.5)	9.2	(2.2)
Netherlands	16-25	6.1 *	(1.8)	16.8	(1.9)	51.1	(3.0)	26.0	(2.5)
	46-55	12.6	(1.7)	35.7	(2.0)	38.0	(2.4)	13.7	(1.8)
New Zealand	16-25	18.3	(2.2)	29.2	(2.2)	31.9	(1.7)	20.6	(1.4)
	46-55	22.3	(2.3)	32.6	(2.7)	28.6	(3.0)	16.5	(1.8)
Poland	16-25	32.2	(2.1)	33.1	(1.8)	26.2	(1.8)	8.5	(.9)
	46-55	55.6	(2.4)	27.0	(2.5)	13.3	(2.0)	4.1 *	(.8)
Sweden	16-25	3.1 *	(0.8)	16.6	(1.9)	39.6	(1.5)	40.7	(1.6)
	46-55	6.8	(1.0)	19.7	(1.8)	43.1	(2.5)	30.3	(2.1)
Switzerland (French)	16-25	8.7 *	(2.0)	24.9	(2.4)	40.4	(3.9)	26.0	(3.8)
	46-55	18.0	(3.3)	29.8	(3.8)	42.4	(3.9)	9.7	(2.0)
Switzerland (German)	16-25	7.1 *	(1.9)	25.7	(4.2)	41.0	(3.7)	26.3	(3.2)
	46-55	21.0	(3.0)	33.8	(3.3)	35.0	(2.4)	10.2 *	(1.6)
United Kingdom	16-25	17.8	(1.7)	26.6	(1.8)	34.1	(2.3)	21.5	(2.0)
	46-55	24.5	(2.3)	28.2	(1.7)	31.1	(2.9)	16.2	(1.5)
United States[1]	16-25	24.7	(2.2)	30.9	(2.8)	28.4	(3.0)	16.1	x
	46-55	21.4	(2.1)	28.2	(2.8)	33.2	(2.1)	17.3	x

*   Unreliable estimate.

[1]   Because of a sampling anomaly, NALS data have been substituted for the group aged 16-25.

Source: International Adult Literacy Survey, 1994-1995.

TABLE 1.7

Mean of socio-economic index score for all students and for students scoring in the lowest 15 per cent, 1990-1991

	Students in the lowest 15 per cent	All students
Canada (British Columbia)	0.269	0.051
Germany (TFDR)[1]	0.557	0.090
Germany (FTFR)[1]	0.671	0.126
Ireland	0.395	0.091
Netherlands	0.341	0.073
New Zealand	0.520	0.105
Sweden	0.454	0.081
Switzerland	0.573	0.118
United States	0.487	0.097

[1]   Germany: TFDR refers to the Territory of the Former Democratic Republic; FTFR refers to the Former Territory of the Federal Republic.

Source: IEA, Reading Literacy Study, 1991.

TABLE 1.8

Mean mathematics achievement scores on a scale with range 0-1 000 points for 8th-grade students by level of parental education, 1994-1995

	Parent's education		
	With lower secondary education or less	Completed upper secondary education	With some tertiary-level education
Australia[1]	510	528	572
Belgium (Flemish Community)	538	572	599
Canada	510	526	544
Germany[1]	504	526	553
Ireland	510	535	564
Netherlands[1]	524	549	570
New Zealand	491	504	543
Sweden	494	524	544
Switzerland	520	552	588
United States	455	494	527

[1] Countries did not meet TIMSS sampling requirements.

Source: IEA, Third International Mathematics and Science Study, 1994-1995.

TABLE 1.9

Proportion of adults at or above prose literacy level 3, by father's educational attainment, adults 16-65 whose own highest educational attainment is upper secondary graduation, 1994-1995

	Father has not completed upper secondary education		Father has completed upper secondary education	
Australia	59.6	(1.4)	65.9	(1.7)
Belgium (Flanders)	59.5	(2.8)	64.5	(3.7)
Canada	65.3	(2.4)	59.8	(9.3)
Germany	57.3	(4.2)	58.9	(5.9)
Ireland	63.8	(2.9)	74.5	(3.4)
Netherlands	71.8	(1.6)	82.8	(2.8)
New Zealand	70.0	(3.0)	68.7	(3.9)
Poland	29.5	(2.1)	36.0	(5.5)
Sweden	71.7	(1.0)	78.6	(1.7)
Switzerland (French)	46.0	(4.3)	58.9	(3.1)
Switzerland (German)	38.0	(4.8)	53.8	(2.6)
United Kingdom	58.8	(3.1)	74.5	(6.4)
United States	47.3	(3.5)	58.1	(2.3)

Source: International Adult Literacy Survey, 1994-1995.

TABLE 1.10

Mean scores by gender and overall standard deviations in reading (students aged 14, 1990-1991) and mathematics[1] (8th-grade, 1994-1995) achievement on a scale with range 0-1 000 points

	Mathematics			Reading		
	Boys Mean	Girls Mean	Standard deviation	Boys Mean	Girls Mean	Standard deviation
Australia[1]	527 (5.1)	532 (4.6)	98	—	—	—
Belgium (Flemish Community)	563 (8.8)	567 (7.4)	92	—	—	—
Canada (All)	526 (3.2)	530 (2.7)	86	—	—	—
Canada (British Columbia)	—	—	—	513 (3.4)	534 (3.3)	81
Germany (All)[1]	512 (5.1)	509 (5.0)	90	—	—	—
Germany (FTFR)[2]	—	—	—	522 (4.4)	526 (4.4)	78
Germany (TFDR)[2]	—	—	—	523 (4.0)	530 (4.0)	73
Ireland	535 (7.2)	520 (6.0)	93	502 (5.1)	525 (5.0)	81
Netherlands[1]	545 (7.8)	536 (6.4)	89	511 (4.9)	520 (5.2)	76
New Zealand	512 (5.9)	503 (5.3)	90	544 (5.9)	549 (5.5)	92
Sweden	520 (3.6)	518 (3.1)	85	540 (3.3)	555 (3.2)	80
Switzerland	548 (3.5)	543 (3.1)	88	535 (3.5)	538 (3.3)	74
United Kingdom (England)	508 (5.1)	504 (3.5)	93	—	—	—
United Kingdom (Scotland)	506 (6.6)	490 (5.2)	87	—	—	—
United States	502 (5.2)	497 (4.5)	91	530 (6.3)	543 (5.9)	85

[1]   Countries did not meet TIMSS sampling requirements.

[2]   Germany: TFDR refers to the Territory of the Former Democratic Republic; FTFR refers to the Former Territory of the Federal Republic.

—   Did not participate in the study.

Source: IEA, Reading Literacy Study, 1991, and IEA, Third International Mathematics and Science Study, 1994-1995.

TABLE 1.11

Mean scores by gender and overall standard deviations on the prose, document and quantitative scales with range 0-500 points, persons aged 16-65, 1994-1995

| | Prose | | | | |
	Men Mean		Women Mean		Standard deviation
Australia	271.3	(1.4)	277.2	(1.3)	64.9
Belgium (Flanders)	274.9	(5.5)	268.9	(3.0)	56.6
Canada	271.3	(5.6)	284.7	(4.9)	64.5
Germany	276.3	(2.1)	274.9	(1.3)	46.8
Ireland	263.2	(5.3)	268.6	(2.3)	59.0
Netherlands	281.1	(1.2)	283.9	(1.3)	45.4
New Zealand	270.9	(1.7)	279.8	(1.7)	59.1
Poland	228.5	(1.0)	230.8	(2.0)	61.2
Sweden	300.3	(2.1)	301.9	(1.9)	52.7
Switzerland (French)	266.7	(2.7)	264.1	(2.1)	56.4
Switzerland (German)	265.4	(1.9)	260.7	(2.4)	55.5
United Kingdom	266.7	(2.1)	266.1	(2.4)	62.8
United States	269.4	(1.7)	276.0	(2.0)	67.9

| | Document | | | | |
	Men Mean		Women Mean		Standard deviation
Australia	275.8	(1.5)	270.8	(1.3)	63.8
Belgium (Flanders)	284.6	(5.4)	272.2	(2.1)	55.9
Canada	279.3	(4.6)	277.9	(3.0)	71.5
Germany	289.3	(2.2)	281.0	(1.4)	46.6
Ireland	261.1	(5.4)	257.3	(2.2)	60.5
Netherlands	290.1	(1.3)	283.0	(1.3)	47.8
New Zealand	271.2	(1.8)	267.6	(1.7)	61.9
Poland	227.1	(1.7)	220.0	(2.6)	73.5
Sweden	310.6	(1.6)	301.4	(1.7)	53.6
Switzerland (French)	278.6	(2.9)	270.9	(2.1)	57.8
Switzerland (German)	274.0	(2.7)	264.3	(2.7)	67.0
United Kingdom	274.2	(2.4)	260.2	(2.4)	68.4
United States	266.6	(1.8)	267.8	(2.2)	70.5

| | Quantitative | | | | |
	Men Mean		Women Mean		Standard deviation
Australia	282.2	(1.5)	269.6	(1.3)	62.8
Belgium (Flanders)	293.1	(6.0)	271.4	(3.3)	62.5
Canada	281.4	(5.4)	279.7	(5.1)	64.6
Germany	299.1	(2.0)	287.7	(1.4)	45.0
Ireland	269.7	(5.5)	259.2	(2.3)	65.4
Netherlands	294.5	(1.5)	279.5	(1.4)	49.1
New Zealand	277.0	(1.9)	265.2	(1.6)	60.7
Poland	240.0	(1.9)	229.9	(2.4)	70.8
Sweden	313.8	(1.6)	298.7	(1.5)	54.7
Switzerland (French)	287.2	(2.6)	274.6	(2.1)	59.6
Switzerland (German)	284.8	(2.6)	272.0	(2.5)	59.3
United Kingdom	278.1	(2.3)	256.0	(2.7)	67.4
United States	279.0	(1.4)	269.7	(2.2)	69.1

Source: International Adult Literacy Survey, 1994-1995.

TABLE 1.12

Mean scores by gender and overall standard deviations on the prose, document and quantitative scales with range 0-500 points, for population with completed upper secondary education, persons aged 16-65, 1994-1995

	Prose				
	Men Mean		Women Mean		Standard deviation
Australia	276.4	(2.1)	285.1	(1.8)	54.9
Belgium (Flanders)	280.5	(3.0)	281.4	(2.5)	44.3
Canada	275.8	(6.4)	292.5	(5.1)	49.7
Germany	283.3	(4.1)	284.3	(1.8)	41.6
Ireland	287.4	(2.8)	288.8	(3.4)	40.8
Netherlands	294.6	(1.4)	299.4	(2.2)	35.0
New Zealand	288.4	(3.1)	292.4	(2.6)	51.9
Poland	253.4	(3.5)	252.1	(1.9)	44.7
Sweden	301.0	(2.9)	303.7	(2.4)	46.4
Switzerland (French)	272.1	(3.2)	276.1	(2.3)	43.6
Switzerland (German)	272.2	(2.7)	274.5	(2.2)	45.4
United Kingdom	279.5	(2.8)	286.4	(5.4)	53.5
United States	261.5	(3.0)	277.5	(3.5)	54.7

	Document				
	Men Mean		Women Mean		Standard deviation
Australia	282.3	(2.1)	281.3	(1.4)	53.4
Belgium (Flanders)	291.4	(2.8)	285.5	(2.6)	44.4
Canada	288.9	(4.7)	287.0	(6.3)	55.1
Germany	299.1	(4.6)	291.5	(1.7)	42.4
Ireland	285.6	(3.4)	276.2	(3.0)	41.7
Netherlands	305.8	(1.8)	298.6	(2.4)	36.9
New Zealand	291.4	(3.2)	283.8	(2.9)	52.7
Poland	256.8	(3.7)	247.7	(2.2)	56.6
Sweden	312.4	(2.1)	303.9	(1.9)	46.4
Switzerland (French)	284.3	(3.2)	282.7	(2.5)	43.2
Switzerland (German)	284.5	(3.0)	281.9	(2.2)	50.1
United Kingdom	287.7	(3.0)	281.3	(4.9)	56.0
United States	260.3	(3.6)	270.3	(3.6)	57.2

	Quantitative				
	Men Mean		Women Mean		Standard deviation
Australia	288.5	(2.0)	279.3	(1.4)	52.2
Belgium (Flanders)	297.0	(3.3)	285.1	(3.0)	50.6
Canada	287.3	(5.6)	283.8	(6.3)	45.0
Germany	305.6	(4.3)	294.6	(2.5)	40.8
Ireland	293.7	(3.8)	279.0	(3.0)	48.6
Netherlands	308.4	(1.9)	291.6	(2.4)	38.4
New Zealand	296.9	(3.0)	280.4	(2.7)	51.0
Poland	270.4	(3.2)	258.0	(2.5)	53.3
Sweden	314.1	(2.1)	300.3	(1.7)	48.3
Switzerland (French)	297.2	(3.2)	289.0	(2.3)	42.9
Switzerland (German)	294.2	(2.3)	285.5	(2.2)	44.7
United Kingdom	289.3	(2.9)	277.1	(4.5)	56.0
United States	270.3	(3.3)	270.0	(3.8)	55.1

Source: International Adult Literacy Survey, 1994-1995.

TABLE 2.1

Rates of return to education, by educational attainment, men and women, short-cut method, 1992 and 1994

| | Upper secondary vs. lower secondary | | | |
| | 1992 | | 1994 | |
	Men	Women	Men	Women
Australia	6.8 [a]	5.6 [a]	5.6 [b]	11.7 [b]
Belgium	5.4	9.4	×	×
Canada	7.8 [a]	13.0 [a]	7.8	11.7
Germany	4.4	6.3	1.0	7.8
Ireland	×	×	10.0	20.4
Netherlands	6.3	12.3	6.3 [b]	9.9 [b]
New Zealand	8.8	9.2	9.4	12.8
Sweden	4.5	2.9	4.5 [b]	2.9 [b]
Switzerland	7.9	12.3	7.9	11.8
United Kingdom	12.5	21.4	13.3	25.8
United States	17.2	17.9	18.8	19.6

| | Tertiary non-university vs. upper secondary | | | |
| | 1992 | | 1994 | |
	Men	Women	Men	Women
Australia	7.0 [a]	8.0 [a]	5.7 [b]	6.7 [b]
Belgium	3.8	9.3	×	×
Canada	3.5 [a]	8.0 [a]	4.5	7.0
Germany	5.3	4.7	5.3	3.7
Ireland	×	×	7.0	7.7
Netherlands	×	×	×	×
New Zealand	-5.0	-1.0	-2.3	-1.0
Sweden	6.0	6.3	5.7 [b]	6.0 [b]
Switzerland	6.8	6.5	6.0	8.8
United Kingdom	10.5	28.0	9.5	25.0
United States	10.0	15.0	8.0	13.5

| | University degree vs. upper secondary | | | |
| | 1992 | | 1994 | |
	Men	Women	Men	Women
Australia	14.5 [a]	18.8 [a]	11.0 [b]	13.0 [b]
Belgium	9.8	12.8	×	×
Canada	15.5 [a]	18.5 [a]	13.0	15.5
Germany	14.0	15.0	13.4	12.4
Ireland	×	×	23.7	29.0
Netherlands	8.0	11.8	9.0 [b]	10.3 [b]
New Zealand	16.0	17.5	14.3	13.8
Sweden	15.0	14.0	16.0 [b]	14.5 [b]
Switzerland	10.4	10.4	8.4	12.0
United Kingdom	23.7	35.3	21.3	34.7
United States	16.0	17.5	17.0	18.8

[a] 1991 data.

[b] 1993 data.

× Data unavailable.

Source: Calculated from data published in OECD (1995 and 1996*a*), by Cohn and Addison (1997).

TABLE 2.2

Proportion of employed people aged 25-65 at each literacy level who are in the top 60 per cent of earners: percentage points difference from level 3, 1994-1995

	Prose			
	Level 1	Level 2	Level 3	Level 4/5
Australia	26.4 (1.8)	43.8 (1.4)	50.8 (1.2)	57.9 (1.7)
Belgium (Flanders)[1]	5.8* (1.2)	13.0* (2.1)	23.0* (1.9)	33.7* (3.7)
Canada	23.5 (6.4)	44.9 (8.4)	56.9 (3.0)	68.9 (7.5)
Germany	35.4 (4.2)	43.7 (2.5)	49.9 (3.5)	55.8 (3.1)
Ireland	23.7 (2.6)	45.0 (3.8)	60.3 (3.0)	75.0 (4.0)
Netherlands	33.0 (4.3)	47.9 (1.7)	60.7 (1.6)	63.3 (3.1)
New Zealand	34.0 (3.0)	53.7 (3.1)	62.9 (2.3)	73.4 (2.3)
Poland	57.3 (2.1)	64.6 (1.5)	74.5 (2.6)	86.9 (4.2)
Sweden	72.3 (6.1)	78.8 (2.4)	81.3 (1.5)	82.6 (1.9)
Switzerland (French)	47.2 (6.1)	56.5 (3.3)	70.1 (2.8)	68.2 (6.2)
Switzerland (German)	47.3 (5.7)	61.6 (3.4)	74.1 (2.8)	72.9 (4.9)
United Kingdom	24.9 (1.9)	42.5 (2.2)	56.5 (1.7)	71.5 (3.0)
United States	13.4 (1.9)	31.6 (2.8)	47.4 (2.6)	60.3 (2.6)

	Document			
	Level 1	Level 2	Level 3	Level 4/5
Australia	23.5 (1.5)	39.5 (1.2)	53.4 (1.3)	63.6 (1.7)
Belgium (Flanders)[1]	3.1* (1.1)	13.5* (2.2)	22.7* (2.1)	29.0* (2.9)
Canada	17.9 (3.7)	46.5 (8.5)	58.3 (5.6)	72.8 (8.2)
Germany	28.3 (2.7)	40.2 (3.6)	50.8 (2.1)	56.4 (5.2)
Ireland	24.6 (3.3)	46.5 (3.7)	63.6 (2.3)	74.4 (5.0)
Netherlands	27.7 (4.4)	45.8 (2.0)	59.9 (1.3)	68.0 (3.0)
New Zealand	32.8 (2.9)	52.6 (3.0)	67.3 (2.0)	76.8 (2.6)
Poland	57.6 (2.0)	66.5 (1.3)	70.6 (2.7)	81.2 (3.4)
Sweden	70.1 (4.2)	72.5 (2.6)	82.9 (1.5)	83.6 (1.4)
Switzerland (French)	37.1 (5.3)	60.9 (3.8)	66.6 (2.8)	72.0 (5.1)
Switzerland (German)	45.2 (4.8)	62.7 (3.2)	70.5 (2.5)	75.8 (4.1)
United Kingdom	22.6 (1.9)	42.1 (2.0)	55.7 (1.7)	75.0 (2.5)
United States	16.6 (1.8)	32.3 (2.6)	47.3 (2.7)	64.9 (2.7)

	Quantitative			
	Level 1	Level 2	Level 3	Level 4/5
Australia	21.0 (1.6)	38.8 (1.3)	51.8 (1.4)	65.8 (1.5)
Belgium (Flanders)[1]	3.3* (1.2)	12.8* (2.0)	18.6* (2.3)	34.9* (3.0)
Canada	20.2 (5.0)	43.1 (8.7)	55.3 (5.8)	75.7 (8.0)
Germany	33.8 (3.8)	36.6 (3.7)	48.9 (2.3)	56.1 (3.2)
Ireland	24.2 (2.8)	42.8 (3.7)	61.6 (3.4)	75.9 (4.0)
Netherlands	25.8 (3.7)	46.2 (2.3)	58.3 (1.3)	70.0 (2.8)
New Zealand	31.2 (3.2)	53.5 (2.7)	65.0 (2.0)	78.2 (2.3)
Poland	55.4 (2.0)	64.4 (1.9)	69.1 (1.9)	86.1 (3.4)
Sweden	63.5 (4.2)	76.0 (3.1)	81.9 (1.8)	83.9 (1.5)
Switzerland (French)	39.0 (6.2)	55.2 (4.4)	66.4 (2.2)	70.3 (4.9)
Switzerland (German)	44.9 (6.6)	55.1 (2.8)	70.0 (2.9)	78.8 (3.3)
United Kingdom	21.6 (1.9)	41.2 (1.7)	53.8 (2.2)	78.1 (1.9)
United States	12.2 (1.9)	29.7 (2.1)	44.9 (3.0)	65.9 (2.3)

* Unreliable estimate.

[1] Belgium (Flanders) is excluded from Figure 2.2 because the data are unreliable.

Source: International Adult Literacy Survey, 1994-1995.

TADLE 2.3

Proportion of native-born vs. foreign-born employed population aged 25-65 in top 60 per cent of earners, by literacy level, document scale, 1994-1995

	Native-born		Foreign-born	
	Level 1/2	Levels 3, 4/5	Level 1/2	Levels 3, 4/5
Australia	33.8 (1.2)	55.1 (1.2)	31.5 (2.0)	62.2 (1.8)
Belgium (Flanders)	9.0* (1.5)	24.5* (1.8)	11.5* (6.7)	33.1* (18.4)
Canada	38.7 (7.3)	61.5 (2.6)	19.7 (6.4)	77.4 (21.8)
Germany	38.8 (2.7)	53.4 (1.9)	28.6* (8.8)	35.5* (15.0)
Ireland	36.3 (3.3)	68.5 (2.7)	38.9* (9.1)	46.6* (6.9)
Netherlands	40.5 (2.0)	62.9 (1.4)	43.2 (6.0)	54.8 (7.0)
New Zealand	45.6 (2.7)	71.2 (1.5)	39.1 (4.2)	67.9 (4.8)
Poland	61.5 (1.2)	73.2 (2.2)	x	x
Sweden	71.1 (2.8)	83.6 (1.1)	76.4 (6.5)	76.4 (3.4)
Switzerland (French)	55.7 (3.5)	68.8 (2.8)	49.4 (5.7)	65.4 (7.6)
Switzerland (German)	57.5 (2.7)	72.7 (1.9)	55.3 (7.0)	64.9* (10.6)
United Kingdom	32.7 (1.6)	62.9 (1.6)	34.8 (4.8)	66.1 (4.8)
United States	26.5 (2.3)	53.7 (1.7)	21.3 (4.1)	60.0 (6.0)

* Unreliable estimate.

Source: International Adult Literacy Survey, 1994-1995.

TABLE 2.4

Expected lifetime pre-tax income from employment by document literacy level and age, 16-65, undiscounted 1994 dollar values

Figure 2.4 is based on Canadian data derived from the International Adult Literacy Survey, 1994.

Source: Bloom *et al.* (1997).

TABLE 2.5

Regression coefficients showing the strength of the direct effect[1] of education on income and of literacy on income net of the effects of background variables[2], 1994-1995

	Educational attainment β coefficient		Literacy proficiency β coefficient	
Belgium (Flanders)	0.484	(0.04)	0.131	(0.03)
Canada	0.356	(0.03)	0.197	(0.03)
Germany	0.244	(0.04)	0.189	(0.03)
Ireland	0.274	(0.04)	0.309	(0.04)
Netherlands	0.272	(0.03)	0.195	(0.03)
Poland	0.374	(0.03)	0.003	(0.03)
Sweden	0.179	(0.03)	0.103	(0.03)
Switzerland[3]	0.304	(0.03)	0.178	(0.03)
United Kingdom	0.243	(0.03)	0.231	(0.03)
United States	0.302	(0.03)	0.296	(0.03)

[1] Direct effect coefficients are standardised maximum-likelihood regression estimates obtained in LISREL path models.

[2] Direct effects of educational attainment and literacy proficiency on income controlling for gender and parental occupation.

[3] Combined sample for the French-speaking and German-speaking communities in Switzerland.

Source: International Adult Literacy Survey, 1994-1995.

TABLE 2.6A

**Rates of labour force participation for population aged 25-65 by low (levels 1-2)
and medium to high (levels 3-5) literacy proficiency, prose scale, 1994-1995**

		In labour force		Not in labour force	
Australia	Level 1/2	67.0	(1.1)	33.0	(1.1)
	Level 3, 4/5	84.0	(0.6)	16.0	(0.6)
Belgium (Flanders)	Level 1/2	63.1	(1.7)	36.9	(1.7)
	Level 3, 4/5	83.4	(1.3)	16.6	(1.3)
Canada	Level 1/2	67.1	(4.2)	32.9	(4.2)
	Level 3, 4/5	81.7	(4.6)	18.3	(4.6)
Germany	Level 1/2	60.9	(3.1)	39.1	(3.1)
	Level 3, 4/5	72.0	(1.3)	28.0	(1.3)
Ireland	Level 1/2	55.5	(1.7)	44.5	(1.7)
	Level 3, 4/5	72.9	(1.3)	27.1	(1.3)
Netherlands	Level 1/2	55.8	(1.6)	44.2	(1.6)
	Level 3, 4/5	77.0	(1.3)	23.0	(1.3)
New Zealand	Level 1/2	70.0	(1.9)	30.0	(1.9)
	Level 3, 4/5	81.4	(1.1)	18.6	(1.1)
Poland	Level 1/2	66.8	(0.7)	33.2	(0.7)
	Level 3, 4/5	81.9	(2.2)	18.1	(2.2)
Sweden	Level 1/2	71.0	(1.7)	29.0	(1.7)
	Level 3, 4/5	87.0	(1.1)	13.0	(1.1)
Switzerland (French)	Level 1/2	73.9	(2.1)	26.1	(2.1)
	Level 3, 4/5	84.7	(1.6)	15.3	(1.6)
Switzerland (German)	Level 1/2	77.3	(2.2)	22.7	(2.2)
	Level 3, 4/5	84.3	(1.6)	15.7	(1.6)
United Kingdom	Level 1/2	67.9	(1.3)	32.1	(1.3)
	Level 3, 4/5	87.0	(0.9)	13.0	(0.9)
United States	Level 1/2	73.8	(1.7)	26.2	(1.7)
	Level 3, 4/5	83.7	(1.3)	16.3	(1.3)

Source: International Adult Literacy Survey, 1994-1995.

TABLE 2.6B

**Rates of labour force participation for population aged 25-65 by low (levels 1-2)
and medium to high (levels 3-5) literacy proficiency, document scale, 1994-1995**

		In labour force		Not in labour force	
Australia	Level 1/2	65.0	(1.2)	35.0	(1.2)
	Level 3, 4/5	86.1	(0.7)	13.9	(0.7)
Belgium (Flanders)	Level 1/2	60.1	(1.8)	39.9	(1.8)
	Level 3, 4/5	83.2	(1.5)	16.8	(1.5)
Canada	Level 1/2	66.3	(3.2)	33.7	(3.2)
	Level 3, 4/5	82.7	(4.9)	17.3	(4.9)
Germany	Level 1/2	59.1	(3.2)	40.9	(3.2)
	Level 3, 4/5	71.9	(1.1)	28.1	(1.1)
Ireland	Level 1/2	55.7	(1.3)	44.3	(1.3)
	Level 3, 4/5	74.6	(1.4)	25.4	(1.4)
Netherlands	Level 1/2	51.6	(1.6)	48.4	(1.6)
	Level 3, 4/5	78.2	(1.2)	21.8	(1.2)
New Zealand	Level 1/2	67.1	(1.8)	32.9	(1.8)
	Level 3, 4/5	85.8	(0.9)	14.2	(0.9)
Poland	Level 1/2	65.2	(0.7)	34.8	(0.7)
	Level 3, 4/5	86.9	(1.5)	13.1	(1.5)
Sweden	Level 1/2	70.6	(2.5)	29.4	(2.5)
	Level 3, 4/5	86.4	(0.9)	13.6	(0.9)
Switzerland (French)	Level 1/2	74.0	(2.1)	26.0	(2.1)
	Level 3, 4/5	83.4	(1.4)	16.6	(1.4)
Switzerland (German)	Level 1/2	77.8	(2.3)	22.2	(2.3)
	Level 3, 4/5	82.8	(1.5)	17.2	(1.5)
United Kingdom	Level 1/2	67.2	(1.1)	32.8	(1.1)
	Level 3, 4/5	87.2	(0.9)	12.8	(0.9)
United States	Level 1/2	72.0	(1.6)	28.0	(1.6)
	Level 3, 4/5	86.1	(1.2)	13.9	(1.2)

Source: International Adult Literacy Survey, 1994-1995.

TABLE 2.6C

Rates of labour force participation for population aged 25-65 by low (levels 1-2) and medium to high (levels 3-5) literacy proficiency, quantitative scale, 1994-1995

		In labour force		Not in labour force	
Australia	Level 1/2	64.0	(1.2)	36.0	(1.2)
	Level 3, 4/5	85.7	(0.7)	14.3	(0.7)
Belgium (Flanders)	Level 1/2	60.1	(1.8)	39.9	(1.8)
	Level 3, 4/5	82.8	(1.4)	17.2	(1.4)
Canada	Level 1/2	67.2	(2.9)	32.8	(2.9)
	Level 3, 4/5	81.6	(4.8)	18.4	(4.8)
Germany	Level 1/2	56.7	(3.0)	43.3	(3.0)
	Level 3, 4/5	71.3	(1.6)	28.7	(1.6)
Ireland	Level 1/2	53.6	(1.4)	46.4	(1.4)
	Level 3, 4/5	75.3	(1.6)	24.7	(1.6)
Netherlands	Level 1/2	51.7	(1.7)	48.3	(1.7)
	Level 3, 4/5	77.5	(1.0)	22.5	(1.0)
New Zealand	Level 1/2	68.7	(1.9)	31.3	(1.9)
	Level 3, 4/5	83.5	(1.0)	16.5	(1.0)
Poland	Level 1/2	64.9	(0.8)	35.1	(0.8)
	Level 3, 4/5	81.5	(1.0)	18.5	(1.0)
Sweden	Level 1/2	72.2	(2.1)	27.8	(2.1)
	Level 3, 4/5	85.7	(1.1)	14.3	(1.1)
Switzerland (French)	Level 1/2	71.7	(2.7)	28.3	(2.7)
	Level 3, 4/5	83.5	(1.2)	16.5	(1.2)
Switzerland (German)	Level 1/2	77.9	(2.8)	22.1	(2.8)
	Level 3, 4/5	82.1	(1.7)	17.9	(1.7)
United Kingdom	Level 1/2	67.7	(1.1)	32.3	(1.1)
	Level 3, 4/5	86.5	(1.0)	13.5	(1.0)
United States	Level 1/2	72.8	(1.6)	27.2	(1.6)
	Level 3, 4/5	84.3	(1.2)	15.7	(1.2)

Source: International Adult Literacy Survey, 1994-1995.

TABLE 2.7

Mean number of weeks worked for people who worked during the year preceding the interview, by literacy level on the quantitative scale, population aged 25-65, 1994-1995

	Mean weeks worked per year			Mean hours worked per week
	Level 1	Level 2 and above	All levels	All levels
Australia	44.5 (0.6)	47.8 (0.2)	47.4 (0.2)	38.7 (0.2)
Belgium (Flanders)	49.4 (0.9)	49.9 (0.3)	49.8 (0.3)	38.1 (0.4)
Canada	38.9 (1.0)	45.8 (0.3)	44.9 (0.3)	38.0 (0.3)
Germany	48.5 (1.2)	50.2 (0.2)	48.2 (0.2)	38.0 (0.4)
Ireland	46.3 (0.9)	48.5 (0.3)	50.1 (0.2)	41.5 (0.5)
Netherlands	46.8 (1.2)	49.0 (0.2)	48.1 (0.3)	35.9 (0.3)
New Zealand	43.5 (0.9)	46.5 (0.3)	48.9 (0.2)	37.5 (0.3)
Poland	47.9 (0.4)	49.2 (0.3)	46.1 (0.3)	45.6 (0.4)
Sweden[1]	48.0 (1.1)	47.3 (0.3)	48.7 (0.2)	— —
Switzerland (French)	47.8 (1.1)	48.0 (0.3)	47.4 (0.3)	36.5 (0.4)
Switzerland (German)	47.8 (0.9)	49.2 (0.3)	48.0 (0.3)	38.0 (0.4)
United Kingdom	47.6 (0.4)	48.3 (0.2)	49.0 (0.3)	36.3 (0.2)
United States	46.4 (0.7)	48.4 (0.2)	48.1 (0.2)	40.9 (0.3)
Average of above	45.8 (0.2)	48.0 (0.1)	47.7 (0.1)	38.5 (0.1)

[1] The Swedish survey did not ask about work-week duration.

Source: International Adult Literacy Survey, 1994-1995.

TABLE 2.8

Unemployment incidence (rate) by level of literacy proficiency for the labour force aged 16-65, document scale, 1994-1995

	Level 1/2		Levels 3, 4/5	
Australia	11.3	(0.8)	4.6	(0.5)
Belgium (Flanders)	17.7	(3.0)	8.0	(1.0)
Canada	17.0	(2.6)	7.2	(1.5)
Germany	16.5	(1.9)	7.2	(1.3)
Ireland	23.4	(2.9)	9.9	(1.6)
Netherlands	9.8	(1.4)	5.2	(0.7)
New Zealand	15.2	(1.6)	3.8	(0.6)
Poland	17.0	(1.1)	11.5	(1.6)
Sweden	12.8	(1.5)	7.0	(0.6)
Switzerland (French)	5.3*	(1.4)	5.2*	(1.3)
Switzerland (German)	3.6*	(1.2)	3.2*	(0.9)
United Kingdom	17.5	(1.4)	7.7	(0.8)
United States	7.1	(1.0)	3.4	(0.9)

* Unreliable estimate.

Source: International Adult Literacy Survey, 1994-1995.

TABLE 2.9

Unemployment predicted by social origin, educational attainment, age and literacy proficiency for white and black men aged 25-59 who are in the labour force, regression estimates, United States, 1992

Effect variables	β		Z-ratio	P-value
Intercept	-0.48	(0.453)	-1.05	0.227
Age	-0.01	(0.004)	-1.94	0.063
Educational attainment	0.02	(0.045)	0.49	0.350
African American	0.65	(0.113)	5.72	0.000
Hispanic	0.11	(0.299)	0.36	0.371
Asian	1.02	(0.436)	2.35	0.028
Spanish language	-0.50	(0.407)	-1.23	0.185
European language	-0.41	(0.206)	-2.00	0.056
Asian language	-1.38	(0.474)	-2.92	0.008
General education diploma	0.22	(0.169)	1.30	0.169
High school diploma	-0.61	(0.205)	-2.99	0.006
Associates degree	-0.23	(0.104)	-2.24	0.035
Bachelors degree	-0.27	(0.200)	-1.33	0.164
Masters degree	-0.59	(0.262)	-2.27	0.033
Literacy proficiency	-0.01	(0.001)	-6.68	0.000
Parent education	0.01	(0.015)	0.63	0.324

Source: Raudenbush, Kasim, Eamsukkawat and Miyazaki (1996).

TABLE 2.10

Adjusted regression coefficients indicating the size of the effect of labour market experience on income, relative to the effects of years of education and literacy skills, 1994-1995

Variance explained in income		β coefficients[1]		
		Literacy	Education	Labour experience
0.413	Belgium (Flanders)	0.131 (.03)	0.484 (.04)	0.352 (.03)
0.279	Canada	0.197 (.03)	0.356 (.03)	0.242 (.03)
0.190	Germany	0.189 (.03)	0.244 (.04)	0.116 (.04)
0.286	Ireland	0.309 (.04)	0.274 (.04)	0.232 (.03)
0.260	Netherlands	0.195 (.03)	0.272 (.03)	0.350 (.03)
0.202	Poland	0.003 (.03)	0.347 (.03)	0.176 (.03)
0.160	Sweden	0.103 (.03)	0.179 (.03)	0.265 (.03)
0.225	Switzerland	0.178 (.03)	0.304 (.03)	0.263 (.03)
0.232	United Kingdom	0.231 (.03)	0.243 (.03)	0.089 (.02)
0.333	United States	0.296 (.03)	0.302 (.03)	0.145 (.02)

[1] See notes to Table 2.5. The β coefficients are adjusted for the amount of variance explained in the dependent variable, pre-tax income.

Source: International Adult Literacy Survey, 1994-1995.

TABLE 2.11

Proportion of labour force aged 16-65 employed in white collar jobs, which are mostly high-skill and high-wage, 1994-1995

	White collar high-skill	White collar low-skill	Blue collar high-skill	Blue collar low-skill
Australia	24.5 (0.5)	6.4 (0.4)	36.8 (0.7)	32.3 (0.8)
Belgium (Flanders)	10.9* (1.6)	2.6* (0.7)	60.3 (3.9)	26.2 (2.3)
Canada	30.1 (3.9)	6.1 (1.4)	33.2 (2.3)	30.6 (2.0)
Germany	27.1 (2.0)	6.4 (0.8)	37.3 (1.3)	29.2 (2.3)
Ireland	20.4 (2.0)	8.6 (0.5)	31.0 (1.6)	40.0 (2.8)
Netherlands	40.4 (0.9)	9.3 (0.7)	31.9 (1.1)	18.5 (0.8)
New Zealand	23.9 (1.1)	7.8 (0.6)	32.1 (1.2)	36.2 (1.1)
Poland	12.1 (1.1)	14.6 (0.7)	14.7 (1.2)	58.6 (1.2)
Sweden	44.5 (1.4)	8.7 (0.9)	34.3 (1.1)	12.6 (0.8)
Switzerland (French)	30.4 (1.5)	12.2 (1.1)	27.7 (1.5)	29.7 (1.4)
Switzerland (German)	30.5 (1.4)	13.1 (1.4)	25.0 (1.7)	31.4 (1.3)
United Kingdom	25.9 (0.9)	9.1 (0.7)	31.1 (0.9)	33.9 (1.1)
United States	27.4 (1.2)	6.9 (0.8)	29.3 (1.2)	36.5 (1.8)

* Unreliable estimate.

Source: International Adult Literacy Survey, 1994-1995.

TABLE 2.12

Proportion of skilled craft workers and machine operators at literacy levels 3-5, document scale, 1994-1995

	Level 1		Level 2		Level 3		Level 4/5	
Australia	20.4	(1.4)	33.6	(1.3)	35.2	(1.6)	10.7	(1.3)
Belgium (Flanders)	18.6	(2.6)	28.8	(3.9)	40.5	(4.0)	12.1	(2.6)
Canada	26.2	(6.3)	30.9	(5.1)	27.6	(5.8)	15.3	(1.6)
Germany	8.1*	(2.6)	37.2	(3.5)	42.6	(3.5)	12.1	(2.5)
Ireland	21.7	(2.6)	35.5	(3.9)	34.8	(3.5)	8.0*	(2.4)
Netherlands	10.5	(1.9)	35.2	(3.0)	38.0	(3.3)	16.3	(2.8)
New Zealand	23.1	(2.9)	35.8	(3.1)	29.9	(2.7)	11.2	(1.7)
Poland	50.6	(1.9)	29.4	(2.1)	15.3	(2.1)	4.7*	(0.9)
Sweden	8.0	(1.3)	18.0	(2.7)	44.8	(4.7)	29.2	(3.3)
Switzerland (French)	23.0	(3.9)	29.9	(4.2)	30.4	(5.0)	16.7*	(4.0)
Switzerland (German)	24.2	(3.7)	34.4	(5.3)	32.3	(3.0)	9.1*	(2.4)
United Kingdom	23.2	(2.0)	37.9	(2.3)	28.2	(2.0)	10.7	(1.7)
United States	33.0	(1.9)	34.6	(2.5)	25.4	(2.2)	7.0	(1.3)

*   Unreliable estimate.

Source: International Adult Literacy Survey, 1994-1995.

TABLE 2.13

Mean literacy proficiency of prison and general household population aged 16-65, mean scores on prose scale with a range of 0-500 points, United States, 1992

	Household population	Prison population
Prose	273 (0.6)	246 (1.9)
Document	267 (0.7)	240 (2.2)
Quantitative	271 (0.7)	236 (3.1)

Source: Haigler *et al.* (1994).

TABLE 2.14

Proportion of the population aged 16-65 who participated in voluntary community activity at least once a month during the year preceding the interview, by prose literacy level, 1994-1995

	Level 1/2		Levels 3, 4/5		All levels	
Australia	20.8	(1.0)	29.4	(0.8)	25.6	(0.8)
Belgium (Flanders)	16.7	(1.5)	30.7	(2.4)	24.1	(1.0)
Canada	13.9	(0.8)	30.2	(3.1)	23.4	(1.8)
Germany	23.4	(2.2)	27.6	(1.4)	25.6	(0.8)
Ireland	24.2	(1.6)	34.2	(2.1)	28.9	(1.6)
Netherlands	27.7	(1.6)	34.2	(1.1)	31.5	(0.9)
New Zealand	29.7	(1.7)	35.6	(1.4)	32.9	(1.2)
Poland	8.4	(0.6)	10.6	(1.7)	8.9	(0.5)
Sweden	40.0	(2.4)	50.0	(0.8)	47.2	(0.9)
Switzerland (French)	17.8	(2.0)	22.6	(1.7)	20.2	(1.4)
Switzerland (German)	18.8	(1.8)	28.0	(2.1)	23.1	(1.3)
United Kingdom	14.5	(0.9)	24.4	(1.4)	19.2	(0.9)
United States	25.2	(2.1)	40.4	(1.7)	33.5	(1.7)

Source: International Adult Literacy Survey, 1994-1995.

TABLE 3.1

Percentage of children aged 4 and 5 from homes with low and high education, who face developmental delays, Canada, 1994-1995

	Delayed development	Advanced development
Below upper secondary	35.0	7.6
Upper secondary education	16.6	10.4
Trade and business school	15.4	12.0
Tertiary education	11.6	22.5

Source: National Longitudinal Survey of Children and Youth; HRDC Bulletin, 1997.

TABLE 3.2

Mean reading scores for schools with high, medium and low levels of parental engagement[1] in school activities, 8th-grade students, United States, 1988

	Parental engagement in schools			
	Low	Medium	High	Total
Mean socio-economic status	-0.067 (.05)	0.010 (.02)	0.887 (.07)	0.090 (.02)
Mean reading scores	-0.043 (.04)	-0.010 (.02)	0.603 (.04)	0.047 (.02)

[1] The 10th and 90th percentiles denote low and high engagement respectively.
Source: National Educational Longitudinal Study, 1988.

TABLE 3.3

Mean document literacy scores for IALS youth aged 16-25 and IEA students aged 14

	IALS document scores 16-25 year-olds	IEA document scores 14-year-olds
Canada	294.1 (4.7)	522 (2.7)
Germany[1]	294.0 (3.9)	532 (3.9)
Ireland	271.6 (2.8)	518 (4.9)
Netherlands	300.3 (2.7)	533 (5.3)
New Zealand	275.3 (3.5)	552 (5.3)
Sweden	314.4 (2.0)	550 (2.4)
Switzerland (French)[2]	291.4 (5.1)	549 (3.0)
Switzerland (German)[2]	294.5 (4.7)	549 (3.0)
United States[3]	278.0 (1.0)	528 (4.0)

[1] Former Territory of the Federal Republic of Germany for IEA literacy scores.
[2] Samples for French- and German-speaking Switzerland are combined for the IEA literacy scores.
[3] Because of a sampling anomaly in the IALS youth data in the United States, National Adult Literacy Survey (1992) data have been substituted.
Source: International Adult Literacy Survey, 1994-1995, and IEA Reading Literacy Survey, 1991.

TABLE 3.4

Net enrolment rates at age 16 and 17, and graduation rates at the typical age of graduation, 1994

	Enrolment		Graduation
	Age 16	Age 17	Population at typical age of graduation[1]
Australia	95.8	92.3	×
Belgium	100.0	100.0	96.7
Canada	94.2	88.1	71.7
Germany	96.3	92.5	88.5
Ireland	93.2	83.2	93.8
Netherlands	97.5	90.6	80.0
New Zealand	94.3	78.7	95.0
Poland	×	×	90.3
Sweden	96.2	94.8	74.6
Switzerland	87.3	83.3	82.1
United Kingdom	87.1	73.6	×
United States	95.4	85.9	75.8
OECD mean[2]	**87.5**	**78.3**	**76.9**

[1] Ratio of upper secondary graduates to population at typical age of graduation (times 100) by type of programme, first educational programme only.

[2] Average for 25 countries.

× Data unavailable.

Source: OECD Education Database.

TABLE 3.5

Mean literacy scores on prose scale of young people aged 20-29 with and without upper secondary graduation, selected countries, 1994-1995

	Without upper secondary education		With upper secondary education	
Australia	264.4	(2.8)	297.6	(1.5)
Canada	228.5	(18.5)	300.7	(7.9)
Germany	270.7	(4.5)	304.4	(5.0)
Netherlands	262.5	(4.6)	308.4	(2.1)
New Zealand	245.0	(5.4)	299.6	(2.9)

Source: International Adult Literacy Survey, 1994-1995.

TABLE 3.6

Unemployment rates by level of educational attainment for persons 25-29 years of age, 1994

	University education	Upper secondary education	Below upper secondary education	Unemployment rate ages 25-29
Australia	5.4	8.2	13.2	9.6
Belgium	8.7	11.1	18.5	11.7
Canada	6.4	12.5	19.5	11.5
Germany	5.8	8.6	18.1	8.7
Ireland	5.1	10.6	25.7	14.2
Netherlands	7.4	5.4	10.0	7.1
New Zealand	2.9*	3.2	11.1	5.8
Poland	7.4	14.4	26.1	14.5
Sweden	5.6	10.6	15.8	9.9
Switzerland	4.2*	3.5*	12.4	4.1
United Kingdom	4.3	10.7	24.2	10.3
United States	3.1	7.8	17.2	7.4

* Unreliable estimate.

Source: OECD Education Database.

TABLE 3.7A

Relationship between prose literacy scores and age, with and without adjustment for level of education, Australia, 1994-1995

	Unstandardised coefficients		Standardised coefficients		
	B	Standard error	β	t-value	Significance
Unadjusted					
(Constant)	0.11	0.02		7.38	0.00
Age (40 years = 0)					
Linear	-0.02	0.00	-0.25	-10.02	0.00
Quadratic	-0.68	0.06	-0.13	-11.58	0.00
Cubic	8.36	4.47	0.05	1.87	0.06
Adjusted					
(Constant)	0.23	0.01		18.10	0.00
Age (40 years = 0)					
Linear	-0.01	0.00	-0.07	-3.41	0.00
Quadratic	-0.25	0.05	-0.05	-5.30	0.00
Cubic	-9.72	3.56	-0.05	-2.73	0.01
Years education (grade 9 = 0)	0.15	0.00	0.48	55.05	0.00
Other language (test language = 0)	-2.06	0.12	-0.78	-17.88	0.00
Years speaking language (20 years = 0)					
Linear	0.13	0.02	1.47	8.39	0.00
Quadratic	0.00	0.00	-1.92	-7.14	0.00
Cubic	0.00	0.00	0.91	6.61	0.00

Source: International Adult Literacy Survey, 1994-1995.

TABLE 3.7B

Relationship between prose literacy scores and age, with and without adjustment for level of education, Canada, 1994-1995

	Unstandardised coefficients		Standardised coefficients		
	B	Standard error	β	t-value	Significance
Unadjusted					
(Constant)	0.20	0.02		10.08	0.00
Age (40 years = 0)					
Linear	-0.01	0.00	-0.14	-4.29	0.00
Quadratic	-0.84	0.08	-0.15	-10.52	0.00
Cubic	-15.24	6.30	-0.08	-2.42	0.02
Adjusted					
(Constant)	0.08	0.02		5.18	0.00
Age (40 years = 0)					
Linear	0.00	0.00	0.02	0.78	0.43
Quadratic	0.06	0.06	0.01	0.87	0.39
Cubic	-26.94	4.79	-0.14	-5.62	0.00
Years education (grade 9 = 0)	0.16	0.00	0.59	51.05	0.00
Other language (test language = 0)	-1.60	0.10	-0.60	-15.46	0.00
Years speaking language (20 years = 0)					
Linear	0.12	0.02	1.39	7.86	0.00
Quadratic	0.00	0.00	-1.83	-6.10	0.00
Cubic	0.00	0.00	0.87	5.34	0.00

Source: International Adult Literacy Survey, 1994-1995.

TABLE 3.7C

Relationship between prose literacy scores and age, with and without adjustment for level of education, Netherlands, 1994-1995

	Unstandardised coefficients		Standardised coefficients		
	B	Standard error	β	t-value	Significance
Unadjusted					
(Constant)	0.21	0.02		11.77	0.00
Age (40 years = 0)					
Linear	-0.02	0.00	-0.38	-9.14	0.00
Quadratic	-0.49	0.07	-0.12	-6.93	0.00
Cubic	15.69	5.55	0.12	2.82	0.00
Adjusted					
(Constant)	0.16	0.02		9.89	0.00
Age (40 years = 0)					
Linear	-0.01	0.00	-0.28	-7.34	0.00
Quadratic	-0.24	0.06	-0.06	-3.74	0.00
Cubic	5.92	4.96	0.04	1.19	0.23
Years education (grade 9 = 0)	0.07	0.00	0.38	22.92	0.00
Other language (test language = 0)	-1.09	0.09	-0.41	-11.50	0.00
Years speaking language (20 years = 0)					
Linear	0.03	0.01	0.30	3.10	0.00
Quadratic	0.00	0.00	0.10	0.55	0.58
Cubic	0.00	0.00	-0.14	-1.22	0.22

Source: International Adult Literacy Survey, 1994-1995.

TABLE 3.7D

Relationship between prose literacy scores and age, with and without adjustment for level of education, United Kingdom, 1994-1995

	Unstandardised coefficients		Standardised coefficients		
	B	Standard error	β	t-value	Significance
Unadjusted					
(Constant)	0.02	0.02		1.40	0.16
Age (40 years = 0)					
Linear	-0.01	0.00	-0.18	-6.21	0.00
Quadratic	-0.68	0.06	-0.13	-10.94	0.00
Cubic	0.32	4.98	0.00	0.06	0.95
Adjusted					
(Constant)	0.07	0.02		4.50	0.00
Age (40 years = 0)					
Linear	-0.01	0.00	-0.19	-6.80	0.00
Quadratic	-0.72	0.06	-0.14	-11.72	0.00
Cubic	2.41	4.86	0.01	0.50	0.62
Years education (grade 9 = 0)	0.01	0.00	0.05	4.52	0.00
Other language (test language = 0)	-3.72	0.31	-0.91	-11.90	0.00
Years speaking language (20 years = 0)					
Linear	0.28	0.04	2.25	7.81	0.00
Quadratic	-0.01	0.00	-2.75	-6.50	0.00
Cubic	0.00	0.00	1.20	5.67	0.00

Source: International Adult Literacy Survey, 1994-1995.

TABLE 3.7E

Relationship between prose literacy scores and age, with and without adjustment for level of education, Switzerland (French), 1994-1995

	Unstandardised coefficients		Standardised coefficients		
	B	Standard error	β	t-value	Significance
Unadjusted					
(Constant)	-0.11	0.03		-3.47	0.00
Age (40 years = 0)					
Linear	-0.02	0.00	-0.26	-4.24	0.00
Quadratic	-0.08	0.13	-0.02	-0.60	0.55
Cubic	10.88	10.75	0.06	1.01	0.31
Adjusted					
(Constant)	0.03	0.03		0.97	0.33
Age (40 years = 0)					
Linear	-0.02	0.00	-0.32	-5.38	0.00
Quadratic	-0.14	0.13	-0.03	-1.12	0.26
Cubic	12.41	10.07	0.07	1.23	0.22
Years education (grade 9 = 0)	-0.01	0.00	-0.27	-10.97	0.00
Other language (test language = 0)	-1.90	0.23	-0.90	-8.25	0.00
Years speaking language "(20 years = 0)					
Linear	0.15	0.03	1.97	4.62	0.00
Quadratic	0.00	0.00	-2.06	-3.14	0.00
Cubic	0.00	0.00	0.77	2.27	0.02

Source: International Adult Literacy Survey, 1994-1995.

TABLE 3.7F

Relationship between prose literacy scores and age, with and without adjustment for level of education, Switzerland (German), 1994-1995

	Unstandardised coefficients		Standardised coefficients		
	B	Standard error	β	t-value	Significance
Unadjusted					
(Constant)	-0.18	0.03		-5.54	0.00
Age (40 years = 0)					
Linear	-0.01	0.00	-0.20	-3.38	0.00
Quadratic	0.14	0.14	0.03	1.04	0.30
Cubic	-5.26	10.53	-0.03	-0.50	0.62
Adjusted					
(Constant)	0.00	0.03		0.06	0.96
Age (40 years = 0)					
Linear	-0.02	0.00	-0.26	-4.98	0.00
Quadratic	-0.06	0.12	-0.01	-0.46	0.65
Cubic	1.17	9.37	0.01	0.12	0.90
Years education (grade 9 = 0)	-0.01	0.00	-0.30	-12.88	0.00
Other language (test language = 0)	-2.56	0.29	-0.95	-8.88	0.00
Years speaking language (20 years = 0)					
Linear	0.15	0.04	1.45	3.37	0.00
Quadratic	0.00	0.00	-1.22	-1.80	0.07
Cubic	0.00	0.00	0.42	1.19	0.23

Source: International Adult Literacy Survey, 1994-1995.

TABLE 3.7G

Relationship between prose literacy scores and age, with and without adjustment for level of education, United States, 1994-1995

	Unstandardised coefficients		Standardised coefficients		
	B	Standard error	β	t-value	Significance
Unadjusted					
(Constant)	0.13	0.03		4.65	0.00
Age (40 years = 0)					
Linear	0.00	0.00	0.04	0.84	0.40
Quadratic	-0.69	0.11	-0.12	-6.29	0.00
Cubic	-3.76	8.61	-0.02	-0.44	0.66
Adjusted					
(Constant)	-0.08	0.02		-3.41	0.00
Age (40 years = 0)					
Linear	0.00	0.00	0.02	0.58	0.56
Quadratic	-0.22	0.09	-0.04	-2.50	0.01
Cubic	-15.45	6.86	-0.08	-2.25	0.02
Years education (grade 9 = 0)	0.18	0.01	0.52	34.15	0.00
Other language (test language = 0)	-1.60	0.17	-0.49	-9.39	0.00
Years speaking language (20 years = 0)					
Linear	0.07	0.02	0.61	3.04	0.00
Quadratic	0.00	0.00	-0.74	-2.21	0.03
Cubic	0.00	0.00	0.42	2.23	0.03

Source: International Adult Literacy Survey, 1994-1995.

TABLE 3.0A

Relationship between document literacy scores and level of education of respondents' parents, for young adults aged 16-25, 1994-1995

	Unstandardised coefficients		Standardised coefficients				
	B	Standard error	β	t-value	Signifi-cance	Mean	Standard error of the mean
Australia							
Constant	-1.03	0.12		-8.68	0.00		
Parents' education	0.10	0.01	0.26	9.83	0.00	11.21	0.06
Belgium (Flanders)							
Constant	-0.90	0.11		-7.94	0.00		
Parents' education	0.11	0.01	0.39	11.29	0.00	10.99	0.10
Canada							
Constant	-1.52	0.14		-10.49	0.00		
Parents' education	0.16	0.01	0.34	12.58	0.00	11.47	0.07
Germany							
Constant	-1.43	0.34		-4.21	0.00		
Parents' education	0.16	0.03	0.27	5.04	0.00	10.74	0.07
Ireland							
Constant	-1.46	0.19		-7.69	0.00		
Parents' education	0.14	0.02	0.30	7.18	0.00	9.62	0.09
Netherlands							
Constant	-0.95	0.21		-4.65	0.00		
Parents' education	0.13	0.02	0.32	6.72	0.00	10.59	0.09
New Zealand							
Constant	-1.68	0.26		-6.45	0.00		
Parents' education	0.15	0.02	0.27	6.58	0.00	11.47	0.08
Poland							
Constant	-2.46	0.23		-10.90	0.00		
Parents' education	0.18	0.02	0.31	8.41	0.00	10.13	0.07
Sweden							
Constant	-0.26	0.16		-1.62	0.10		
Parents' education	0.08	0.01	0.23	5.55	0.00	10.95	0.10
Switzerland (French)							
Constant	-0.77	0.29		-2.62	0.01		
Parents' education	0.10	0.03	0.26	3.82	0.00	11.37	0.16
Switzerland (German)							
Constant	-1.29	0.38		-3.35	0.00		
Parents' education	0.14	0.03	0.32	4.39	0.00	12.13	0.14
United Kingdom							
Constant	-1.31	0.31		-4.27	0.00		
Parents' education	0.12	0.03	0.18	4.26	0.00	10.78	0.07
United States[1]							
Constant	-1.90	0.05		-35.78	0.00		
Parents' education	0.15	0.00	0.46	36.19	0.00	12.44	0.04

[1] Because of a sampling anomaly in the IALS youth data in the United States, National Adult Literacy Survey (1992) data have been substituted.

Source: International Adult Literacy Survey, 1994-1995.

TABLE 3.8B

Relationship between document literacy scores and level of education of respondents' parents, for the entire adult population aged 26-65, 1994-1995

	Unstandardised coefficients		Standardised coefficients				Standard error of the mean
	B	Standard error	β	t-value	Signifi-cance	Mean	
Australia							
Constant	-1.19	0.04		-28.07	0.00		
Parents' education	0.13	0.00	0.38	31.52	0.00	9.86	0.04
Belgium (Flanders)							
Constant	-0.71	0.06		-10.96	0.00		
Parents' education	0.09	0.01	0.33	13.06	0.00	8.75	0.08
Canada							
Constant	-1.31	0.05		-24.72	0.00		
Parent's education	0.15	0.01	0.47	28.84	0.00	9.42	0.06
Germany							
Constant	-1.00	0.18		-5.65	0.00		
Parents' education	0.12	0.02	0.17	6.96	0.00	10.33	0.03
Ireland							
Constant	-1.73	0.09		-18.91	0.00		
Parents' education	0.18	0.01	0.39	17.46	0.00	8.71	0.05
Netherlands							
Constant	-1.10	0.07		-14.67	0.00		
Parents' education	0.14	0.01	0.35	18.05	0.00	9.49	0.04
New Zealand							
Constant	-1.08	0.07		-15.33	0.00		
Parents' education	0.11	0.01	0.33	16.97	0.00	10.22	0.05
Poland							
Constant	-2.10	0.07		-29.85	0.00		
Parents' education	0.17	0.01	0.40	20.47	0.00	8.03	0.05
Sweden							
Constant	-0.64	0.06		-9.97	0.00		
Parents' education	0.13	0.01	0.39	18.76	0.00	9.03	0.05
Switzerland (French)							
Constant	-0.99	0.08		-12.35	0.00		
Parents' education	0.10	0.01	0.38	13.94	0.00	10.27	0.08
Switzerland (German)							
Constant	-1.81	0.12		-15.69	0.00		
Parents' education	0.17	0.01	0.44	16.51	0.00	10.93	0.07
United Kingdom							
Constant	-1.85	0.10		-19.24	0.00		
Parents' education	0.19	0.01	0.28	20.01	0.00	10.06	0.02
United States							
Constant	-1.96	0.10		-19.18	0.00		
Parents' education	0.18	0.01	0.40	20.49	0.00	11.21	0.05

Source: International Adult Literacy Survey, 1994-1995.

TABLE 3.8C

Relationship between document literacy scores and level of education of respondents' parents, for the employed population aged 26-65, 1994-1995

	Unstandardised coefficients		Standardised coefficients				
	B	Standard error	β	t-value	Signifi-cance	Mean	Standard error of the mean
Australia							
Constant	-0.68	0.05		-14.35	0.00		
Parents' education	0.10	0.00	0.31	20.99	0.00	10.11	0.04
Belgium (Flanders)							
Constant	-0.41	0.09		-4.76	0.00		
Parents' education	0.08	0.01	0.27	8.62	0.00	9.33	0.09
Canada							
Constant	-0.97	0.06		-14.89	0.00		
Parents' education	0.14	0.01	0.43	21.58	0.00	9.88	0.07
Germany							
Constant	-0.66	0.21		-3.11	0.00		
Parents' education	0.10	0.02	0.15	4.77	0.00	10.36	0.03
Ireland							
Constant	-1.38	0.12		-11.35	0.00		
Parents' education	0.16	0.01	0.38	12.30	0.00	9.02	0.07
Netherlands							
Constant	-0.73	0.09		-8.09	0.00		
Parents' education	0.11	0.01	0.31	12.62	0.00	9.70	0.04
New Zealand							
Constant	-0.73	0.08		-8.69	0.00		
Parents' education	0.09	0.01	0.27	11.80	0.00	10.36	0.06
Poland							
Constant	-1.83	0.10		-19.25	0.00		
Parents' education	0.16	0.01	0.36	14.32	0.00	8.45	0.06
Sweden							
Constant	-0.36	0.08		-4.75	0.00		
Parents' education	0.11	0.01	0.32	13.42	0.00	9.22	0.06
Switzerland (French)							
Constant	-0.89	0.10		-9.24	0.00		
Parents' education	0.10	0.01	0.35	11.21	0.00	10.42	0.09
Switzerland (German)							
Constant	-1.66	0.13		-12.92	0.00		
Parents' education	0.16	0.01	0.43	14.06	0.00	10.99	0.08
United Kingdom							
Constant	-1.47	0.11		-13.84	0.00		
Parents' education	0.17	0.01	0.27	16.18	0.00	10.15	0.02
United States							
Constant	-1.78	0.11		-15.53	0.00		
Parents' education	0.17	0.01	0.39	17.63	0.00	11.37	0.05

Source: International Adult Literacy Survey, 1994-1995.

TABLE 3.9

Distribution of home engagement in literacy index scores by level of prose literacy, 1994-1995

	Mean	Standard error of the mean	Minimum	25th percentile	Median	75th percentile	Maximum
Australia							
Level 1	-0.45	0.02	-1.64	-1.27	-0.61	0.12	2.75
Level 2	-0.17	0.02	-1.64	-0.99	-0.32	0.59	2.88
Level 3	0.19	0.02	-1.64	-0.61	0.22	1.00	2.93
Level 4/5	0.55	0.02	-1.64	-0.06	0.59	1.20	2.75
Belgium (Flanders)							
Level 1	-0.83	0.04	-1.64	-1.45	-0.92	-0.52	1.85
Level 2	-0.65	0.04	-1.64	-1.36	-0.88	-0.06	2.38
Level 3	-0.21	0.03	-1.64	-0.94	-0.26	0.47	2.38
Level 4/5	0.17	0.05	-1.64	-0.54	0.19	0.91	2.30
Canada							
Level 1	-0.57	0.02	-1.64	-1.20	-0.79	-0.15	2.43
Level 2	-0.20	0.03	-1.64	-1.07	-0.26	0.47	2.93
Level 3	0.09	0.02	-1.64	-0.61	0.02	0.83	3.07
Level 4/5	0.50	0.03	-1.64	-0.35	0.47	1.22	2.75
Germany							
Level 1	-0.40	0.05	-1.64	-1.07	-0.52	0.08	2.47
Level 2	-0.24	0.03	-1.64	-0.91	-0.34	0.34	2.38
Level 3	0.05	0.03	-1.64	-0.71	-0.06	0.67	2.61
Level 4/5	0.35	0.06	-1.64	-0.34	0.30	1.11	2.48
Ireland							
Level 1	-0.39	0.04	-1.64	-1.07	-0.52	0.19	2.50
Level 2	-0.04	0.04	-1.64	-0.77	-0.09	0.59	2.93
Level 3	0.27	0.03	-1.64	-0.43	0.22	0.95	3.32
Level 4/5	0.60	0.06	-1.64	-0.15	0.59	1.40	2.93
Netherlands							
Level 1	-0.57	0.04	-1.64	-1.32	-0.88	0.02	2.93
Level 2	-0.33	0.03	-1.64	-1.23	-0.52	0.38	2.38
Level 3	0.11	0.03	-1.64	-0.71	0.04	0.91	2.93
Level 4/5	0.32	0.05	-1.64	-0.43	0.30	1.03	2.75
New Zealand							
Level 1	-0.05	0.04	-1.64	-0.91	-0.22	0.75	2.95
Level 2	0.15	0.03	-1.64	-0.63	0.11	0.81	3.05
Level 3	0.47	0.03	-1.64	-0.24	0.47	1.22	2.93
Level 4/5	0.78	0.03	-1.64	0.30	0.83	1.48	3.00
Poland							
Level 1	-0.51	0.02	-1.64	-1.04	-0.71	-0.15	2.93
Level 2	-0.11	0.03	-1.64	-0.80	-0.28	0.52	2.57
Level 3	0.19	0.04	-1.64	-0.62	0.04	0.92	2.93
Level 4/5	0.67	0.10	-1.64	-0.16	0.66	1.42	2.81
Sweden							
Level 1	-0.28	0.04	-1.64	-0.92	-0.36	0.37	2.24
Level 2	-0.12	0.03	-1.64	-0.80	-0.26	0.49	2.72
Level 3	0.09	0.03	-1.64	-0.54	0.04	0.74	2.75
Level 4/5	0.38	0.03	-1.64	-0.26	0.39	1.02	2.75
Switzerland (French)							
Level 1	-0.47	0.06	-1.64	-1.17	-0.61	0.04	2.75
Level 2	-0.20	0.04	-1.64	-0.95	-0.34	0.34	2.75
Level 3	0.20	0.04	-1.64	-0.52	0.12	0.81	2.75
Level 4/5	0.51	0.08	-1.64	-0.07	0.39	1.20	2.75
Switzerland (German)							
Level 1	-0.50	0.05	-1.64	-1.08	-0.51	0.02	1.65
Level 2	-0.24	0.04	-1.64	-0.99	-0.35	0.30	2.30
Level 3	0.12	0.04	-1.64	-0.54	0.04	0.67	2.75
Level 4/5	0.53	0.08	-1.36	-0.15	0.47	1.19	2.75

TABLE 3.9 (concluded)

Distribution of home engagement in literacy index scores by level of prose literacy, 1994-1995

	Mean	Standard error of the mean	Minimum	25th percentile	Median	75th percentile	Maximum
United Kingdom							
Level 1	-0.47	0.02	-1.64	-1.22	-0.67	0.15	2.75
Level 2	-0.06	0.02	-1.64	-0.81	-0.15	0.59	2.75
Level 3	0.27	0.02	-1.64	-0.52	0.29	1.03	2.93
Level 4/5	0.54	0.03	-1.64	-0.15	0.60	1.20	2.75
United States							
Level 1	-0.38	0.04	-1.64	-1.01	-0.52	0.22	3.06
Level 2	-0.16	0.03	-1.64	-0.91	-0.24	0.55	2.38
Level 3	0.20	0.03	-1.64	-0.47	0.19	0.81	2.57
Level 4/5	0.30	0.04	-1.64	-0.35	0.30	0.85	2.75

Source: International Adult Literacy Survey, 1994-1995.

TABLE 3.10

Percentage of respondents reading a book at least once a week, writing a letter at least once a month, and mean number of hours per day spent watching television, by level of education, 1994-1995

	Reading books	Writing letters	Television hours Mean
Australia[1]			
Primary education or less	36.7 (0.02)	27.4 (0.02)	— —
Lower secondary education	45.7 (0.01)	42.9 (0.01)	— —
Upper secondary education	57.1 (0.01)	61.1 (0.01)	— —
Non-university tertiary education	54.6 (0.01)	53.7 (0.01)	— —
University education	72.7 (0.01)	77.3 (0.01)	— —
Belgium (Flanders)			
Primary education or less	14.2 (0.02)	11.5 (0.02)	2.72 (0.08)
Lower secondary education	22.0 (0.02)	19.1 (0.02)	2.16 (0.06)
Upper secondary education	31.1 (0.02)	26.5 (0.02)	1.99 (0.05)
Non-university tertiary education	38.6 (0.03)	33.6 (0.03)	1.46 (0.07)
University education	44.1 (0.04)	47.4 (0.04)	1.28 (0.07)
Canada			
Primary education or less	33.4 (0.02)	15.2 (0.01)	3.12 (0.08)
Lower secondary education	47.1 (0.02)	33.5 (0.02)	2.54 (0.05)
Upper secondary education	49.7 (0.01)	36.3 (0.01)	2.15 (0.04)
Non-university tertiary education	50.3 (0.02)	41.4 (0.02)	1.86 (0.05)
University education	72.4 (0.02)	57.0 (0.02)	1.42 (0.04)
Germany			
Primary education or less	19.4*(0.10)	25.1*(0.10)	3.06*(0.43)
Lower secondary education	35.8 (0.01)	40.2 (0.02)	2.90 (0.05)
Upper secondary education	55.0 (0.02)	63.1 (0.02)	2.30 (0.07)
Non-university tertiary education	62.4 (0.06)	72.6 (0.05)	2.19 (0.15)
University education	81.6 (0.03)	76.6 (0.03)	1.91 (0.09)
Ireland			
Primary education or less	35.0 (0.02)	36.4 (0.02)	2.93 (0.08)
Lower secondary education	46.2 (0.02)	41.0 (0.02)	2.72 (0.06)
Upper secondary education	60.6 (0.02)	59.6 (0.02)	2.36 (0.06)
Non-university tertiary education	73.3 (0.03)	66.4 (0.03)	2.16 (0.11)
University education	79.0 (0.03)	77.0 (0.03)	1.66 (0.09)
Netherlands[2]			
Primary education or less	32.9 (0.02)	23.1 (0.02)	3.11 (0.07)
Lower secondary education	37.4 (0.02)	25.2 (0.02)	2.70 (0.05)
Upper secondary education	46.5 (0.02)	40.5 (0.01)	2.21 (0.04)
University education	61.0 (0.02)	59.0 (0.02)	1.56 (0.05)

TABLE 3.10 (concluded)

Percentage of respondents reading a book at least once a week, writing a letter at least once a month, and mean number of hours per day spent watching television, by level of education, 1994-1995

	Reading books	Writing letters	Television hours Mean
New Zealand			
Primary education or less	49.4 (0.05)	43.4 (0.05)	2.95 (0.18)
Lower secondary education	54.6 (0.01)	45.2 (0.01)	2.73 (0.04)
Upper secondary education	65.7 (0.02)	58.6 (0.02)	2.58 (0.05)
Non-university tertiary education	69.5 (0.02)	59.0 (0.02)	2.30 (0.06)
University education	79.2 (0.02)	76.4 (0.02)	1.83 (0.07)
Poland			
Primary education or less	18.7 (0.01)	17.6 (0.01)	2.42 (0.06)
Lower secondary education	35.6 (0.01)	28.9 (0.01)	2.34 (0.04)
Upper secondary education	46.5 (0.02)	37.0 (0.02)	2.04 (0.05)
Non-university tertiary education	68.2 (0.03)	47.8 (0.03)	1.63 (0.09)
University education	69.6 (0.03)	53.4 (0.03)	1.60 (0.07)
Sweden[1]			
Primary education or less	39.4 (0.03)	21.4 (0.02)	— —
Lower secondary education	45.9 (0.03)	29.6 (0.02)	— —
Upper secondary education	48.9 (0.02)	32.6 (0.01)	— —
Non-university tertiary education	69.5 (0.03)	45.8 (0.03)	— —
University education	71.3 (0.03)	53.6 (0.03)	— —
Switzerland (French)			
Primary education or less	40.8 (0.04)	31.3 (0.04)	2.19 (0.12)
Lower secondary education	45.9 (0.04)	27.3 (0.03)	2.15 (0.11)
Upper secondary education	53.2 (0.02)	45.4 (0.02)	1.90 (0.05)
Non-university tertiary education	62.3 (0.04)	54.0 (0.05)	1.39 (0.11)
University education	76.7 (0.03)	75.8 (0.03)	1.31 (0.09)
Switzerland (German)			
Primary education or less	39.1*(0.07)	26.3*(0.06)	2.15 (0.20)
Lower secondary education	29.2 (0.03)	22.5 (0.03)	1.81 (0.11)
Upper secondary education	56.2 (0.02)	45.7 (0.02)	1.37 (0.04)
Non-university tertiary education	58.2 (0.04)	49.1 (0.04)	1.26 (0.10)
University education	89.0 (0.03)	70.0 (0.05)	1.08 (0.12)
United Kingdom			
Primary education or less	34.9 (0.02)	40.4 (0.02)	3.24 (0.08)
Lower secondary education	40.4 (0.01)	35.3 (0.01)	3.15 (0.03)
Upper secondary education	48.3 (0.01)	44.1 (0.01)	2.80 (0.04)
Non-university tertiary education	65.7 (0.02)	56.5 (0.02)	2.34 (0.06)
University education	73.5 (0.02)	68.3 (0.02)	2.05 (0.05)
United States			
Primary education or less	32.4 (0.03)	28.4 (0.03)	2.72 (0.12)
Lower secondary education	43.2 (0.03)	47.9 (0.03)	2.92 (0.11)
Upper secondary education	46.4 (0.01)	33.5 (0.01)	2.48 (0.05)
Non-university tertiary education	60.8 (0.02)	47.4 (0.02)	2.15 (0.08)
University education	61.4 (0.02)	52.3 (0.02)	1.79 (0.05)

[1] Australia and Sweden did not ask about television viewing.

[2] Non-university tertiary education does not apply in the Netherlands.

* Unreliable estimate.

Source: International Adult Literacy Survey, 1994-1995.

TABLE 3.11

Distribution of index scores for engagement in literacy activities at work by level of educational attainment, 1994-1995

	Literacy engagement at work						
	Mean	Standard error of the mean	Mini-mum	25th per-centile	Median	75th per-centile	Maxi-mum
Australia							
Lower secondary education or less	-0.54	0.02	-1.63	-1.26	-0.68	0.09	1.89
Upper secondary education	-0.27	0.03	-1.63	-1.06	-0.30	0.44	1.89
Non-university tertiary education	-0.01	0.02	-1.63	-0.66	0.02	0.65	1.89
University education	0.33	0.02	-1.63	-0.15	0.40	0.89	1.89
Belgium (Flanders)							
Lower secondary education or less	-0.78	0.04	-1.63	-1.53	-1.05	-0.21	1.89
Upper secondary education	-0.25	0.04	-1.63	-0.95	-0.35	0.43	1.82
Non-university tertiary education	0.06	0.05	-1.63	-0.50	0.02	0.59	1.89
University education	0.50	0.06	-1.63	-0.05	0.54	1.10	1.89
Canada							
Lower secondary education or less	-0.51	0.04	-1.63	-1.34	-0.80	0.24	1.89
Upper secondary education	-0.10	0.03	-1.63	-0.90	-0.19	0.59	1.89
Non-university tertiary education	0.31	0.04	-1.63	-0.39	0.23	0.96	1.89
University education	0.53	0.03	-1.63	0.01	0.58	1.20	1.89
Germany							
Lower secondary education or less	0.03	0.04	-1.63	-0.68	0.14	0.73	1.89
Upper secondary education	0.31	0.05	-1.63	-0.33	0.42	0.95	1.89
Non-university tertiary education	0.44	0.13	-1.34	-0.43	0.56	1.09	1.80
University education	0.42	0.06	-1.25	-0.09	0.55	0.96	1.89
Ireland							
Lower secondary education or less	-0.64	0.04	-1.63	-1.49	-0.86	-0.03	1.89
Upper secondary education	-0.07	0.05	-1.63	-0.95	-0.08	0.85	1.89
Non-university tertiary education	0.29	0.07	-1.63	-0.35	0.45	0.92	1.81
University education	0.45	0.06	-1.63	-0.09	0.54	1.08	1.89
Netherlands[1]							
Lower secondary education or less	-0.51	0.04	-1.63	-1.34	-0.57	0.17	1.89
Upper secondary education	0.00	0.03	-1.63	-0.61	-0.01	0.69	1.89
University education	0.38	0.04	-1.63	-0.17	0.43	0.99	1.89
New Zealand							
Lower secondary education or less	-0.17	0.03	-1.63	-1.12	-0.24	0.70	1.89
Upper secondary education	0.01	0.04	-1.63	-0.83	0.08	0.79	1.89
Non-university tertiary education	0.39	0.04	-1.63	-0.21	0.44	1.05	1.89
University education	0.60	0.05	-1.63	0.15	0.69	1.14	1.89
Poland							
Lower secondary education or less	-1.17	0.02	-1.63	-1.63	-1.41	-0.93	1.70
Upper secondary education	-0.34	0.04	-1.63	-1.03	-0.38	0.27	1.71
Non-university tertiary education	-0.34	0.07	-1.63	-0.87	-0.44	0.11	1.62
University education	0.10	0.05	-1.63	-0.39	0.08	0.59	1.89
Sweden							
Lower secondary education or less	-0.32	0.04	-1.63	-1.10	-0.34	0.31	1.89
Upper secondary education	0.01	0.03	-1.63	-0.63	0.04	0.68	1.89
Non-university tertiary education	0.26	0.05	-1.63	-0.18	0.25	0.79	1.89
University education	0.40	0.05	-1.63	-0.09	0.46	0.96	1.89
Switzerland (French)							
Lower secondary education or less	-0.38	0.06	-1.63	-1.16	-0.41	0.37	1.73
Upper secondary education	0.09	0.04	-1.63	-0.48	0.12	0.69	1.89
Non-university tertiary education	0.50	0.07	-1.63	0.04	0.56	1.07	1.89
University education	0.42	0.07	-1.63	-0.08	0.42	1.01	1.89

TABLE 3.11 (concluded)

Distribution of index scores for engagement in literacy activities at work by level of educational attainment, 1994-1995

	Literacy engagement at work						
	Mean	Standard error of the mean	Mini-mum	25th per-centile	Median	75th per-centile	Maxi-mum
Switzerland (German)							
Lower secondary education or less	-0.65	0.07	-1.63	-1.34	-0.70	0.00	1.42
Upper secondary education	0.24	0.03	-1.63	-0.30	0.32	0.85	1.89
Non-university tertiary education	0.66	0.06	-1.63	0.06	0.72	1.22	1.89
University education	0.68	0.08	-1.01	0.19	0.74	1.15	1.89
United Kingdom							
Lower secondary education or less	-0.33	0.02	-1.63	-1.14	-0.41	0.39	1.89
Upper secondary education	0.07	0.03	-1.63	-0.69	0.08	0.86	1.89
Non-university tertiary education	0.32	0.04	-1.63	-0.22	0.38	0.90	1.89
University education	0.54	0.03	-1.56	0.13	0.61	1.03	1.89
United States							
Lower secondary education or less	-0.87	0.06	-1.63	-1.63	-1.18	-0.37	1.89
Upper secondary education	-0.13	0.03	-1.63	-0.98	-0.18	0.69	1.89
Non-university tertiary education	0.41	0.05	-1.63	-0.21	0.51	1.12	1.89
University education	0.60	0.03	-1.63	0.16	0.70	1.19	1.89

[1] Non-university tertiary education does not apply in the Netherlands.

Source: International Adult Literacy Survey, 1994-1995.

TABLE 3.12

Index scores for engagement in literacy activities at work by industrial groups for Germany and the United States, 1994-1995

	Literacy engagement at work						
	Mean	Standard error of the mean	Mini-mum	25th per centile	Median	75th per centile	Maxi-mum
Germany							
Agriculture and mining	-0.29	0.20	-1.63	-1.63	-0.07	0.68	1.47
Manufacturing	0.20	0.06	-1.63	-0.46	0.30	0.86	1.89
Construction and transport	-0.10	0.07	-1.63	-0.86	-0.08	0.55	1.89
Trade and hospitality	0.26	0.07	-1.63	-0.48	0.38	1.01	1.89
Financial services	0.72	0.07	-1.63	0.39	0.74	1.17	1.89
Personal services	0.16	0.04	-1.63	-0.34	0.22	0.74	1.89
United States							
Agriculture and mining	-0.27	0.16	-1.63	-1.38	-0.35	0.72	1.89*
Manufacturing	-0.15	0.06	-1.63	-1.10	-0.22	0.75	1.89
Construction and transport	0.04	0.06	-1.63	-0.84	0.14	0.96	1.89
Trade and hospitality	0.02	0.06	-1.63	-0.95	0.02	1.05	1.89
Financial services	0.37	0.06	-1.63	-0.22	0.54	1.06	1.89
Personal services	0.12	0.03	-1.63	-0.60	0.27	0.86	1.89

* Unreliable estimate.

Source: International Adult Literacy Survey, 1994-1995.

TABLE 4.1

Per cent of population aged 16-65[1] participating in adult education and training during the year preceding the interview, by document literacy level, 1994-1995

	Total participation rate	Level 1	Level 2	Level 3	Level 4/5
Australia	38.8 (0.7)	13.6 (1.2)	29.3 (1.2)	46.5 (1.2)	62.4 (1.5)
Belgium (Flanders)	21.2 (1.1)	4.4* (1.3)	15.1 (2.4)	25.6 (1.6)	37.2 (3.2)
Canada	37.7 (1.0)	16.6 (6.2)	29.4 (2.4)	39.6 (2.9)	60.4 (2.2)
Ireland	24.3 (2.3)	10.1 (2.0)	19.6 (2.3)	34.2 (2.8)	47.3 (4.2)
Netherlands	37.4 (1.2)	16.8 (2.3)	27.0 (1.6)	41.6 (1.8)	53.4 (3.1)
New Zealand	47.5 (1.2)	28.7 (2.3)	40.8 (2.3)	55.2 (2.0)	68.3 (1.9)
Poland	13.9 (0.9)	8.4 (1.0)	14.8 (1.8)	22.8 (2.4)	31.9 (6.2)
Sweden	52.5 (1.1)	29.3 (5.2)	40.1 (2.2)	54.5 (1.8)	61.6 (1.3)
Switzerland (French)	33.7 (2.1)	20.4 (3.6)	24.3 (3.5)	40.9 (1.9)	46.4 (4.4)
Switzerland (German)	44.7 (1.1)	20.2 (3.3)	37.3 (3.0)	50.7 (2.0)	68.9 (4.3)
United Kingdom	43.9 (0.9)	21.8 (1.7)	33.6 (1.8)	53.9 (1.8)	70.7 (2.0)
United States	39.7 (1.4)	17.3 (2.1)	32.3 (1.8)	49.0 (1.8)	59.1 (3.0)

*   Unreliable estimate.

[1]   Full-time students aged 16-24 and people who obtained less than 6 hours of training are excluded.

Source: International Adult Literacy Survey, 1994-1995.

TABLE 4.2

Per cent of population[1] aged 16-65 participating in adult education and training during the year preceding the interview, by level of educational attainment, 1994-1995

	Primary education or less	Lower secondary education	Upper secondary education	Non-university tertiary education	University education
Australia	8.4* (1.8)	28.8 (1.0)	41.9 (1.4)	50.0 (2.4)	60.8 (1.7)
Belgium (Flanders)	4.6* (2.2)	13.3 (2.2)	22.0 (1.6)	37.8 (2.2)	45.6 (3.3)
Canada	15.4 (4.0)	25.6 (4.0)	33.9 (2.4)	51.8 (7.0)	59.5 (8.7)
Ireland	8.6 (1.2)	17.6 (2.9)	29.4 (2.4)	44.1 (4.5)	51.0 (4.0)
Netherlands[2]	17.2 (2.8)	29.0 (2.4)	44.5 (1.9)	—	51.4 (2.1)
New Zealand	6.8* (3.4)	37.8 (1.9)	52.0 (2.4)	60.4 (2.3)	71.5 (2.9)
Poland	2.7* (0.6)	9.9 (1.2)	20.6 (2.3)	32.5 (4.8)	34.3 (3.0)
Sweden	27.0 (2.1)	46.7 (3.3)	52.8 (1.9)	66.6 (2.7)	70.4 (1.9)
Switzerland (French)	9.5* (4.8)	15.0* (3.3)	35.7 (3.1)	51.0 (6.5)	51.0 (4.0)
Switzerland (German)	6.7* (4.3)	22.9* (4.4)	48.0 (2.0)	59.1 (4.5)	63.4 (4.7)
United Kingdom	23.4 (2.9)	34.2 (1.3)	53.2 (3.1)	60.7 (3.2)	73.7 (2.1)
United States	10.3 (3.0)	21.0 (3.8)	30.7 (2.3)	54.9 (2.4)	64.2 (2.2)

*   Unreliable estimate.

[1]   Full-time students aged 16-24 and people who obtained less than 6 hours of training are excluded.

[2]   The tertiary non-university category does not apply in the Netherlands.

Source: International Adult Literacy Survey, 1994-1995.

TABLE 4.3

Adjusted odds[a,b] ratios indicating the likelihood of adults aged 16-65 receiving adult education and training during the year preceding the interview, by level of educational attainment, 1994-1995

	Primary education or less	Lower secondary education	Upper secondary education	Non-university tertiary education	University education
Australia	1.00	2.6 [1] (.19)	4.3 [1] (.19)	7.6 [1] (.20)	11.2 [1] (.20)
Belgium (Flanders)	1.00	3.2 [1] (.31)	5.9 [1] (.29)	12.8 [1] (.31)	17.0 [1] (.32)
Canada	1.00	1.4 [2] (.16)	1.9 [1] (.14)	4.4 [1] (.15)	6.5 [1] (.15)
Ireland	1.00	1.9 [1] (.20)	3.4 [1] (.19)	6.8 [1] (.22)	9.7 [1] (.22)
Netherlands[c]	1.00	1.8 [1] (.16)	3.2 [1] (.15)	—	4.5 [1] (.16)
New Zealand	1.00	5.3 [1] (.47)	8.1 [1] (.47)	14.0 [1] (.47)	21.7 [1] (.48)
Poland	1.00	2.8 [1] (.26)	7.8 [1] (.26)	14.9 [1] (.29)	16.7 [1] (.28)
Sweden	1.00	2.1 [1] (.18)	2.8 [1] (.15)	4.7 [1] (.18)	5.6 [1] (.19)
Switzerland (French)	1.00	1.6 [3] (.39)	3.9 [1] (.34)	7.6 [1] (.38)	7.4 [1] (.37)
Switzerland (German)	1.00	3.6 [2] (.61)	10.7 [1] (.59)	18.0 [1] (.61)	24.0 [1] (.62)
United Kingdom	1.00	1.3 [2] (.14)	2.5 [1] (.14)	4.4 [1] (.16)	7.1 [1] (.16)
United States	1.00	2.1 [1] (.29)	3.6 [1] (.22)	9.8 [1] (.23)	15.7 [1] (.22)

[a]   Odds are adjusted for gender and age.

[b]   Standard errors are for the logarithm of the odds ratio.

[c]   The non-university tertiary category does not apply in the Netherlands.

[1] $p < .01$.

[2] $p < .05$.

[3] $p > .05$ not statistically significant.

Source: International Adult Literacy Survey, 1994-1995.

TABLE 4.4

Per cent of population aged 16-65 participating in adult education and training during the year preceding the interview, by 10-year age intervals, 1994-1995

	Age	Participation rate	
Australia	16-25	58.5	(1.4)
	26-35	40.2	(1.5)
	36-45	39.3	(1.5)
	46-55	30.1	(1.5)
	56-65	16.8	(1.5)
Belgium (Flanders)	16-25	19.3	(5.4)
	26-35	24.6	(1.9)
	36-45	22.1	(1.9)
	46-55	22.9	(2.5)
	56-65	11.8	(2.2)
Canada	16-25	57.6	(3.8)
	26-35	39.2	(2.6)
	36-45	40.7	(3.3)
	46-55	32.7	(5.3)
	56-65	14.7	(3.6)
Ireland	16-25	34.6	(3.6)
	26-35	27.0	(2.7)
	36-45	25.0	(3.5)
	46-55	18.4	(3.7)
	56-65	9.1*	(1.9)
Netherlands	16-25	49.3	(3.2)
	26-35	45.1	(1.6)
	36-45	39.5	(1.9)
	46-55	30.3	(2.0)
	56-65	17.0	(2.5)
New Zealand	16-25	66.6	(2.8)
	26-35	49.9	(2.0)
	36-45	47.6	(1.9)
	46-55	40.3	(2.6)
	56-65	26.1	(3.6)
Poland	16-25	17.2	(2.1)
	26-35	17.0	(1.1)
	36-45	17.7	(1.6)
	46-55	10.9	(1.5)
	56-65	2.8*	(0.9)
Sweden	16-25	45.6	(3.3)
	26-35	57.0	(2.7)
	36-45	60.7	(2.3)
	46-55	57.1	(1.8)
	56-65	34.7	(2.8)
Switzerland (German)	16-25	56.2	(4.0)
	26-35	51.4	(2.5)
	36-45	44.8	(4.0)
	46-55	40.9	(2.6)
	56-65	28.0	(4.7)
Switzerland (French)	16-25	44.7	(6.4)
	26-35	40.2	(2.9)
	36-45	38.3	(4.6)
	46-55	28.5	(3.3)
	56-65	13.5*	(2.6)
United Kingdom	16-25	59.0	(2.9)
	26-35	48.9	(1.4)
	36-45	49.3	(2.1)
	46-55	39.3	(1.9)
	56-65	18.1	(1.9)
United States	16-25	45.8	(6.1)
	26-35	43.5	(2.8)
	36-45	41.2	(2.0)
	46-55	41.5	(2.1)
	56-65	24.6	(2.9)

*   Unreliable estimate.

Source: International Adult Literacy Survey, 1994-1995.

TABLE 4.5

Mean hours of study by age groups, participants aged 16-65, 1994-1995

	Age	Mean hours of training per participant	Standard error of the mean
Australia	16-25	492.4	15.7
	26-35	201.6	11.6
	36-45	151.6	10.0
	46-55	145.2	14.6
	56-65	112.5	19.0
Belgium (Flanders)	16-25	184.8	59.5
	26-35	118.4	15.6
	36-45	142.4	26.8
	46-55	115.1	24.1
	56-65	104.2	43.9
Canada	16-25	731.3	41.1
	26-35	248.2	21.0
	36-45	141.8	13.7
	46-55	240.3	27.8
	56-65	116.3	17.8
Ireland	16-25	611.4	58.2
	26-35	262.9	32.7
	36-45	196.5	33.7
	46-55	184.4	42.2
	56-65	127.0	58.3
Netherlands	16-25	525.5	46.3
	26-35	243.3	24.6
	36-45	154.2	21.7
	46-55	99.6	13.8
	56-65	80.1	10.9
New Zealand	16-25	534.9	30.2
	26-35	299.9	27.2
	36-45	186.6	18.8
	46-55	103.2	14.0
	56-65	125.1	27.7
Poland	16-25	216.5	37.6
	26-35	178.8	25.7
	36-45	115.7	20.4
	46-55	104.0	25.4
	56-65	126.1	46.2
Sweden[1]	16-25	—	—
	26-35	—	—
	36-45	—	—
	46-55	—	—
	56-65	—	—
Switzerland (German)	16-25	245.6	42.7
	26-35	154.5	20.7
	36-45	86.6	10.5
	46-55	119.3	20.8
	56-65	58.4	6.9
Switzerland (French)	16-25	255.6	46.1
	26-35	181.2	30.3
	36-45	105.7	19.3
	46-55	95.5	16.4
	56-65	72.9	13.1
United Kingdom	16-25	526.7	22.4
	26-35	145.5	13.1
	36-45	139.5	10.8
	46-55	76.4	7.5
	56-65	49.5	5.0
United States	16-25	441.3	43.3
	26-35	160.7	21.5
	36-45	130.2	19.6
	46-55	62.0	6.0
	56-65	53.8	10.6

* Unreliable estimate.

[1] The Swedish survey did not collect information on training duration.

Source: International Adult Literacy Survey, 1994-1995.

TABLE 4.6

Share of employer- or non-employer-sponsored courses in total adult education and training provision, and average hours, for the employed and general adult population aged 16-65, by gender, 1994-1995

| | Per cent courses | | | | | |
| | Employer-sponsored | | | Non-employer-sponsored | | |
	Total	Men	Women	Total	Men	Women
Australia						
Employed	54.4	33.7	20.7	45.6	20.3	25.3
General population	49.1	30.4	18.7	50.9	22.1	28.7
Belgium (Flanders)						
Employed	55.8	37.7	18.1	44.2	24.9	19.3
General population	48.1	32.1	16.0	51.9	23.0	28.9
Canada						
Employed	52.6	29.6	23.1	47.4	24.6	22.8
General population	45.1	25.2	19.9	54.9	25.4	29.5
Ireland						
Employed	51.5	31.8	19.7	48.5	21.9	26.6
General population	40.4	24.3	16.0	59.6	23.4	36.3
Netherlands						
Employed	62.4	43.6	18.8	37.6	18.8	18.9
General population	50.6	35.1	15.5	49.4	19.6	29.8
New Zealand						
Employed	59.7	32.4	27.3	40.3	17.6	22.6
General population	52.4	28.1	24.3	47.6	19.6	28.0
Poland						
Employed	66.7	39.9	26.8	33.3	14.9	18.4
General population	59.5	35.0	24.5	40.5	19.3	21.1
Sweden						
Employed	88.3	43.0	45.3	11.7	5.5	6.2
General population	79.4	38.5	40.9	20.6	9.5	11.1
Switzerland (German)						
Employed	47.8	29.9	17.9	52.2	23.5	28.7
General population	42.4	26.0	16.4	57.6	23.2	34.4
Switzerland (French)						
Employed	51.3	31.6	19.7	48.7	26.9	21.8
General population	45.6	28.1	17.5	54.4	26.4	28.0
United Kingdom						
Employed	73.0	41.5	31.5	27.0	12.6	14.4
General population	66.9	38.2	28.7	33.1	14.8	18.3
United States						
Employed	63.3	33.3	30.1	36.7	16.9	19.8
General population	60.3	31.1	29.3	39.7	16.7	23.0

TABLE 4.6   (concluded)

Share of employer- or non-employer-sponsored courses in total adult education and training provision, and average hours, for the employed and general adult population aged 16-65, by gender, 1994-1995

| | Average hours | | | | | |
| | Employer-sponsored | | | Non-employer-sponsored | | |
	Total	Men	Women	Total	Men	Women
Australia						
Employed	121.3	138.8	91.1	351.6	352.4	351.0
General population	120.5	137.4	91.5	358.2	393.1	331.6
Belgium (Flanders)						
Employed	84.6	86.0	81.7	153.3	157.2	149.1
General population	84.3	85.9	81.1	165.3	158.5	169.7
Canada						
Employed	91.8	97.8	84.4	429.8	471.8	379.6
General population	99.9	113.0	83.7	476.5	520.4	437.3
Ireland						
Employed	192.0	178.1	215.0	304.0	313.9	296.0
General population	195.6	179.0	221.5	349.2	408.8	313.0
Netherlands						
Employed	159.9	142.1	202.0	320.6	366.3	271.7
General population	158.7	141.7	198.4	323.8	444.5	242.9
New Zealand						
Employed	112.5	129.7	91.1	430.4	420.3	438.2
General population	119.7	140.9	93.8	444.9	458.0	435.7
Poland						
Employed	117.0	126.9	101.7	195.9	183.9	206.4
General population	117.2	126.3	103.7	202.0	208.9	195.6
Sweden[1]						
Employed	—	—	—	—	—	—
General population	—	—	—	—	—	—
Switzerland (German)						
Employed	102.2	116.7	78.6	121.6	115.3	126.4
General population	103.4	118.2	80.3	153.0	132.8	165.7
Switzerland (French)						
Employed	84.3	100.7	56.8	165.5	230.6	82.0
General population	94.5	117.2	56.1	194.8	247.6	145.7
United Kingdom						
Employed	92.4	117.8	59.2	352.3	323.5	377.3
General population	93.3	117.0	62.3	410.2	427.6	396.3
United States						
Employed	73.7	95.3	49.3	286.7	360.3	225.3
General population	76.8	95.9	56.1	323.4	450.1	235.1

[1]   The Swedish survey did not ask about training duration.

Source: International Adult Literacy Survey, 1994-1995.

TABLE 4.7

Per cent of participants in adult education and training who receive financial support[1] from various sources, by gender, for the general population and employed population aged 16-65, 1994-1995

			General population	Employed population
Australia	Self or family	Men	22.5	22.7
		Women	29.5	27.7
	Employers	Men	28.4	32.3
		Women	18.0	20.3
	Government	Men	8.3	6.6
		Women	7.3	5.7
	Other	Men	3.7	3.7
		Women	3.8	3.5
Belgium (Flanders)	Self or family	Men	21.0	23.6
		Women	27.0	18.6
	Employers	Men	33.1	40.1
		Women	17.3	20.0
	Government	Men	7.3*	8.2*
		Women	5.9*	4.3*
	Other	Men	4.1*	4.6*
		Women	6.0*	3.6*
Canada	Self or family	Men	22.9	25.7
		Women	27.7	23.9
	Employers	Men	25.9	31.9
		Women	19.8	24.2
	Government	Men	9.8	8.2
		Women	13.9	10.3
	Other	Men	6.0	5.9
		Women	5.2	5.3
Ireland	Self or family	Men	13.8	13.9
		Women	27.3	21.1
	Employers	Men	21.4	29.2
		Women	16.3	21.0
	Government	Men	9.5	8.0*
		Women	7.6	6.0*
	Other	Men	4.7*	5.1*
		Women	5.2	3.1*
Netherlands	Self or family	Men	17.4	18.3
		Women	29.6	20.6
	Employers	Men	34.0	43.6
		Women	16.5	20.6
	Government	Men	6.5	6.0
		Women	5.3	4.0
	Other	Men	3.5	3.1*
		Women	2.9	1.6*
New Zealand	Self or family	Men	18.8	20.6
		Women	27.2	23.4
	Employers	Men	27.6	32.9
		Women	24.5	28.6
	Government	Men	11.3	9.6
		Women	13.3	11.5
	Other	Men	5.6	6.0
		Women	7.8	6.1
Poland	Self or family	Men	16.1	12.8
		Women	19.3	18.1
	Employers	Men	34.0	39.3
		Women	23.8	26.6
	Government	Men	3.3*	2.2*
		Women	3.7*	2.6*
	Other	Men	7.5*	7.7*
		Women	5.7*	5.6*

TABLE 4.7 (concluded)

Per cent of participants in adult education and training who receive financial support[1] from various sources, by gender, for the general population and employed population aged 16-65, 1994-1995

			General population	Employed population
Sweden	Self or family	Men	—	—
		Women	—	—
	Employers	Men	48.5	48.7
		Women	51.5	51.3
	Government	Men	—	—
		Women	—	—
	Other	Men	—	—
		Women	—	—
Switzerland (French)	Self or family	Men	25.8	27.4
		Women	28.3	24.0
	Employers	Men	30.2	34.8
		Women	17.5	19.9
	Government	Men	9.3	8.6
		Women	5.9*	4.5*
	Other	Men	4.7*	5.0*
		Women	4.6*	3.2*
Switzerland (German)	Self or family	Men	25.8	27.7
		Women	34.4	28.4
	Employers	Men	27.8	32.1
		Women	19.9	21.6
	Government	Men	8.0	7.5
		Women	8.6	8.2
	Other	Men	3.1*	3.2*
		Women	4.8*	4.6*
United Kingdom	Self or family	Men	9.6	9.2
		Women	14.4	11.8
	Employers	Men	37.8	42.4
		Women	29.2	32.8
	Government	Men	9.6	7.8
		Women	10.6	8.2
	Other	Men	5.2	5.1
		Women	3.7	3.2
United States	Self or family	Men	16.1	17.1
		Women	21.1	17.8
	Employers	Men	32.4	35.4
		Women	30.1	31.3
	Government	Men	4.8	5.1
		Women	6.5	5.9
	Other	Men	3.2	3.2
		Women	5.0	4.5

*   Unreliable estimate.

[1]   Respondents could indicate more than one source of financial support so totals may exceed 100 per cent for a country. The Swedish survey only asked about employer-sponsored training.

Source: International Adult Literacy Survey, 1994-1995.

TABLE 4.8

Per cent of non-employer-sponsored and employer-sponsored courses taken for job-related reasons, persons aged 16-65, 1994-1995

	Non-employer sponsored	Employer sponsored
Australia	70.4	94.8
Belgium (Flanders)	56.3	89.1
Canada	71.0	91.1
Ireland	60.2	93.5
Netherlands	46.9	81.5
New Zealand	63.2	93.0
Poland	58.2	92.8
Sweden[1]	—	—
Switzerland (French)	54.1	79.2
Switzerland (German)	45.9	79.7
United Kingdom	63.8	93.7
United States	75.6	95.4

[1] Sweden is excluded from this table because the wording of the question asked in that country's survey differed.

Source: International Adult Literacy Survey, 1994-1995.

TABLE 4.9

Odds and adjusted odds[a,b] of participating in employer-sponsored adult education and training by firm size, persons aged 16-65, 1994-1995

	20 or fewer employees	20-99 employees	100-199 employees	200-499 employees	500 or more employees
Australia					
Odds ratio	1.00	3.22 [1] (.11)	4.19 [1] (.15)	5.35 [1] (.14)	6.62 [1] (.09)
Adjusted odds	1.00	2.44 [1] (.12)	3.05 [1] (.16)	3.32 [1] (.15)	4.03 [1] (.10)
Canada					
Odds ratio	1.00	3.32 [1] (.16)	1.30 [3] (.22)	3.85 [1] (.20)	4.78 [1] (.13)
Adjusted odds	1.00	3.44 [1] (.18)	0.98 [3] (.25)	2.73 [1] (.21)	3.47 [1] (.15)
Ireland					
Odds ratio	1.00	2.47 [1] (.32)	4.23 [1] (.36)	4.73 [1] (.32)	4.73 [1] (.25)
Adjusted odds	1.00	2.61 [1] (.37)	2.93 [1] (.43)	3.16 [1] (.39)	3.45 [1] (.30)
New Zealand					
Odds ratio	1.00	3.29 [1] (.14)	3.51 [1] (.19)	5.69 [1] (.18)	5.3 [1] (.12)
Adjusted odds	1.00	2.65 [1] (.15)	3.37 [1] (.21)	4.25 [1] (.20)	4.53 [1] (.13)
Poland					
Odds ratio	1.00	3.43 [1] (.23)	4.76 [1] (.28)	3.00 [1] (.30)	4.90 [1] (.22)
Adjusted odds	1.00	1.93 [1] (.26)	2.34 [1] (.32)	1.67 [3] (.34)	3.09 [1] (.27)
Switzerland (French)					
Odds ratio	1.00	2.04 [2] (.32)	2.65 [1] (.29)	3.29 [1] (.31)	4.62 [1] (.23)
Adjusted odds	1.00	1.77 [3] (.39)	3.27 [1] (.35)	3.66 [1] (.39)	4.78 [1] (.30)
Switzerland (German)					
Odds ratio	1.00	1.51 [3] (.24)	1.68 [2] (.25)	2.47 [1] (.29)	3.39 [1] (.19)
Adjusted odds	1.00	1.29 [3] (.27)	1.36 [3] (.29)	2.23 [2] (.33)	2.69 [1] (.22)
United Kingdom					
Odds ratio	1.00	3.15 [1] (.15)	3.03 [1] (.18)	6.82 [1] (.18)	6.98 [1] (.13)
Adjusted odds	1.00	2.35 [1] (.17)	2.40 [1] (.20)	4.16 [1] (.21)	5.62 [1] (.14)
United States					
Odds ratio	1.00	2.04 [1] (.19)	1.93 [1] (.24)	3.44 [1] (.20)	5.38 [1] (.14)
Adjusted odds	1.00	1.76 [1] (.20)	1.91 [1] (.27)	3.05 [1] (.22)	4.28 [1] (.16)

[a] Odds are adjusted for occupational status, industry classification, literacy engagement at work, and full- or part-time work.

[b] Standard errors are of the logarithm of the odds ratio.

[1] $p < .01$.

[2] $p < .05$.

[3] $p > .05$ not statistically significant.

Note: Belgium (Flanders), Netherlands and Sweden are excluded because the surveys did not ask about firm size.

Source: International Adult Literacy Survey, 1994-1995.

TABLE 4.10

Odds and adjusted odds[a,b] of participating in employer-sponsored adult education and training, by occupational status, persons aged 16-65, 1994-1995

	Blue-collar worker[c]	Clerk	Services worker	Manager	Technician	Professional
Australia						
Odds ratio	1.00	1.97 [1] (.09)	0.88 [3] (.11)	2.62 [1] (.11)	2.49 [1] (.11)	3.31 [1] (.09)
Adjusted odds	1.00	1.14 [3] (.11)	0.85 [3] (.14)	1.37 [2] (.14)	1.23 [3] (.13)	1.35 [1] (.12)
Canada						
Odds ratio	1.00	2.06 [1] (.15)	1.47 [2] (.16)	2.52 [1] (.17)	3.24 [1] (.15)	4.8 [1] (.13)
Adjusted odds	1.00	1.39 [3] (.19)	2.07 [1] (.22)	1.91 [1] (.21)	2.95 [1] (.21)	2.41 [1] (.19)
Ireland						
Odds ratio	1.00	3.22 [1] (.23)	1.46 [3] (.29)	2.05 [2] (.33)	3.42 [1] (.26)	3.01 [1] (.23)
Adjusted odds	1.00	1.69 [3] (.35)	1.43 [3] (.39)	1.88 [3] (.42)	2.10 [2] (.34)	1.72 [3] (.35)
Netherlands[d]						
Odds ratio	1.00	1.41 [3] (.19)	0.73 [3] (.22)	1.09 [3] (.20)	1.86 [1] (.15)	2.45 [1] (.16)
Adjusted odds	1.00	0.96 [3] (.22)	0.83 [3] (.26)	0.72 [3] (.23)	0.85 [3] (.19)	0.97 [3] (.21)
New Zealand						
Odds ratio	1.00	2.20 [1] (.14)	0.97 [3] (.15)	2.44 [1] (.14)	3.07 [1] (.15)	3.59 [1] (.15)
Adjusted odds	1.00	1.10 [3] (.18)	0.76 [3] (.20)	1.32 [3] (.18)	1.23 [3] (.19)	1.55 [2] (.21)
Poland						
Odds ratio	1.00	3.43 [1] (.26)	0.63 [3] (.37)	2.92 [1] (.31)	2.80 [1] (.20)	4.79 [1] (.22)
Adjusted odds	1.00	1.59 [3] (.32)	0.62 [3] (.44)	1.47 [3] (.36)	1.40 [3] (.26)	1.89 [2] (.30)
Sweden[d]						
Odds ratio	1.00	1.76 [1] (.22)	1.53 [1] (.17)	2.46 [1] (.24)	3.32 [1] (.14)	3.45 [1] (.13)
Adjusted odds	1.00	0.99 [3] (.25)	1.31 [3] (.21)	1.35 [3] (.27)	2.10 [1] (.18)	2.15 [1] (.17)
Switzerland (French)						
Odds ratio	1.00	1.26 [3] (.29)	1.43 [3] (.31)	3.40 [1] (.28)	3.13 [1] (.24)	2.12 [1] (.27)
Adjusted odds	1.00	0.78 [3] (.37)	1.42 [3] (.46)	2.85 [1] (.37)	2.20 [1] (.31)	1.38 [3] (.36)
Switzerland (German)						
Odds ratio	1.00	1.53 [3] (.28)	1.34 [3] (.26)	2.65 [1] (.27)	2.52 [1] (.21)	2.86 [1] (.24)
Adjusted odds	1.00	0.97 [3] (.33)	0.97 [3] (.34)	1.49 [3] (.31)	1.51 [3] (.25)	1.48 [3] (.30)
United Kingdom						
Odds ratio	1.00	2.02 [1] (.09)	1.51 [1] (.09)	2.29 [1] (.10)	2.90 [1] (.13)	4.37 [1] (.10)
Adjusted odds	1.00	0.96 [3] (.12)	1.57 [1] (.14)	1.40 [2] (.14)	1.77 [1] (.17)	1.91 [1] (.14)
United States						
Odds ratio	1.00	3.11 [1] (.16)	1.11 [3] (.16)	3.44 [1] (.16)	4.54 [1] (.25)	4.79 [1] (.16)
Adjusted odds	1.00	1.34 [3] (.20)	1.07 [3] (.21)	1.54 [2] (.20)	2.10 [1] (.30)	1.90 [1] (.21)

[a] Odds are adjusted for literacy engagement at work, industry classification, firm size, and full- or part-time work.

[b] Standard errors are of the logarithm of the odds ratio.

[c] Blue-collar workers include skilled agricultural and fishery workers, craft and related trades workers, plant and machine operators and assemblers, and elementary occupations.

[d] Odds are not adjusted for firm size because the country omitted this question.

[1] $p < .01$.

[2] $p < .05$.

[3] $p > .05$ not statistically significant.

Note: Belgium (Flanders) is excluded because the survey did not ask about occupation in a comparable way.

Source: International Adult Literacy Survey, 1994-1995.

TABLE 4.11

Odds and adjusted odds[a,b] of receiving employer-sponsored adult education and training by the level of literacy engagement[c] at work, employed persons aged 16-65, 1994-1995

	1st quartile	2nd quartile	3rd quartile	4th quartile
Australia				
Odds ratio	1.00	1.95 [1] (.11)	5.06 [1] (.10)	8.74 [1] (.11)
Adjusted odds	1.00	1.57 [1] (.12)	2.96 [1] (.12)	3.93 [1] (.13)
Canada				
Odds ratio	1.00	2.03 [1] (.18)	5.42 [1] (.15)	8.98 [1] (.16)
Adjusted odds	1.00	1.37 [3] (.20)	2.85 [1] (.18)	4.76 [1] (.19)
Ireland				
Odds ratio	1.00	1.79 [2] (.26)	3.30 [1] (.23)	5.33 [1] (.23)
Adjusted odds	1.00	1.74 [3] (.33)	2.61 [1] (.32)	4.32 [1] (.33)
Netherlands[d]				
Odds ratio	1.00	2.44 [1] (.19)	5.33 [1] (.18)	7.01 [1] (.19)
Adjusted odds	1.00	2.31 [1] (.20)	4.34 [1] (.20)	5.27 [1] (.22)
New Zealand				
Odds ratio	1.00	2.83 [1] (.15)	5.40 [1] (.14)	6.55 [1] (.16)
Adjusted odds	1.00	2.49 [1] (.16)	3.56 [1] (.16)	3.56 [1] (.18)
Poland				
Odds ratio	1.00	2.66 [1] (.21)	3.58 [1] (.21)	7.90 [1] (.22)
Adjusted odds	1.00	1.67 [2] (.24)	2.04 [1] (.25)	3.55 [1] (.28)
Sweden[d]				
Odds ratio	1.00	2.03 [1] (.18)	4.10 [1] (.17)	6.56 [1] (.17)
Adjusted odds	1.00	1.73 [1] (.19)	2.80 [1] (.18)	4.35 [1] (.18)
Switzerland (French)				
Odds ratio	1.00	3.22 [1] (.36)	4.66 [1] (.34)	5.17 [1] (.35)
Adjusted odds	1.00	2.18 [3] (.41)	2.83 [1] (.40)	2.18 [3] (.42)
Switzerland (German)				
Odds ratio	1.00	2.73 [2] (.45)	6.42 [1] (.40)	10.20 [1] (.40)
Adjusted odds	1.00	3.16 [2] (.51)	5.37 [1] (.47)	8.76 [1] (.47)
United Kingdom				
Odds ratio	1.00	2.89 [1] (.11)	6.74 [1] (.10)	11.92 [1] (.11)
Adjusted odds	1.00	2.79 [1] (.13)	4.98 [1] (.13)	6.69 [1] (.14)
United States				
Odds ratio	1.00	4.25 [1] (.20)	9.29 [1] (.18)	13.01 [1] (.18)
Adjusted odds	1.00	3.41 [1] (.21)	5.70 [1] (.20)	6.83 [1] (.21)

[a]   Odds are adjusted for occupational status, industry classification, firm size, and full- or part-time work.

[b]   Standard errors are of the logarithm of the odds ratio.

[c]   The literacy engagement at work index is constructed using frequencies of nine literacy tasks – reading magazines or journals; manuals or reference books; diagrams or schematics; reports or articles; reading or writing letters or memos; bills, invoices or budgets; writing reports or articles; estimates or technical specifications; and calculating prices, costs or budgets. The 1st quartile represents workers who use workplace literacy skills the least; the 4th quartile represents workers who use workplace literacy skills the most.

[d]   Odds are not adjusted for firm size because the country omitted this question.

[1]   p < .01.

[2]   p < .05.

[3]   p > .05 not statistically significant.

Note: Data for Switzerland (French) are not shown in Figure 4.9 because the estimates are unreliable.

Source: International Adult Literacy Survey, 1994-1995.

Annex D

Participants in the Project

International management and co-ordination

Mr. T. Scott Murray, International Study Director
Statistics Canada, Ottawa

Mr. Albert Tuijnman
Organisation for Economic Co-operation and
Development, Paris

International survey and production team

Ms. Danielle Baum
Statistics Canada, Ottawa

Ms. Colleen Bolger
Statistics Canada, Ottawa

Ms. Nancy Darcovich
Statistics Canada, Ottawa

Mr. Richard Desjardins
Statistics Canada, Ottawa

Mr. Doug Giddings
Human Resources Development Canada, Hull

Mr. Stan Jones
Statistics Canada, Yarmouth

Mr. Irwin Kirsch
Educational Testing Service, Princeton

Ms. Johanne Lussier
Human Resources Development Canada, Hull

Ms. Marlène Mohier
Organisation for Economic Co-operation and
Development, Paris

Mr. Jim Page
Human Resources Development Canada, Hull

Mr. Jean Pignal
Statistics Canada, Ottawa

Ms. Cindy Sceviour
Statistics Canada, Ottawa

Ms. Marla Waltman Daschko
Human Resources Development Canada, Hull

Mr. Kentaro Yamamoto
Educational Testing Service, Princeton

National study managers

Australia	Mr. Mel Butler Australian Bureau of Statistics, Canberra
Belgium	Mr. Luc van de Poele University of Ghent, Ghent
Canada	Mr. Jean Pignal Statistics Canada, Ottawa
Germany	Mr. Rainer Lehmann Humboldt University, Berlin
Great Britain	Ms. Siobhán Carey Office for National Statistics, London
Ireland	Mr. Mark Morgan St. Patrick's College, Dublin
Netherlands	Mr. Willem Houtkoop Max Goote Expert Center, Amsterdam
New Zealand	Mr. Hans Wagemaker Ministry of Education, Wellington
Northern Ireland	Mr. Kevin Sweeney Central Survey Unit, Belfast
Poland	Mr. Ireneusz Bialecki Warsaw University, Warsaw
Sweden	Mr. Mats Myrberg Linköping University, Linköping
Switzerland	Mr. Philipp Notter University of Zürich, Zürich
	Mr. François Stoll University of Zürich, Zürich
United States	Ms. Marilyn Binkley National Center for Education Statistics, Washington, DC.

Authors

Ms. Nancy Darcovich
Statistics Canada, Ottawa

Mr. Stan Jones
Statistics Canada, Yarmouth

Mr. Irwin Kirsch
Educational Testing Service, Princeton

Mr. Henry M. Levin
Russell Sage Foundation, New York

Mr. T. Scott Murray
Statistics Canada, Ottawa

Mr. Kjell Rubenson
University of British Columbia, Vancouver

Mr. Albert Tuijnman (Editor)
OECD, Paris

Mr. J. Douglas Willms
University of New Brunswick, Fredericton

MAIN SALES OUTLETS OF OECD PUBLICATIONS
PRINCIPAUX POINTS DE VENTE DES PUBLICATIONS DE L'OCDE

AUSTRALIA – AUSTRALIE
D.A. Information Services
648 Whitehorse Road, P.O.B 163
Mitcham, Victoria 3132   Tel. (03) 9210.7777
                             Fax: (03) 9210.7788

AUSTRIA – AUTRICHE
Gerold & Co.
Graben 31
Wien I   Tel. (0222) 533.50.14
                        Fax: (0222) 512.47.31.29

BELGIUM – BELGIQUE
Jean De Lannoy
Avenue du Roi, Koningslaan 202
B-1060 Bruxelles   Tel. (02) 538.51.69/538.08.41
                             Fax: (02) 538.08.41

CANADA
Renouf Publishing Company Ltd.
5369 Canotek Road
Unit 1
Ottawa, Ont. K1J 9J3   Tel. (613) 745.2665
                             Fax: (613) 745.7660

Stores:
71 1/2 Sparks Street
Ottawa, Ont. K1P 5R1   Tel. (613) 238.8985
                             Fax: (613) 238.6041

12 Adelaide Street West
Toronto, QN M5H 1L6   Tel. (416) 363.3171
                             Fax: (416) 363.5963

Les Éditions La Liberté Inc.
3020 Chemin Sainte-Foy
Sainte-Foy, PQ G1X 3V6   Tel. (418) 658.3763
                             Fax: (418) 658.3763

Federal Publications Inc.
165 University Avenue, Suite 701
Toronto, ON M5H 3B8   Tel. (416) 860.1611
                             Fax: (416) 860.1608

Les Publications Fédérales
1185 Université
Montréal, QC H3B 3A7   Tel. (514) 954.1633
                             Fax: (514) 954.1635

CHINA – CHINE
Book Dept., China National Publications
Import and Export Corporation (CNPIEC)
16 Gongti E. Road, Chaoyang District
Beijing 100020   Tel. (10) 6506-6688 Ext. 8402
                             (10) 6506-3101

CHINESE TAIPEI – TAIPEI CHINOIS
Good Faith Worldwide Int'l. Co. Ltd.
9th Floor, No. 118, Sec. 2
Chung Hsiao E. Road
Taipei   Tel. (02) 391.7396/391.7397
                             Fax: (02) 394.9176

**CZECH REPUBLIC –
RÉPUBLIQUE TCHÈQUE**
National Information Centre
NIS – prodejna
Konviktská 5
Praha 1 – 113 57   Tel. (02) 24.23.09.07
                         Fax: (02) 24.22.94.33
E-mail: nkposp@dec.niz.cz
Internet: http://www.nis.cz

DENMARK – DANEMARK
Munksgaard Book and Subscription Service
35, Nørre Søgade, P.O. Box 2148
DK-1016 København K   Tel. (33) 12.85.70
                             Fax: (33) 12.93.87

J. H. Schultz Information A/S,
Herstedvang 12,
DK – 2620 Albertslung   Tel. 43 63 23 00
                             Fax: 43 63 19 69
Internet: s-info@inet.uni-c.dk

EGYPT – ÉGYPTE
The Middle East Observer
41 Sherif Street
Cairo   Tel. (2) 392.6919
                             Fax: (2) 360.6804

FINLAND – FINLANDE
Akateeminen Kirjakauppa
Keskuskatu 1, P.O. Box 128
00100 Helsinki

Subscription Services/Agence d'abonnements :
P.O. Box 23
00100 Helsinki   Tel. (358) 9.121.4403
                          Fax: (358) 9.121.4450

*FRANCE
OECD/OCDE
Mail Orders/Commandes par correspondance :
2, rue André-Pascal
75775 Paris Cedex 16   Tel. 33 (0)1.45.24.82.00
                        Fax: 33 (0)1.49.10.42.76
                        Telex: 640048 OCDE
Internet: Compte.PUBSINQ@oecd.org

Orders via Minitel, France only/
Commandes par Minitel, France exclusivement :
36 15 OCDE

OECD Bookshop/Librairie de l'OCDE :
33, rue Octave-Feuillet
75016 Paris   Tel. 33 (0)1.45.24.81.81
                          33 (0)1.45.24.81.67

Dawson
B.P. 40
91121 Palaiseau Cedex   Tel. 01.89.10.47.00
                          Fax: 01.64.54.83.26

Documentation Française
29, quai Voltaire
75007 Paris   Tel. 01.40.15.70.00

Economica
49, rue Héricart
75015 Paris   Tel. 01.45.78.12.92
                          Fax: 01.45.75.05.67

Gibert Jeune (Droit-Économie)
6, place Saint-Michel
75006 Paris   Tel. 01.43.25.91.19

Librairie du Commerce International
10, avenue d'Iéna
75016 Paris   Tel. 01.40.73.34.60

Librairie Dunod
Université Paris-Dauphine
Place du Maréchal-de-Lattre-de-Tassigny
75016 Paris   Tel. 01.44.05.40.13

Librairie Lavoisier
11, rue Lavoisier
75008 Paris   Tel. 01.42.65.39.95

Librairie des Sciences Politiques
30, rue Saint-Guillaume
75007 Paris   Tel. 01.45.48.36.02

P.U.F.
49, boulevard Saint-Michel
75005 Paris   Tel. 01.43.25.83.40

Librairie de l'Université
12a, rue Nazareth
13100 Aix-en-Provence   Tel. 04.42.26.18.08

Documentation Française
165, rue Garibaldi
69003 Lyon   Tel. 04.78.63.32.23

Librairie Decitre
29, place Bellecour
69002 Lyon   Tel. 04.72.40.54.54

Librairie Sauramps
Le Triangle
34967 Montpellier Cedex 2 Tel. 04.67.58.85.15
                           Fax: 04.67.58.27.36

A la Sorbonne Actual
23, rue de l'Hôtel-des-Postes
06000 Nice   Tel. 04.93.13.77.75
                          Fax: 04.93.80.75.69

GERMANY – ALLEMAGNE
OECD Bonn Centre
August-Bebel-Allee 6
D-53175 Bonn   Tel. (0228) 959.120
                       Fax: (0228) 959.12.17

GREECE – GRÈCE
Librairie Kauffmann
Stadiou 28
10564 Athens   Tel. (01) 32.55.321
                             Fax: (01) 32.30.320

HONG-KONG
Swindon Book Co. Ltd.
Astoria Bldg. 3F
34 Ashley Road, Tsimshatsui
Kowloon, Hong Kong   Tel. 2376.2062
                             Fax: 2376.0685

HUNGARY – HONGRIE
Euro Info Service
Margitsziget, Európa Ház
1138 Budapest   Tel. (1) 111.60.61
                             Fax: (1) 302.50.35
E-mail: euroinfo@mail.matav.hu
Internet: http://www.euroinfo.hu//index.html

ICELAND – ISLANDE
Mál og Menning
Laugavegi 18, Pósthólf 392
121 Reykjavik   Tel. (1) 552.4240
                             Fax: (1) 562.3523

INDIA – INDE
Oxford Book and Stationery Co.
Scindia House
New Delhi 110001   Tel. (11) 331.5896/5308
                             Fax: (11) 332.2639
E-mail: oxford.publ@axcess.net.in

17 Park Street
Calcutta 700016   Tel. 240832

INDONESIA – INDONÉSIE
Pdii-Lipi
P.O. Box 4298
Jakarta 12042   Tel. (21) 573.34.67
                             Fax: (21) 573.34.67

IRELAND – IRLANDE
Government Supplies Agency
Publications Section
4/5 Harcourt Road
Dublin 2   Tel. 661.31.11
                             Fax: 475.27.60

ISRAEL – ISRAËL
Praedicta
5 Shatner Street
P.O. Box 34030
Jerusalem 91430   Tel. (2) 652.84.90/1/2
                             Fax: (2) 652.84.93

R.O.Y. International
P.O. Box 13056
Tel Aviv 61130   Tel. (3) 546 1423
                             Fax: (3) 546 1442
E-mail: royil@netvision.net.il

Palestinian Authority/Middle East:
INDEX Information Services
P.O.B. 19502
Jerusalem   Tel. (2) 627.16.34
                             Fax: (2) 627.12.19

ITALY – ITALIE
Libreria Commissionaria Sansoni
Via Duca di Calabria, 1/1
50125 Firenze   Tel. (055) 64.54.15
                             Fax: (055) 64.12.57
E-mail: licosa@ftbcc.it

Via Bartolini 29
20155 Milano   Tel. (02) 36.50.83

Editrice e Libreria Herder
Piazza Montecitorio 120
00186 Roma   Tel. 679.46.28
                             Fax: 678.47.51

Libreria Hoepli
Via Hoepli 5
20121 Milano   Tel. (02) 86.54.46
                             Fax: (02) 805.28.86

Libreria Scientifica
Dott. Lucio de Biasio 'Aeiou'
Via Coronelli, 6
20146 Milano   Tel. (02) 48.95.45.52
                                Fax: (02) 48.95.45.48

JAPAN – JAPON
OECD Tokyo Centre
Landic Akasaka Building
2-3-4 Akasaka, Minato-ku
Tokyo 107   Tel. (81.3) 3586.2016
                                Fax: (81.3) 3584.7929

KOREA – CORÉE
Kyobo Book Centre Co. Ltd.
P.O. Box 1658, Kwang Hwa Moon
Seoul   Tel. 730.78.91
                                Fax: 735.00.30

MALAYSIA – MALAISIE
University of Malaya Bookshop
University of Malaya
P.O. Box 1127, Jalan Pantai Baru
59700 Kuala Lumpur
Malaysia   Tel. 756.5000/756.5425
                                Fax: 756.3246

MEXICO – MEXIQUE
OECD Mexico Centre
Edificio INFOTEC
Av. San Fernando no. 37
Col. Toriello Guerra
Tlalpan C.P. 14050
Mexico D.F.   Tel. (525) 528.10.38
                                Fax: (525) 606.13.07
E-mail: ocde@rtn.net.mx

NETHERLANDS – PAYS-BAS
SDU Uitgeverij Plantijnstraat
Externe Fondsen
Postbus 20014
2500 EA's-Gravenhage   Tel. (070) 37.89.880
Voor bestellingen: Fax: (070) 34.75.778

Subscription Agency/   Agence d'abonnements :
SWETS & ZEITLINGER BV
Heereweg 347B
P.O. Box 830
2160 SZ Lisse   Tel. 252.435.111
                                Fax: 252.415.888

**NEW ZEALAND –
NOUVELLE-ZÉLANDE**
GPLegislation Services
P.O. Box 12418
Thorndon, Wellington   Tel. (04) 496.5655
                                Fax: (04) 496.5698

NORWAY – NORVÈGE
NIC INFO A/S
Ostensjoveien 18
P.O. Box 6512 Etterstad
0606 Oslo   Tel. (22) 97.45.00
                                Fax: (22) 97.45.45

PAKISTAN
Mirza Book Agency
65 Shahrah Quaid-E-Azam
Lahore 54000   Tel. (42) 735.36.01
                                Fax. (42) 5/6.37.14

PHILIPPINE – PHILIPPINES
International Booksource Center Inc.
Rm 179/920 Cityland 10 Condo Tower 2
HV dela Costa Ext cor Valero St.
Makati Metro Manila   Tel. (632) 817 9676
                                Fax: (632) 817 1741

POLAND – POLOGNE
Ars Polona
00-950 Warszawa
Krakowskie Prezdmiescie 7   Tel. (22) 264760
                                Fax: (22) 265334

PORTUGAL
Livraria Portugal
Rua do Carmo 70-74
Apart. 2681
1200 Lisboa   Tel. (01) 347.49.82/5
                                Fax: (01) 347.02.64

SINGAPORE – SINGAPOUR
Ashgate Publishing
Asia Pacific Pte. Ltd
Golden Wheel Building, 04-03
41, Kallang Pudding Road
Singapore 349316   Tel. 741.5166
                                Fax: 742.9356

SPAIN – ESPAGNE
Mundi-Prensa Libros S.A.
Castelló 37, Apartado 1223
Madrid 28001   Tel. (91) 431.33.99
                                Fax: (91) 575.39.98
E-mail: mundiprensa@tsai.es
Internet: http://www.mundiprensa.es

Mundi-Prensa Barcelona
Consell de Cent No. 391
08009 – Barcelona   Tel. (93) 488.34.92
                                Fax: (93) 487.76.59

Libreria de la Generalitat
Palau Moja
Rambla dels Estudis, 118
08002 – Barcelona
                    (Suscripciones) Tel. (93) 318.80.12
                    (Publicaciones) Tel. (93) 302.67.23
                                Fax: (93) 412.18.54

SRI LANKA
Centre for Policy Research
c/o Colombo Agencies Ltd.
No. 300-304, Galle Road
Colombo 3   Tel. (1) 574240, 573551-2
                                Fax: (1) 575394, 510711

SWEDEN – SUÈDE
CE Fritzes AB
S–106 47 Stockholm   Tel. (08) 690.90.90
                                Fax: (08) 20.50.21

For electronic publications only/
Publications électroniques seulement
STATISTICS SWEDEN
Informationsservice
S-115 81 Stockholm   Tel. 8 783 5066
                                Fax: 8 783 4045

Subscription Agency/Agence d'abonnements :
Wennergren-Williams Info AB
P.O. Box 1305
171 25 Solna   Tel. (08) 705.97.50
                                Fax: (08) 27.00.71

Liber distribution
Internatinal organizations
Fagerstagatan 21
S-163 52 Spanga

SWITZERLAND – SUISSE
Maditec S.A (Books and Periodicals/Livres
et périodiques)
Chemin des Palettes 4
Case postale 266
1020 Renens VD 1   Tel. (021) 635.08.65
                                Fax: (021) 635.07.80

Librairie Payot S.A.
4, place Pépinet
CP 3212
1002 Lausanne   Tel. (021) 320.25.11
                                Fax: (021) 320.25.14

Librairie Unilivres
6, rue de Candolle
1205 Genève   Tel. (022) 320.26.23
                                Fax: (022) 329.73.18

Subscription Agency/Agence d'abonnements :
Dynapresse Marketing S.A.
38, avenue Vibert
1227 Carouge   Tel. (022) 308.08.70
                                Fax: (022) 308.07.99

See also – Voir aussi :
OECD Bonn Centre
August-Bebel-Allee 6
D-53175 Bonn (Germany)   Tel. (0228) 959.120
                                Fax: (0228) 959.12.17

THAILAND – THAÏLANDE
Suksit Siam Co. Ltd.
113, 115 Fuang Nakhon Rd.
Opp. Wat Rajbopith
Bangkok 10200   Tel. (662) 225.9531/2
                                Fax: (662) 222.5188

**TRINIDAD & TOBAGO, CARIBBEAN
TRINITÉ-ET-TOBAGO, CARAÏBES**
Systematics Studies Limited
9 Watts Street
Curepe
Trinidad & Tobago, W.I.   Tel. (1809) 645.3475
                                Fax: (1809) 662.5654
E-mail: tobe@trinidad.net

TUNISIA – TUNISIE
Grande Librairie Spécialisée
Fendri Ali
Avenue Haffouz Imm El-Intilaka
Bloc B 1 Sfax 3000   Tel. (216-4) 296 855
                                Fax: (216-4) 298.270

TURKEY – TURQUIE
Kültür Yayinlari Is-Türk Ltd.
Atatürk Bulvari No. 191/Kat 13
06684 Kavaklidere/Ankara
                        Tel. (312) 428.11.40 Ext. 2458
                        Fax : (312) 417.24.90
Dolmabahce Cad. No. 29
Besiktas/Istanbul   Tel. (212) 260 7188

UNITED KINGDOM – ROYAUME-UNI
The Stationery Office Ltd.
Postal orders only:
P.O. Box 276, London SW8 5DT
Gen. enquiries   Tel. (171) 873 0011
                                Fax: (171) 873 8463

The Stationery Office Ltd.
Postal orders only:
49 High Holborn, London WC1V 6HB
Branches at: Belfast, Birmingham, Bristol,
Edinburgh, Manchester

UNITED STATES – ÉTATS-UNIS
OECD Washington Center
2001 L Street N.W., Suite 650
Washington, D.C. 20036-4922 Tel. (202) 785.6323
                                Fax: (202) 785.0350
Internet: washcont@oecd.org

Subscriptions to OECD periodicals may also be
placed through main subscription agencies.

Les abonnements aux publications périodiques de
l'OCDE peuvent être souscrits auprès des
principales agences d'abonnement.

Orders and inquiries from countries where Distribu-
tors have not yet been appointed should be sent to:
OECD Publications, 2, rue André-Pascal, 75775
Paris Cedex 16, France.

Les commandes provenant de pays où l'OCDE n'a
pas encore désigné de distributeur peuvent être
adressées aux Éditions de l'OCDE, 2, rue André-
Pascal, 75775 Paris Cedex 16, France.

12-1996